The Burden of German History 1919–45

Essays for the Goethe Institute

The Burden of German History 1919–45

Essays for the Goethe Institute

Edited by Michael Laffan

Methuen London

First published in Great Britain 1988
by Methuen London Ltd
11 New Fetter Lane, London EC4P 4EE

Printed in Great Britain by
Redwood Burn Ltd,
Trowbridge, Wiltshire

British Library Cataloguing in Publication Data
The Burden of German History 1919–45:
Essays for the Goethe Institute.
1. Germany – History – 1919–1933
2. Germany – History – 1933–1945
I. Laffan, Michael II. Goethe-Institute (*Dublin*)
943.085 DD237

ISBN 0 413 40560 5

Contents

The Contributors

Imanuel Geiss, Professor of Modern History in the University of Bremen, is the author of *German Foreign Policy, 1871–1914*, *July 1914: the Outbreak of the First World War*, *The Pan-African Movement*, a six-volume world history, and numerous other publications.

Peter Hoffmann, after an academic career in Germany and the United States, is now Professor of German History in McGill University, Montreal. He is the author of the standard *History of the German Resistance, 1933–1945* as well as of many articles on the resistance movement.

Eberhard Jäckel is Professor of Modern History in the University of Stuttgart. His publications include *Hitler in History*, *Hitler's Weltanschauung: a Blueprint for Power*, *Frankreich in Hitlers Europa*, and *Hitlers Herrschaft*.

Peter Labanyi was formerly German editor of the *Times Literary Supplement* and now lectures in the National Institute of Higher Education, Limerick. He has published articles on several German writers and is at present editing and translating Alexander Kluge's *Öffentlichkeit*.

Michael Laffan lectures in University College, Dublin. He has researched and lectured on aspects of Weimar German history, and is the author of *The Partition of Ireland, 1911–1925*, as well as of several articles. He is Secretary of the Irish Historical Society.

J. Joseph Lee, Professor of Modern History in University College, Cork, is the author of *The Modernization of Irish Society, 1848–1918* as well as of studies on Labour in German Industrialization, Urbanization and Economic Development in Germany, and German Agriculture during the First World War.

Hans Mommsen is Professor of Modern History in the University of Bochum. His many publications include *Klassenkampf oder Mitbestimmung: zum Problem der Kontrolle wirtschaftlicher Macht in der Weimarer Republik*, *Beamtentum im Dritten Reich* and *Sozialdemokratie zwischen Klassenbewegung und Volkspartei*.

Hugh Ridley, Professor of German in University College, Dublin, is the author of *Images of Imperial Rule* and *Industrie und deutsche Literatur* as well as of studies on writers such as Thomas Mann, Ernst Jünger, Gottfried Benn and Walter Benjamin.

Eda Sagarra is Professor of German in Trinity College, Dublin. Her publications include *An Introduction to Nineteenth-Century Germany*, *German Literature and Society, 1830–1890*, and *A Social History of Germany, 1648–1914*.

Kurt Sontheimer, Professor of Political Science in the University of Munich, is the author of many books on modern German Politics and Society, among them *Antidemokratisches Denken in der Weimarer Republik, Das Elend unserer Intellektuellen* and *The Government and Politics of West Germany*.

Introduction

The twelve articles in this collection are based on papers delivered to a conference on 'Weimar Germany and National Socialism, 1919–1945', which was held in University College, Dublin, in March 1986. The conference was the result of an initiative by the Goethe Institute Dublin, and it was organized and presented jointly by the Institute and by the Department of Modern History, University College, Dublin, under the direction of Dr Dietrich Kreplin and Professor Kevin B. Nowlan.

The widespread interest which it provoked, the large attendance at the lectures, and numerous requests for the text of the papers, all reinforced the organizers' wish to publish the proceedings of the conference. This volume is the result.

The contributors are Irish and German scholars who belong to several different disciplines and represent a wide range of approaches to their subjects. Some of them break new ground while others synthesize recent research and interpretations. However, one theme runs through most of the chapters: the strong lines of continuity which link different phases of German history and which both underlie and transcend the dramatic changes of regime. The importance of symbolic dates such as 1918/19, 1930/33 or 1945/49 can be exaggerated, and a concentration on 'turning-points' can distract attention from long-term movements or trends.

At the most basic level Germany has been conditioned by her geographical position in the heart of Europe, with the result that any change in her status – unification, expansion, contraction or division – has important consequences for all her many neighbours. This Continent-wide sensitivity to German developments goes back many centuries.

Some of the moods and ideas normally associated with the Weimar Republic are also characteristic of the Wilhelmine Empire, while others re-emerged with the defeat of the Third Reich.

Similarly, anti-democratic attitudes normally associated with the Nazi years frequently had their origins in the 1920s or even earlier.

Such continuities can be seen both in Germany's artistic and literary achievements and in her social, political, economic and military history. 'Weimar culture' was not merely an explosion of novelty and innovation which characterized the 'Golden Twenties'; most of its distinguishing features had already emerged long before the collapse of the monarchy, and although they flourished briefly in a more favourable environment after 1919, republican Germany remained in most respects a conservative society. New styles and new ideas provoked widespread opposition, while the simplistic and chauvinistic *Blut und Boden* (Blood and Soil) literature retained its traditional popularity. Even the educated élite tended to disparage modern art and literature. Hostility towards experimentation and towards what was seen as the anarchic abuse of new freedoms, attempts to maim and destroy 'Weimar culture', and a tepid defence of democracy and freedom by the *avant-garde*, were all patterns evident long before 1933. Intellectuals lacked public support and in return most of them did little to support the Republic.

Weimar was ambivalent in its political as well as in its cultural life. The new system emerged less as a result of any positive action by those who believed in democracy or republicanism than because of their predecessors' failure. The revolution was half-hearted, and the Republic was divided and polarized from the beginning, crippled both by external circumstances such as its legacy of defeat in the First World War and by its own structural faults and weaknesses. Its many powerful enemies were confronted by too few committed defenders, and as early as 1920 it was rejected by the electorate. Ironically, less than two years after Germany became a modern democracy with a government dependent on parliamentary and electoral support, the democratic parties lost the majority which they had won in every election for the past thirty years. They never regained it. For the next decade there was deadlock, followed by a collapse into autocratic rule and then a further repudiation of democracy; in July 1932, 52 per cent of the electorate voted for totalitarian parties of the extreme right or the extreme left.

The Republic failed to disarm its enemies and it was undermined by the efforts of social, military and industrial groups to undo the limited achievements of the revolution. Its foreign policy failed to strengthen democratic government and even contributed towards its collapse. The economic difficulties of the late 1920s – reduced industrial competitiveness, reduced investment and high taxation – were reinforced by the Depression of the early 1930s. The result was paralysis, a combination of economic and political problems which, in the view of many historians, made the state almost ungovernable.

Loud and insistent calls for a national dictatorship were being made long before Hitler was able to gratify them. The drift towards conservative authoritarianism in the years after 1928, the reaction against a system widely associated with drabness, crisis and failure, and the ability of a small reactionary clique to entrench itself in office, meant that in many respects the Republic had already committed suicide before its Nazi enemies were strong enough to murder it.

There was nothing predestined about Hitler's triumph in 1933. Like the democrats in 1918, the National Socialists came to power more because of their enemies' weakness and failures than because of their own strength. In the late 1920s and early 1930s they had shown little consistency in membership and had no clear-cut programme which distinguished them from other parties or groups on the far right. Apart from his nationalism Hitler's appeal was basically negative, and he won the support of those who felt alienated or threatened by modern society and its upheavals. The Nazis' energy and discipline, and the votes of one-third of the electorate, would not have brought them to office without the help of favourable circumstances. It was above all the misguided efforts of the ruling faction to exploit and tame Hitler which enabled him to outmanœuvre his new allies and establish his dictatorship.

Once securely in power, Hitler lost no time in implementing his policies. As the regime began its campaign to dominate the people's hearts, minds and actions, internal opposition was crushed and those perceived as 'enemies', particularly the Jews, were persecuted. A powerful and dominant Germany was to emerge from the wreckage of Weimar democracy. The new Reich would be a work of art, grandiose at one level and middlebrow at another, in which monumental feats of architecture and engineering would glorify the Führer. Propaganda and spectacle could distract attention from internal contradictions and failures.

The desire for *Lebensraum*, territorial conquest and settlement in the East, was central to Hitler's objectives. He was not alone in such expansionism and he had already been anticipated by Italy and

Japan, but the Nazis' particular brutality and the limitlessness of their ambitions marked them off from their allies. Piecemeal annexations culminated in a war which, despite the lack of enthusiasm shown by the German people, proceeded inexorably from one enemy and one campaign to the next.

As the slaughter continued, both on the battlefronts and in the concentration camps, the Gestapo's grip on the country ensured that only the army had any chance of overthrowing the regime and ending the bloodshed. Against overwhelming odds, and with virtually no chance of success, a group of officers tried to redeem some of Germany's honour by assassinating the Führer. The failure of their attempt was followed within a year by the defeat and conquest of the Third Reich.

The year 1945 marked the end of certain patterns of German history: Prussia and her Junkers disappeared, and the unity which Bismarck had brought about was ended after less than three-quarters of a century. 1945 also saw the re-emergence of other patterns, of ideas and values which had survived or flourished during the Weimar Republic, and of the river Elbe as a dividing line between Eastern and Western Germany. Even the events of 1945–9 revealed continuity as well as disruption.

The contributors to this book examine all these developments, as well as many others. Their articles reflect many of the insights and much of the understanding of those who study German art, literature and history during the first half of the twentieth century, and in particular during the traumatic decades between the end of the Second Reich and the end of the Third.

Michael Laffan

ONE

Weimar Culture

KURT SONTHEIMER

The short-lived Weimar Republic has an ambiguous and contradictory reputation. In *political* terms it is generally seen as a tragedy, as the agonizing drama of Germany's first liberal democracy which ended in Hitler's brutal dictatorship. In *cultural* terms it is considered to have been one of the richest, most exciting and most fruitful periods of the general history of the twentieth century. But the legend or even the myth of Weimar culture was born only after the Republic's death and was not really experienced during the 1920s. On the contrary, when they viewed their country's cultural variety, German contemporaries felt that they lived in difficult and crisis-ridden times, in a chaotic age filled with tensions and contradictions.

In some respects this is hardly surprising. Far from being a distinct phenomenon which can easily be described and analysed, Weimar culture was bewildering, irritating and often unclear in its main tendencies and currents. It was neither unified nor harmonious. But its internal contradictions and tensions have not really impaired the positive image which it still enjoys. While the historical fate of the Weimar Republic as a political system serves as one of the most telling examples of how a democracy can be ruined within a very short time, we usually associate its cultural life with some of the most important creative achievements in modern German history.

Weimar Germany's cultural achievements were in large part brought about by the work of those who were forced out of Germany in 1933. These artistic and intellectual achievements were so important and so enduring that they simply could not be ignored by the outside world or by subsequent generations. This was especially the case after 1945 when, at the end of German barbarism, after the ravages of National Socialism and of Hitler's war, German culture had to find a new basis. Moreover, most of the intellectuals, scientists and artists who had been forced to leave Germany because of Hitler's totalitarian regime represented Weimar culture at its best. These emigrés did all they could to praise the achievements of the society and period to which they belonged, and, particularly in the United States, they proved to be effective representatives of the best of Weimar culture.

The democratic Republic lasted a mere fourteen years and this was too short a period in which to create so many lasting works and outstanding achievements in the cultural field. The roots of Weimar culture reach back into Germany's more immediate past, through the hectic war years and through the two previous decades, back as far as the mood and style of the *fin de siècle.* What happened in the Weimar period was what a French author has aptly called 'the explosion of modernity', but this explosion was being prepared for many years before 1919.

The excitement and activity of the Weimar years resulted from the synthesis between a ripe new culture and a new political system in which freedom of art and expression could flourish as never before. It was a constellation which witnessed a fierce struggle between on the one side the old and conventional, the tradition of the *Obrigkeitsstaat* or the authoritarian state, and on the other the new and revolutionary, the free and equal democratic Republic. In the field of culture the new forces tried to impose themselves in the new constitutional setting. In the early phase of the Republic they were supported by a common spirit of freedom, emancipation, hope for a new future and a strong belief in the liberating and humanizing effects of republican and democratic government.

But the authoritarian state of Wilhelmine Germany was not, after all, a pure dictatorship. Even under the Empire there was a certain freedom of cultural expression, and a strong modernist current opposed official cultural expectations and conventional patterns. Peter Gay, one of the great analysts of Weimar culture, claims that: 'There can be no doubt: the Weimar style was born before the Weimar Republic. The war gave it a political cast and a strident tone, and saddled it with a deadly quarrel; the revolution gave it unprecedented opportunities. But the Republic created little; it liberated what was already there.'[1]

The Weimar style not only preceded the Republic, it also

extended far beyond Germany. 'Both in the Empire and in the Republic, German painters, poets, playwrights, psychologists, philosophers, composers, architects, even humorists were engaged in a free international commerce of ideas. They were part of a Western community on which they drew and which, in turn, they fed; chauvinism was not merely offensive to the Weimar style, it would have been fatal.'[2]

If Weimar culture is in a sense more enduring and profound than what was achieved under the auspices of German democracy in the 1920s, it must also be stressed that Weimar culture was very much a minority affair. It was a playground for specialized élites. As Professor Hagen Schulze put it in his important book on the Weimar Republic,

> Everything takes place in a layer (*Schicht*) of writers, painters, musicians, thinkers, supporters, elevated culture-consumers and journalists, that is between the *Bildungsbürgertum* and the *Bohème*. It is a deeply bourgeois culture which is at the same time very much petit bourgeois. It is a generation which was born in the *fin de siècle* and which experienced the *belle époque* (or *Wilhelmismus*) as an age of philistine materialism, silly boasting, bourgeois bad taste and stylistic impotence.[3]

Industrialization and the creation of a new mass civilization have often provoked a deep cultural shock, and in part Weimar culture was a reaction against the social, economic and technical revolution of the industrial age. Artists and philosophers began to articulate the new and widespread feelings of alienation and estrangement.

The revolt against bourgeois society and the bourgeois way of life, a revolt which began long before the collapse of the Empire, took many different artistic and intellectual forms. On the one hand some observers saw in the Weimar Republic and its constitution the framework for a new society, composed of equal men and women who were working together for a new social and democratic life in a free republic. On the other hand were those who believed that Weimar was a weak and contemptible state in which only the worst elements of bourgeois society and ideology could flourish. It should therefore be attacked and overthrown in the name of the true or real German state, a modern, corporate *wahre Staat* which would emphasize discipline and authority.

The real Republic, as it actually existed, was far removed from both these ideals. The intellectual left tried in vain to find in the Weimar system a true expression of their ideas of a living, democratic Germany. Its more radical elements believed that it would be necessary to destroy the bourgeois incarnation of a weak liberal democracy which, in their view, did not conform to German traditions and German needs.

Left-wing intellectuals, represented by important writers such as Brecht and Heinrich Mann, and constantly animated by great satirical writers like Kurt Tucholsky, experienced bitter disappointment between 1919 and 1930. They discovered that the Republic did not fulfil their expectations, and that its day-to-day realities were far removed from the ideals of social and democratic republicanism which the left had dreamed of after the war.

The radical right, represented by aggressive writers like Ernst Jünger, Oswald Spengler and many others, was quite unwilling to make its peace with the existing Republic. It did everything it could to overthrow Weimar democracy in order to install a new, strong and *unliberal* system of German government.

In between were those intellectuals, such as the historian Friedrich Meinecke, who called themselves *Vernunftrepublikaner*, or rational republicans. They did not fight for the Republic; they simply made their peace with it since they did not see any better solution. But they were neither strong nor united in their support of German democracy and they felt helpless when finally it came under heavy attack by the nationalist movement. Writing of this category of intellectuals, Peter Gay remarked that their

> cool rationalism had its own characteristic virtues and vices: it was better equipped to discover defects than excellences; it was more likely to elicit dispassionate analysis of past errors than passionate loyalty to new possibilities. . . . The *Vernunftrepublikaner* were reasonable men who had been willing to learn the first lesson of modernity but not the second: they acknowledged that nostalgia for the Empire was ridiculous, but they could not see that the Republic might deserve wholehearted support – or, rather, it might become deserving if enough deserving people supported it.[4]

The rational republicans were isolated intellectuals; they were left to themselves and did not form an active political group, let alone co-operate with a particular party. In this respect it is surprising to find that one of the most prominent intellectual figures of the Weimar Republic, Thomas Mann, exhorted the German bourgeoisie to support the Social Democrats. This was after the disastrous elections of September 1930 when he made his 'Appeal for Reason' in which he tried to explain, at least in part, the Nazis' dramatic success by their ability to exploit a strong contemporary irrational current or mood. Thomas Mann himself was a *Vernunftrepublikaner* at the beginning and he had to liberate himself from the extreme nationalist stance he had taken on behalf of the Wilhelmine state at the outbreak of the First World War. But he converted to the new democratic system openly and with great courage when, in 1922, he proclaimed his love for Weimar and declared that the new democracy could be reconciled with the best in Germany's romantic tradition.

Weimar culture was not only rich and varied, it was also dramatic, provocative and polarized. It provided the arena for a remarkable left-wing intelligentsia which lived in and around Berlin, as well as for an even stronger and steadily growing intelligentsia on the right. Members of this group, who hated intellectuals and did not wish to be regarded as such, enjoyed a widening appeal among the German public. In their attacks against the democratic Republic they were backed more or less directly by the National Socialists. The rational republicans were positioned between these two rival camps, but they were not strongly united and did not really fight for the defence of the Republic against its enemies. They were full of goodwill but lacked the means to influence events.

The left-wing intellectuals rejected the existing Weimar Republic because it had not realized their early dreams of good and democratic government. They were, of course, right in attacking the perseverance of old structures and of the old authorities in the bureaucracy, the army and the economy. Some authors have criticized them for their rejection of the Republic as they experienced it, and have even held them responsible for the later success of the National Socialists. This claim is exaggerated and it is indeed hard to see how men and women who held republican and radical convictions such as theirs could have been won over to the defence of a system which was, from 1925 onwards, represented by an elderly field marshal of the First World War. It is difficult to judge whether another attitude on the part of many left-wing intellectuals would have helped the Weimar Republic to withstand the attacks of the right, but it is at least good to know that the generation after the Second World War fully accepted the satirical and critical attitude of writers such as Tucholsky. He, especially, enjoyed a great comeback after 1945 and he is now an established figure of German democratic culture.

It makes little sense to accuse left-wing intellectuals of having undermined the Weimar Republic. By themselves they could not have changed the course of events. In Walter Laqueur's words,

> It was after all Hitler, not Tucholsky, who buried the Weimar Republic. Even if the Left intellectuals had been less embittered about the fact that their noble dream had not been realized in Weimar, even if their perspective had not been dictated by utopian visions and moral absolutes, even if they had all rallied to the defence of the Republic, the outcome would most probably have been the same. The political parties through which they should have worked would still have rejected them. A hundred years of German history could not be undone in so short a time.[5]

The German right was in a much stronger position. It had, of course, to accept defeat in the First World War, but it was quite certain why this defeat had come about: the Germans had not been faithful enough to the great national values that made for a good German state.

At the beginning of the Weimar Republic the mood on the right of the intellectual spectrum was gloomy. Oswald Spengler had set the tone with his pessimistic interpretation of *The Decline of the West.* He prophesied the advent of a new type of Caesarian regime which would overcome the grave weaknesses of liberal democracy. He pointed to the Prussian idea of socialism as the ideological foundation for a true and successful German state. His idea of socialism had nothing to do with social justice or with an equal distribution of wealth and opportunities, but only with a collective unity and with a disciplined order to which everybody should give his full service and complete devotion. Spengler anticipated the National Socialist idea of *Volksgemeinschaft* under the guidance of an inspired Führer.

Spengler's was one of the most strident voices in a loud and agitated chorus. There were many others who shared his views, especially among the younger generation which had undergone the experience of the First World War. This had taught them a new kind of heroism, utterly opposed to the values of liberal humanitarianism; *Kriegserlebnis*, or war experience, had profound political implications.

Many intellectuals of the right had little direct influence but they made, of course, an important contribution to the general climate of opinion. In a certain sense they undermined their own intellectual position and thus gave way to the real forces of 'blood and iron' that finally overcame the Weimar Republic. To quote Walter Laqueur again: 'For once it had been established that the life force, blood, myth, the will to power were the central forces, and that it was pointless to subject them to critical analysis, it followed that intellectual interpreters were no longer needed . . . everybody was his own ideologist – and the Führer the ultimate arbiter.'[6]

There were indeed many who contributed to a climate of opinion which was deeply hostile to the values of liberal and parliamentary democracy. This was especially true in academic circles where authors like Carl Schmitt and many others paved the intellectual path for the overthrow of the Weimar system. For many of these right-wing thinkers Nazism was too crude and vulgar, too much of a mass movement; nevertheless they found it acceptable that the Weimar Republic should be attacked so savagely by the German fascists. They hated Weimar and its representatives more than they hated Hitler, an enemy whom they and the Republic shared in common.

One of the most interesting phenomena in the intellectual history of the twentieth century is that there were so many German intellectuals on the political right who questioned reason and preached a bloody irrationalism. They justified their stance by the philosophical belief in the priority of life and action over the processes of adjustment and negotiation.

It is clear that from such points of view the new culture of the Weimar Republic was unacceptable to the right, which condemned it fiercely as *Kulturbolschewismus*, or cultural bolshevism. Such critics never said precisely what they understood by *Kulturbolschewismus*, but prominent among their dislikes were the new kind of modernism, the new freedom of expression and form. They saw in the new culture of the Republic an expression of atomization, fragmentation and disorientation. To the pessimists of that age the spirit of Weimar appeared as an expression of cultural and social anarchy, as an attack on the ideas of beauty and proportion.

The enemies of 'cultural bolshevism' were ultimately successful, and they then had under Hitler the chance to demonstrate what their own form of German culture would be like. The result was pathetic, a scandal and a shame.

When we talk about Weimar culture today, we normally think of the very great achievements in the arts and sciences which were first attacked by the right and in the end liquidated under National Socialism. The positive idea of Weimar culture is associated with great names in literature like the brothers Mann, Bertolt Brecht and Hermann Hesse, and many others who were later forced to leave the country. It is also associated with great stage performances; in the 1920s Berlin was the undisputed centre of European theatre. Weimar culture is also connected with bold new efforts to interpret the world through new approaches in philosophy, theology and the social sciences. It was in these years that the philosophy of existence as represented by Jaspers and Heidegger came into being; it was in the Weimar period that psychoanalysis eased its way into the public consciousness; it was in this time that great sociologists such as Max and Alfred Weber, Karl Mannheim and many others made their great impact on the Western mind. One should not forget that it was towards the end of the Weimar Republic that the critical theory of society which was later to become the 'Frankfurt School' made its first steps into the intellectual world.

The Weimar Republic was also the time in which literature was represented by some of the greatest German authors of the twentieth century. In 1926 republican Prussia founded a literature section within the Prussian Academy of Arts. The list of its members contains some of the most important modern German authors, among them Gerhard Hauptmann, Thomas and Heinrich Mann, Arno Holz, Georg Kaiser, Ricarda Huth, Rene Schickele, Arthur Schnitzler, Jakob Wassermann, Hans Werfel, Gottfried Benn, Alfred Döblin and many others. Heinrich Mann was representative of the large group of leftist writers who put their faith in the Republic and who later complained about its lack of democratic liberty and social values. Thomas Mann became representative of those writers who, after a time of adjustment to the new circumstances, became rational republicans and in the end convinced partisans of the new political order. Thomas Mann is to me an example of the traditional German intelligentsia, especially in academic circles, and of what they could have become if they had been loyal to the idea of reason, freedom and humanity.

The positive image of Weimar culture is due to the fact that we see in it primarily those artistic and intellectual beginnings and developments which are still important to us today and which have survived the difficult years of the Nazi period. We should not forget, however, that in the situation of the Weimar Republic these positive aspects of Weimar culture were by no means so visible, so undisputed or so widely respected as they are today.

The representatives of the great developments in the fields of art and thought were, during the Weimar years, not always aware of the fact that they lived in such a propitious intellectual climate. Most of the intellectuals and artists, whether those of the left or those of the right, did not really feel at home in the atmosphere of the 1920s. On the whole the Republic was a difficult, tedious and uninspiring affair, whereas the spirit of the time was busy, hectic and constantly trying to overcome difficulties and limitations. Weimar culture did little to support the Republic when it came under pressure and was driven into its final agony.

The only consolation we have is that many of the acts, thoughts and intellectual and artistic undertakings of the period extended far beyond the Weimar Republic in their cultural importance. Fortunately, the second German democracy, that of Bonn, has been much more successful than that of Weimar. But the legacy of the 1920s consists of more than a mere negative list of mistakes which must be avoided. To a certain extent it was through Weimar culture that post-Nazi Germany has been able to rediscover and recreate a full and substantial cultural life. It is Weimar's cultural and intellectual achievements that have remained alive and inspiring to the present day. Weimar culture represented, for a brief period, the most fascinating variety of cultural achievements in the twentieth century; it belongs to the great heritage of the modern world. Its significance is more than national – it is a lasting contribution to the richness of Western civilization.

Notes

1. Peter Gay, *Weimar Culture* (Harmondsworth, 1974), p. 6.
2. ibid.

3. Hagen Schulze, *Die Weimarer Republik* (Berlin, 1982), p. 125.
4. Gay, op. cit., pp. 25–6.
5. Walter Laqueur, *Weimar: a Cultural History* (London, 1974), p. 71.
6. ibid., p. 90.

TWO

The Culture of Weimar: Models of Decline

HUGH RIDLEY

Quite apart from their intrinsic merit, the literature and culture of the Weimar Republic have much to offer the historian of the period. Even when the task is to explore Weimar from the perspective of its decline, its replacement by the barbarism of Hitler's regime, the study of the development of literature and culture has much to contribute. Not simply for the light which individual figures, by their works, shed on conditions and events of the time – how much poorer our understanding of the Weimar Republic without George Grosz, or Lion Feuchtwanger – nor indeed just for writers' contribution to public debate on political issues – although the role of the intellectuals (that 'intellectual proletariat' whose growing influence had been diagnosed by Bismarck) was nowhere greater than in Weimar. Although such contributions were influential (primarily within intellectual circles), the indirect role of writers and intellectuals in shaping the reaction of public consciousness to events which featured more explicitly in political discussion is of greater importance still.

One thinks, for instance, of the part played by writers in shaping attitudes to the defeat of 1918, and in giving credence to the image of the 'stab in the back', the legend that the German armies had been undefeated on the field of battle and betrayed by the 'Jews and socialists' at home. The massive sales of the militaristic war-novels (by Ernst Jünger, Werner Beumelburg and others) were not without influence in the acceptance of this politically fateful lie. 'It happened to you,' comments one of Thomas Mann's artist-heroes, 'yet it will be I [the writer] who will for the first time lift it for you to the level of an experience.'[1] So it was often. Many of the ideas essential to National Socialist propaganda – the ideal of the

Germanic race, the *Volksgemeinschaft* or the negative stereotypes of the Jew and socialist – were imaginative constructs, albeit from a poverty of imagination, with all but no basis in reality. Whether or not the imaginative writers accepted all features of National Socialist ideology (and very few did), merely by creating or using these images they contributed tangibly to the acceptance of political ideas of great consequence. Not for nothing had Oscar Wilde spoken of literature as a form of lying (he bemoaned its demise as such); in an age of political liars, the writer as liar had a particularly important function.

This was exacerbated by a situation in which, as has often been observed, Germany, an unpolitical nation without any particular tradition of democratic republicanism, was suddenly thrust by the defeat of 1918 into the status of a democracy – but one without democrats. The intellectuals, few of whom had shown much enthusiasm in fighting for a republic, found themselves in a republic ('without republicans') where the fight was for the minds of the public, to make the ideas, abstractions, values and ambitions of the new republic seem valuable to a population which had never really aspired to them. The way in which writers reacted, even if they stayed within the relatively abstract dimension of cultural and philosophical ideas, could make a real contribution to political events.

In this essay, I shall attempt to outline the development of Weimar culture from a standpoint accessible to the historian. In doing this, rather than sampling the cultural richness of the period, or giving interpretations of individual works and writers, I prefer to work with broad hermeneutic paradigms, to suggest their equivalents in the historiography of the period and their usefulness for the historian.

All historical enquiry – more or less consciously – operates within overall interpretative structures to make sense of the past, and, equally obviously, these paradigms are formulated more or less explicitly in reference to the social-political situation of the historian. Paradigms evolve not only, as Kuhn has shown, in response to perceived anomalies within existing paradigms: they evolve also in response to the social and historical situation of the historians themselves.[2] This general tendency is more pronounced with reference to the Weimar Republic than to other, less troubled historical periods. Of course, in order to interpret individual phenomena in the past – whether of a cultural or a political kind – we need a sense of the direction in which a period was moving, a direction which appears as a common thread or as an understood 'background' to a period of culture. For many periods, what is commonly called literary history is felt to be adequate, a sense that intellectual and cultural movements have autonomy and continuity, passing on some intellectual or artistic message from one period to the next, as between specialist hands, uninterrupted by external agencies. But it is clear that in Weimar the self-identity of an autonomous literary history (especially in a period in which the various self-confessed literary movements, the 'isms', had apparently come to their end[3]) would have had to be enormous to rescue literary works from the gravitational pull of the collapse of Weimar into Hitler's Third Reich. There are few times when the questions as to the development of literature and culture, in isolation from the development of the political context, seem more irrelevant than in the Weimar Republic. Over the end of Weimar hangs the shadow of Hitler, no less strongly over the culture than over the political institutions of the period, and the question which may primarily interest historians in this process is whether the culture of Weimar, like the political system itself, ended in National Socialism by any form of inherent logic, whether it arrived by accident, like Pontius Pilate in the Creed (in Brecht's phrase), or by external extra-literary agencies.

The discussion of fascism among historians (recently summarized for English-language readers by Roger Kershaw[4]) has focused on issues such as the appropriateness of the terms 'totalitarianism' and 'fascism' to denote National Socialism, on the role of traditional élites in the rise of Hitler, the importance of social-structural and demographic change in Germany (in particular the various forces of 'modernization', or the new social classes of a mass-society), and on the continuities in German policy from 1871 to 1939, or in foreign policy from Weimar into the Third Reich. Kershaw shows, as others have done, that the paradigms underlying such interpretations have evolved considerably during the years since the discussions began in the 1930s, initially in response to the fight against fascism in Europe, but subsequently under the pressures caused by the division of Europe and more specifically of Germany itself.

We may identify at one time a tendency to see the relationship between Weimar and Hitler in clear-cut terms: a thriving democracy, with a model constitution, being taken over – as Bullock implies – by 'the gutter'. Other views have seen in the Weimar Republic a state anything but exemplary for liberalism, dominated by an executive unchanged from the Second Reich and succumbing to its own tendency to the right. This view of the state can certainly be found behind views of Weimar as a continuous conspiracy of German capital to protect itself against the winds of change blowing from a class-conscious proletariat; German capital, accepting the Republic in 1919 as the internationally most acceptable form in which to continue its dominance, and turning, under the pressures of the world economic crisis at the end of the 1920s, to the National Socialist party (its 'agent') for a type of support which had come to be seen as necessary for the survival of capitalism. Such interpretations argue for a continuity between Weimar and the Third Reich, and – albeit in a rather different form – this is the picture that emerges from Karl Dietrich Bracher's monumental *Die Auflösung der Weimarer Republik* – the paradigm of a republic that cuts its own throat in September 1930 (rather than being assassinated three years later), when Brüning ceases to depend on a parliamentary majority and governs by means of presidential decrees, a republic which dies before Hitler buries it, which implodes without having to be smashed from outside.

Evidently some of this discussion can be directly paralleled in accounts of the literature and culture of the Weimar Republic, while other accounts of the disintegration of the Weimar Republic's political structures clearly cannot be extended into overall interpretations of the literature and culture of Weimar. In the outer contours of their history, both the political and the cultural development of Weimar follow identical paths: born out of an incomplete revolution and snuffed out in the muddled combination of backstairs intrigue, populism and 'revolution' of 1933. But while certain historical discussions (for instance, on the relationship between conservative and dynamic elements in National Socialist ideology) obviously relate closely to the situation of culture in Weimar, it cannot be assumed that the specialist analysis of political historians will apply to intellectual and cultural life, even though both cultural and political movements belong essentially to the superstructure. Where, for instance, in cultural history can there be an equivalence of key concepts such as unemployment or inflation? Nevertheless, it may be helpful in assessing the particular nature of the cultural process in Weimar if we make in this chapter an attempt at matching up historical and cultural paradigms, and try to present the literature and culture of the Weimar Republic in long shot, rather than close focus.

The model of the Weimar Republic being smashed by a barbaric right wing speaks for itself as we read the list of writers who were forced into emigration by the National Socialist takeover in 1933. Those who left Germany were the cream of the intellectual life of Europe, the outstanding lyricists, dramatists, novelists, essayists, historians and sociologists. They had created by their very existence an intellectual-cultural world of great richness, and – without needing to cite the Einsteins and Freuds – they make clear by their fate the role of Hitler as a destructive and impoverishing outside force, smashing the successes of the Weimar Republic. The bonfires which burned in May 1933, onto which the National Socialist students, and (to their shame) their professors too, threw the quality literature of the Weimar Republic of which they disapproved, demonstrate that the Nazis arrived as a violent ending of a cultural period.

It was in the light of these bonfires (reflected, if not in tranquillity, then at least in peace-time) that the myth of the 'Golden Twenties' was born. The myth was partly an idea of the emigré writers, born of the contrast between an idealized past and the horrors which followed it. But it was taken up in West Germany after the war for reasons which were only marginally associated with nostalgia. The historical paradigm of the 'Golden Twenties' served (as many critics, recently Hermand and Trommler, have shown) as an escape from the ideological polarities which notoriously featured so prominently in Weimar. This escape was very appealing to a West German cultural establishment reluctant to face any problematic elements in its own status and ideals and determined (through the further, more narrowly historical paradigm of the equation of fascism and communism in the concept of totalitarianism), to give central prominence to positive aspects of democracy. This model involved a focusing on the unproblematic concept of cultural richness, particularly in the area of formal innovation, at the expense of a recognition of the major ideological conflicts of these years. Weimar and the 'Golden Twenties' were a carefully selective picture and anything but value-free, emphasizing Weimar 'as the culture of stabilized capitalism, of cultural opulence, of the "good

Europeans", of political understanding and reconciliation, in short as the culture of bourgeois modernism'.[5] The use of this paradigm reminds us that the 'art of inheriting' (for many years rightly the subject of much discussion in the German Democratic Republic) is also practised in the Federal Republic. It is the cultural equivalent of the type of historical simplification which regards the Weimar Republic as 'good' (as democracy) and National Socialism as extraneous 'evil'.

The paradigm of violent destruction cannot conceal the fact that the destruction of the Weimar Republic's culture was prepared. It did not happen out of the blue. Just as Hitler took years to achieve power, so the takeover of cultural power was long prepared for, both organizationally and intellectually. The organizational preparation is a subject on its own, involving the machinations of Alfred Rosenberg's *Kampfbund für deutsche Kultur*, and its various mindless henchmen, and it is more interesting (precisely because more problematic) to look at elements in the preparation process that were intellectual, and indeed respectable. For examples of this we may take the debates between Thomas Mann and his brother Heinrich which ushered in the Weimar Republic.

Thomas Mann's apparent glorification of war in the essay 'Thoughts in Time of War' (1914) and the positive attitude towards German militarism shown in the story 'Frederick and the Great Coalition' (1915) had not escaped his brother's attention. Four years Thomas's senior, Heinrich Mann had gradually moved away from the common literary pursuits of the 1900s and become the spokesman of a radical young generation of writers opposed to traditional society, to the war and committed to political change in Germany. In an essay on Zola, published in an Expressionist journal in 1915, Heinrich Mann violently attacked his brother's position: this attack in turn provoked Thomas to long justifications of his own political stance as a writer.[6]

Thomas Mann's reply, formulated in 1918 in the lengthy *Reflections of a Nonpolitical Man*, provides a good summary of many of the deeply held but largely unconsidered convictions which the German intellectuals of the Second Reich held concerning their political and social function. It is a crucial text for the transfer of pre-1914 attitudes into the Weimar Republic, whose establishment coincided with the book's appearance, and for demonstrating the continuity of conservative ideology across the divide of the war. It owed nothing to the new climate of the Republic, but it developed ideas which were going to be crucially important to the Republic's cultural life, and in particular contributed to the intellectual armoury of the reaction which was to engulf its attempts at a democratic literature. We may briefly summarize four elements in the work:

i The artist is concerned with the timelessly human and with the traditional rather than with the modern or with the ephemeral, time-serving issues of politics. Put another way: the writer is naturally close to the *Volk* rather than to the unstable and shifting masses.

ii Art is concerned with (and in its origins connected with) the demonic, the irrational. It is never a natural ally of rationalism (this had been a central implication of Mann's celebrated story 'Death in Venice' of 1911), or of purely rational political forms such as democracy, or a republic.

iii Politics is a professional activity, and amateurs – especially intellectuals and artists – cause chaos when they become involved. Frederick the Great said that if he ever wanted to punish a state he would appoint a writer as its governor, and Mann certainly had these words in mind as he considered the events in Munich during the short-lived Soviet Republic, when writers and intellectuals found themselves briefly at the helm of state.

iv These views are 'unpolitical' – that is to say traditionally German. The political view is, of itself, 'left-wing' and (incidentally) inimical to the German tradition, un-German.

Put so baldly, these arguments show themselves to be very close to many later National Socialist statements about the writer's position in society, and it is also clear that, in his attempt to defend himself against his brother's counter-example, Zola, Mann had provided weapons for the right wing to use against the writers who supported the Republic. Zola is seen as a second-rate hack-writer (Mann's phrase for him, which became established in the political language of the Weimar Republic, was a *Zivilisationsliterat*), a *Literat* rather than *Dichter* (the foreign word itself a clear value-judgement); Mann defined this social role in a way which was not merely closer to that of the journalist, and therefore artistically light-weight, but also out of keeping with the German tradition, not really 'German' at all: a word to which Mann's essay all but lends racialist overtones. Thomas Mann's views on republican writers became part of the 'conservative revolution' in the Weimar Republic, part of the stream of increasingly aggressive 'anti-democratic thought' whose historian is Professor Sontheimer.[7] With the increasing political power of the right wing and the increasing threat to the Weimar system, these stereotypes played their part in the gradual erosion of democratic elements in Weimar culture, and in their ultimate destruction by the National Socialists in 1933. They belong in our first paradigm.

One often-remarked-upon example of this revanchist element in Weimar culture is the dispute that shook the literary section of the prestigious Prussian Academy of Arts in the years 1927 to 1933. Among the various problems of this section – to which the cream of Weimar's intellectual life belonged – was a petty-sounding argument about the rights of members living in Berlin as against those in the provinces. The occasion for the argument was as trivial as any golf-club argument about weekend order of play. But thanks to the widespread currency of the polarized language in which the Mann brothers had defined two irreconcilable positions, the parties to the dispute fell almost automatically into political stances, and – despite the fact that the two sides had, at one time, some respect for each other – they moved inexorably to the extremes. So the provincial writers (the producers of the novels of 'Blood and Soil') claimed themselves to be the true poets of the real Germany, and felt (or at least claimed to feel) close to the soil of Germany – an honour which, as has elegantly been pointed out, they 'shared with the slugs and grasshoppers'.[8] They regarded the writers in Berlin (among them people like Heinrich Mann and Alfred Döblin, author of the classic big-city novel in Germany, *Berlin Alexanderplatz*) as rootless internationalists, traitors to art, and out of touch with their people. When they added the notion of being un-German, the provincials were not only following the pattern of Mann's original argument but were announcing a plan of action which was fully revealed only when the National Socialists took over the institutions of the state after 1933 (in Prussia their control over these institutions was particularly strong) and found in the Academy a group of writers more than anxious to participate in purging the Academy of all 'Jewish' elements, in other words anticipating the repression which the new state was about to introduce. They defined these elements which they wished to purge from the Academy according to the direct terms in which their previous argument had been waged. It was not only in the political arena that 1933 saw a settling of old scores.[9]

By this time the Mann brothers had resolved their quarrel, and Thomas Mann had become one of the most committed republicans. In 1922, in an act of some courage, he converted publically to the cause of Weimar democracy, in his own words 'to the cause of the Republic, to democracy or – as I prefer to call it – humanity'. He attempted (as his choice of one of the key words of German idealism made clear) to show the reality which had lurked behind the choice of the title of the Republic: namely the continuity in tradition from German classicism to the modern form of republicanism. Aware that the irrational had too much support and that it was reason – not unreason – which needed the committed support of writers and intellectuals, aware too of the blind alley of political extremism and violence into which the conservative 'non-political' position he had put forward was being steered, Mann changed camp, and immediately felt the power of his own ideas turned against him, recognizing the force of his own arguments as a weapon against republicanism. He was vilified as 'a Judas', betraying the German spirit to political pragmatism, selling out his artistic vocation 'to the times and to Father Ebert'. His great novel, *The Magic Mountain*, which contains the first artistic expression of his change of heart, attracted, among others, a revealing review from within those conservative circles in which Mann would previously have been respected. The review concluded with a chilling sentence which sums up the determination to destroy both the Weimar Republic and the culture and intellectuals identified with it: 'May the day soon dawn when a group of brave young men, with splendid axes, long-handled and broad-bladed, smashes the whole magic mountain into splintering ruins.'[10]

We may take this review as a sign that, already in 1928, the axes were swinging which would later destroy Weimar culture finally. They were fuelled by traditional right-wing ideas which had not been adapted to the new circumstances and to the new understandings of nationalism which the Weimar Republic's situation required, and their momentum would destroy Weimar. That, very abbreviatedly, is our first model.

We examine next, briefly, the appropriateness of that type of historical interpretation which we referred to above: that the Weimar Republic was one form of the dominance of the bourgeoisie and that the Third Reich, although a more radical form, was simply another. This model can, of course, be traced in much of the writing of Stalinist critics and historians about German culture in the Weimar Republic, the view that the system simply pointed towards fascism from the start and that nothing significantly changed in 1933. It was, as is well known, the theory of Trotsky that, in terms of political argument, Stalin's casual equation between Brüning and Hitler was a catastrophe, that the differences between the anti-parliamentarian authoritarianism of the bourgeoisie and the open dictatorship of Hitler were (since they involved the destruction of the organized German working-class movement) rather more important than the similarities.[11] The sort of dismissiveness which Stalin showed to these differences can be found at various places in the writings of Georg Lukács, especially in the famous 'Expressionism debates' in which Lukács argued that the pacifism of the Expressionists (which was, as we saw, closely associated with the ideas of Heinrich Mann in the 'Zola' essay) was not merely ineffective 'romantic anti-capitalism' but ultimately part of the movement towards fascism. Lukács's principal essay ended: 'Just as fascism is the necessary consequence of the November treason of SPD and USPD, so fascism is able to take over the literary heritage of November [i.e. Expressionism].'[12]

More interesting than pursuing this paradigm is to indicate not only the magnificent work of Ernst Bloch immediately after the demise of the Weimar Republic, in trying to 'rescue' from the hands of fascism those elements of bourgeois culture in Weimar which had heedlessly been thrown out by Stalin, but also to suggest that precisely these more discriminating approaches to an understanding of fascism are those adopted in recent work on the culture of this period in the German Democratic Republic. Günter Hartung's exciting publications on the literature of the Third Reich and on the 'tradition' to which it relates, show precisely that readiness to distinguish between a bourgeois literature that, in Marcuse's sense, 'affirms' its society and the literature which will develop into fascism in supplying, beyond this affirmation, 'types of anti-liberal attack' and '"positive" alternative values'.[13] While therefore it is clear that there was once a paradigm which did not distinguish in culture or politics between the Weimar Republic and the Third Reich, and while it is clear that such a paradigm can be useful in counteracting the unpoliticized 'Golden Twenties' image (it served in the German Democratic Republic a similar function to that served in the Federal Republic by the 'Golden Twenties' model, in that it completely isolated the Communist Party from any complicity in Weimar or its collapse, and appeared to bode well for the future of the new state based on uncontaminated principles), we might follow the lead of Bloch and Hartung and be careful about what is in the bathwater we intend to throw out.

Let us return to Heinrich Mann briefly, and to his picture of the artist. Heinrich Mann's fine biographical essay on the writer Emile Zola had been a tribute to the heroic campaigner in the Dreyfus affair, the champion of truth, justice and democracy against the forces of nationalism and militarism. It was particularly appropriate to the Wilhelmine state, which – as intellectuals had complained – had managed to achieve only the first two of the famous trio 'blood, iron and spirit' and which was no less prone than pre-war France to irrational and unthinking attacks on the liberty of intellectuals and on the civil rights of Jews. The essay portrays Zola as the first hero of democratic literature and a model for the republican Germany of the future. In praising Zola, Heinrich Mann had unflattering words for the type of writer enshrined in the figure of his own brother. He called such writers 'intellectual parasites' feeding off a corrupt society, untroubled by thoughts of justice and fairness, aesthetes for whom beauty justifies anything. They are not artists at all, Heinrich claimed, but 'traitors to the spirit'. It is clear that this idea of spirit (*Geist*) was a moral rather than aesthetic or merely intellectual category, and that the elevated notion of spirit was represented in those values which the politically active intellectuals wished to introduce into society.

This eloquent model for the democratic writer corresponded closely to the ideals of the left-of-centre intellectuals around 1918. It appealed to the Expressionists and to many more who held moderate republican positions. It was the inspiration of activists like Kurt Hiller, looking to create a society in which intellectuals were able to realize their ideas of spirit, and to create an intellectual élite, a *Herrschaft des Geistes* (rule of the spirit). But it is also clear, as one looks across the developing culture of the Weimar Republic, that there were many movements on the left which defined their own social position in ways which deliberately repudiated this model. Such views went so far as to see even the model of the intellectual as champion of pure spirit as a mere sop to the realities of society, much as the post-war writers in the *Gruppe 47* came increasingly to see that their role as 'conscience of the nation' amounted to little more than glorified social irrelevance. As the political tensions of the Republic became more acute and as writers felt ever more urgently the need to contribute tangibly towards the halting of National Socialism, the Zola model was increasingly abandoned by those who might once have supported it. Hermann Haarmann has rightly commented that 'the Republic lacked an institutionalized understanding of democracy to which left-wing intellectuals felt committed'.[14] The Zola model of Mann could have had this function, and the effect of devaluing the model of the democratic writer in the Republic forms an aspect of our second paradigm.

Two brief examples may be suggested, the one originating from a writer who was emphatically not a member of the KPD (Communist Party) and the other from the official ranks of the Communist intellectuals, the so-called BPRS (*Bund proletarisch-revolutionärer Schrifststeller*, the Federation of Proletarian-Revolutionary Writers). Walter Benjamin stood Heinrich Mann's argument on its head when (partly as a response to the work in the theatre, reportage and documentary of his friends Bertolt Brecht in Germany and Sergej Tret'jakow in the Soviet Union) he argued that intellectuals could relate to the cause of the proletariat (i.e. to the anti-fascist forces in Germany at the time) not by means of an intellectual process – what they thought *about* the proletariat – but by a recognition of where they, as writers, stood *in* the production process. This theme that even socially critical intellectuals were part of the system of Weimar (or – in the language of the Frankfurt School, which has been one of the few cultural cross-currents from Weimar into the Federal Republic – of the 'Culture Industry', that network of apparent pluralism with which bourgeois societies ensure their safety from intellectual attack) cut completely across Heinrich Mann's arguments. The spirit is not outside society, judging it and following the dictates of a suprasocietal 'spirit'; it is itself a product of society, and it must therefore assume the forms which are appropriate to the particular political struggle in which it is engaged, or it will be merely ineffective.

The BPRS attacked Heinrich Mann's model no less vigorously. Politically, of course, they disapproved of the Weimar Republic with which Mann was identified and were engaged in that fateful campaign against the 'social fascists' (i.e. Social Democrats). So they were equally dismissive of any type of intellectual independence within the cultural sphere, the claim to be 'above the mêlée' of party politics. Already in 1924 Johannes R. Becher (former Expressionist lyricist and later to be a minister in the German Democratic Republic) had attacked as 'a parasite exuding pink-red mimicry'[15] the intellectual who thinks (s)he knows best in politics, and this attack on intellectual politics was continued in the early 1930s as the celebrated periodical of the BPRS, the *Linkskurve*, set about attacking not merely the right-wing future assassins of Weimar culture, but precisely those writers who had most clearly identified themselves with democratic strands within republicanism. The three most telling of these attacks were on the Expressionist dramatist Ernst Toller, who had opposed war with more civil courage than many and who had become committed to elements in the organized trade union movement in Weimar; on the modernist novelist Alfred Döblin, who had committed himself to a democratic independent socialism and encouraged others – even in the face of the crisis of the Republic – to do the same; and, last but not least, the doyen of the Republic's culture, Heinrich Mann.[16]

It is at this point that the close parallels with the third historical paradigm – that of a Republic which destroys itself before fascism comes to bury it – can be seen most clearly. It can be individualized instantly by pointing out that the victims of these attacks by the BPRS – Heinrich Mann and Döblin – had just been attacked in the Academy (no less sharply, if for different reasons) by the hard right, those flat-earthers from the provinces who could not wait to make them pay for being un-German. From historical writing we are familiar with the model of the Weimar Republic as a system eroded equally from both left and right, in which the democratic/republican centre was hollowed away. We are shown this repeatedly in models of the parliamentary elections, as the Communists and National Socialists increased their votes and left the centre hollowed out, and we are familiar with the image of the parliament of the Republic, the *Reichstag* itself, not as a semi-circle (as in traditional models of parliamentary democracy, where the centre is closest to the two wings of politics, and where the extremes are furthest apart) but as a horseshoe, where the extremes are closest to each other and the rest of the parameter (the centre) is out of touch with the extremes. This model has an obvious application to the cultural scene in Weimar.

This perspective on cultural developments was already well known to the observers of the Weimar Republic, and the hollowing-out of the role of the intellectual was a matter of much debate at the time. We may follow these debates in many sources. Perhaps the best known example is provided in an essay published in France in 1927 and widely influential then and since, outside and inside Germany. In his essay 'La trahison des clercs', the French intellectual Julien Benda diagnosed the crisis of the times in these terms. His essay argued that intellectuals formed a kind of spiritual élite in society – hence Benda's use of the term 'clercs' and his natural sympathy for the Zola model as put forward by Heinrich Mann. Intellectuals should follow spiritual and moral absolutes and should be indifferent to the 'passions' and 'material virtues' praised by 'laymen'. Benda saw the pursuit of secular passion (i.e. political and national causes) and the enslavement of intellectuals in 'securing empires' as 'the great betrayal',[17] and he regretted that this malaise affected writers on both right and left. Weimar clearly illustrated Benda's thesis, with the simultaneous evolution not only of the committed writers of the nationalist cause – the nadir of this development was the appointment of former Expressionist writer and subsequently president of Goebbels's literary apparatus, Hanns Johst, as an officer of the SS – but also of the Communist intellectuals committed to partiality (*Parteilichkeit*) rather than to any idea of absolute truth. Karl Mannheim too argued that the problem of his age was the destruction of the transcendent, 'Utopian' element in intellectual positions – he discussed in particular the movement of *Neue Sachlichkeit* [New Sobriety] under this heading – in favour of the purely pragmatic and partisan. He too saw this as a fundamental diminution of the role and social importance of the intellectual, and as damaging to society. Although Mannheim in no way equated the assaults of the left with those of the right, and although he could not be accused (as perhaps Benda might in the application of his thesis to the situation in Germany towards the end of the 1920s) of remaining unaware of the uniquely direct threat to the Republic from the right (although even Mannheim spoke of the situation in 1929 as 'tensionless'[18]), both of them operated with this paradigm of a Republic hollowed out in its essence from both right and left, and both believed that the redefinition of the intellectuals' role in society mirrored and indeed exacerbated this erosion of the democratic humanist centre.

Despite reservations, this paradigm – the self-destruction of the republican intellectual centre-ground – occupies an important place in attempts to classify Weimar culture. John Willett's excellent history of *Neue Sachlichkeit* summarizes the final years of Weimar as follows: 'So the polarization of German life, cultural as well as political, had to continue, and all broadly democratic organizations . . . must be penetrated or split, even at the cost of demolishing them.'[19] The view that the Republic was swamped in polarized, self-destructive violence extends even to the notable landmark with which Hitler's cultural policy announced itself: the ritual book-burning on 10 May 1933. For George Mosse the burning of the books is less a symbol of the barbarians encroaching into the groves of academe than a sobering enactment of 'the educated middle-classes burning their own books'. (Volker Dahm insisted in the subsequent debate at this conference that the book-burning was a purely political action without the overtones of cultural self-destruction.)[20] Hans Mommsen is not alone in speaking (as Benda had) of an historically fateful *sacrificium intellectus*.[21] As we watch the provincial group in the Academy claiming (with all the perverse energy of the in-group argument) that they were not interested in freedom of speech, which was one of the 'destructive' liberties of the city; as we watch Gottfried Benn, arguably the most talented writer to remain in Germany after 1933, openly sneering at the intellectuals against whom the new state had been erected ('the New State has been established against the Intellectuals'[22]); as we read Ernst Jünger's chilling remark that 'it belongs to the sublime and cruel pleasures of this age to participate in the high treason of spirit against spirit'[23] – the idea of the Weimar Republic's culture, like its political system, cutting its own throat before Hitler had time to murder it, has much to commend it. So it is that Michael Stark, in a recent study of German intellectuals from 1910 to 1933, speaks of the final years of the Republic as years of 'self-criticism and self-silencing',[24] an anxiety to bend the neck under the axes of the new masters. Furthermore, the standard history of the Weimar Republic's culture in the German Democratic Republic, without resorting to the Stalinist paradigm which I mentioned above, focuses on such remarks with telling force and tends 'to show the cultural collapse towards the end of the Weimar Republic as the beginning of its final destruction'.[25]

This paradigm has nothing to say about intention. In other words, one cannot necessarily assume that, even in their apparent failure to defend the core of republican culture, the various writers and groups hostile to Weimar deliberately intended to destroy it (although some clearly did), still less that they understood destruction in a similar way. Indeed, it is very evident that their explicit intentions were very divergent. This divergence of intention highlights a weakness in this paradigm, in that it so focuses on theoretical constructs in the light of final effects – this at the expense of intentions – that it is able to bring together (as the totalitarianism theses of the 1950s did) two so polarly opposed movements as communism and fascism. If this is odd in the political arena, then in the cultural discussions it is more questionable still, since – whatever one may say about common responses in relation to the liberal middle-ground – the methodology of the writers of the left (with their attempt to bring scientific, rational method into literature) could not have been further removed from the literary method based on intuition, imagination and rootedness in the soil [*Bodenständigkeit*] beloved of the right. Bringing writers together from any perspective which ignores literary technique – both as conventionally understood or, as Benjamin argued for it, the techniques with which literature relates to the production mechanisms of its day – is a problematical activity. Nevertheless, this basis of comparison (and its faults) lie behind the final paradigm with which we are concerned here, and which corresponds to those historians' paradigms which stress the moments of continuity in the relationship between the National Socialist period and the sweep of a wider historical period.

In brief, the paradigm is that there was a movement in German literature and thought towards the end of the 1920s which was turning – independently of political developments – to a kind of unpolitical conservatism. It is possible, as some have suggested, that this was in response to a feeling that the very substance of perceptual knowledge, science too, was in a state of crisis; or that it was (as Hans Dieter Schäfer in a series of highly influential essays has argued[26]) a sense of tiredness with the period of experimentation which had dominated German literature since around 1910, and a readiness to return to more traditional, inward forms and themes – a tendency which Schäfer traces no less strongly in the type of 'German' realism of the National Socialist writers than in the movements emanating from the Soviet Union and modelled on the nineteenth-century novel which became Socialist Realism; or that (as Erhard Schütz, in what remains one of the clearest accounts of the overall trends of Weimar has suggested)[27] writers merely became disillusioned with their ineffectiveness in a society increasingly dominated by other media. At all events recent years have seen an increasing tendency to identify an overall change of direction at the end of the 1920s, and to group together otherwise disparate elements as moving away from Weimar culture in its generally understood sense. It was as if the entire experiment of Weimar culture, and not just the experimental elements *in* Weimar culture gave way to a form of resigned, apolitical conservatism, which watched unmoved as the Weimar Republic was swept aside.

Quite clearly Schäfer's model has much to be said for it, and it has considerably changed attitudes to the great cesurae of German literary history, 1933 and 1945. It has enabled us to see – based on the work of recent scholars, and also on Hans Klieneberger's pioneering studies of the literature of 'inner emigration'[28] – that there is a deep continuity in literary development over these troubled years. Evidently Schäfer's model has many flaws: it is extraordinary (to put it no stronger) seemingly to ignore the fact that *Neue Sachlichkeit* contained formally innovative and experimental strands, or to put it in a category of conservatism with a tendency towards *metaphysics*[29] – the very antithesis of everything that *Neue Sachlichkeit* was about. It blurs distinctions which are of the very essence of the period, between tradition and the exploitation of tradition in the name of inhumanity. Nevertheless, it has been productive in one area of discussion on which, although it breaks the time-scale of this essay, it is nevertheless appropriate to end.

The myth of the 'Golden Twenties', isolated between the Kaiser's war and Hitler's Germany, was associated with an age that saw itself (for understandable reasons of recent history) standing in equal isolation from the period preceding it. The idea that there was once a golden age of German culture was generated in a society which believed that it too had suspended history, by stopping it completely in 1945, in that moment – the so-called zero hour, the

Stunde Null – when the National Socialist period came to an end and the Federal Republic might be born, starting politically and culturally from scratch, with a *tabula rasa*. This was, as is well known, in marked contrast to the intentions on the other side of the German divide, for the German Democratic Republic began with an open commitment to aligning itself with progressive elements in the German past, including the Weimar Republic's positive ideas. There is no doubt that the work which has recently been done to undermine this notion of the absolute cultural break, and to show among other things the great continuity which exists in the work of those writers such as Andersch, Eich and Koeppen who were to be so influential in the early years of the Federal Republic between the Third Reich and the post-1945 years, would have been unlikely to take place without the encouragement of an historical paradigm that not only broke the rigid divisions set up by arbitrary dates (1914, 1933, 1945) but also restated elements of historical evolution which go beyond ideological divides. Schäfer appears to lack what, for instance, Ernst Bloch's idea of *Ungleichzeitigkeit* [uncontemporaneity] provided – an overall historical theory within which the disharmonies of the historical moment might be reconciled. Nevertheless, his paradigm deserves our attention, no less than the others, and the interest which it arouses in contemporary discussion proves that which is at the heart of our involvement with this period, and indeed with all periods of culture: namely that the past is not dead, it is not even past.

Notes

1. T. Mann, 'Tristan', *Stories of a Lifetime*, 2nd edn (London, 1971), p. 133.
2. Interesting on this theme, the collection by Q. Skinner (ed.), *The return of Grand Theory* (Cambridge, 1985), esp. pp. 12f., 88–90.
3. Hermand and Trommler rightly speak of an 'absence of isms' (*Ismenlosigkeit*) as one of the principal features of Weimar literature (*Die Kultur der Weimarer Republik* (Munich, 1978), pp. 108f.).
4. R. Kershaw, *The National Socialist Dictatorship. Problems and Perspectives of Interpretation* (London, 1985), esp. pp. 1–42; see also Klaus Hildebrand, *Das dritte Reich*, 2nd edn (Munich/Vienna, 1980), pp. 187–94.
5. Hermand/Trommler, op. cit., p. 8.
6. The controversy can be followed most easily through Nigel

Hamilton's *The Brothers Mann: The lives of Heinrich and Thomas Mann 1871–1950 & 1875–1955* (London, 1978). *Reflections of a Nonpolitical Man* has recently been published in English translation (tr. Walter D. Morris, New York, 1983). Heinrich Mann's essay has not been translated, save in 1937 into French. For a differentiation between the ideas expressed in this book and those of the National Socialists, see my own 'Thomas Mann and the dilemma of German Nationalism', *Twentieth Century Studies*, vol. 1 (Leeds, 1969), pp. 18–37. More recent is Keith Bullivant's essay on Mann's political stance in Weimar (K. Bullivant, 'Thomas Mann and politics in the Weimar Republic', in K.B. (ed.), *Culture and Society in the Weimar Republic* (Manchester, 1977), pp. 24–38; discussed by M. Swales, 'In Defence of Weimar: Thomas Mann and the Politics of Republicanism' in A. Bance (ed.), *Writer and society in the Weimar Republic* (Edinburgh, 1982), pp. 1–13).

7. cf. *Antidemokratisches Denken in der Weimarer Republik* (Stuttgart, 1962).
8. Antisthenes, quoted in J. Benda, *The Great Betrayal*, tr. Richard Aldington (London, 1928), p. 48.
9. These debates are recorded in the archive of the Akademie der Künste in Berlin, and have been discussed in I. Jens, *Dichter zwischen rechts und links. Die Geschichte der Sektion für Dichtkunst der Preußischen Akademie der Künste* (Munich, 1971), esp. pp. 93–137.
10. F. G. Jünger, 'Der entzauberte Berg', *Der Tag. Unterhaltungs-Rundschau* (7.3.1928). Other reactions to Mann's change of heart can be found conveniently in K. Schröter (ed.), *Thomas Mann im Urteil seiner Zeit* (Hamburg, 1969), esp. pp. 99ff.
11. *Basic writings of Trotsky*, ed. Irving Howe (London, 1963), pp. 234–66.
12. The debate is fully documented in H. J. Schmitt, *Die Expressionismusdebatte* (Frankfurt/M., 1976). An excellent account of the debate, together with selected documents, is given by F. Jameson (ed.), *Aesthetics and Politics* (London, 1977). This quotation is the last sentence of Lukács's essay 'Greatness and Decline of Expressionism'.
13. G. Hartung, *Literatur und Ästhetik des deutschen Faschismus* (Berlin, 1983).
14. H. Haarmann, 'Literatur unter der Oberfläche', *"Das war ein Vorspiel nur . . .". Bücherverbrennung Deutschland 1933. Voraussetzung und Folgen*, Akademie der Künste (Akademie-Katalog No. 137) (Berlin and Vienna, 1933), p. 75.
15. Quoted by M. Stark, *Deutsche Intellektuelle 1910–1933* (Heidelberg, 1984), p. 276.
16. Rob Burns's essay on the BPRS remains one of the clearest guides to this range of problems ('Theory and organisation of revolutionary working-class literature in the Weimar Republic' in Bullivant, *Culture and Society in the Weimar Republic*, pp. 122–49).

17. This was Aldington's title for the translation of 'La trahison des clercs', cf. ed. cit., pp. 39f., 42 (on Germany), 111f., 117f.
18. K. Mannheim, *Ideology and Utopia* (1929), tr. Edward Shils (new edn, London, 1972), p. 230.
19. J. Willett, *The New Sobriety: Art and Politics in the Weimar Period 1917–33* (London, 1978), p. 204.
20. cf. Horst Denkler and Eberhard Lämmert (ed.), *'Das war ein Vorspiel nur . . .'. Berliner Colloquium zur Literaturpolitik im 'Dritten Reich'* (Berlin, 1985), pp. 35f., 50f.
21. Quoted by Hermann Haarmann, 'Bücherverbrennung 1933', *Arbitrium* (1985), pp. 85f.
22. G. Benn, *Gesammelte Werke*, vol. i (Wiesbaden, 1959), p. 440.
23. E. Jünger, *Der Arbeiter. Herrschaft und Gestalt*, 2nd edn (Hamburg, 1932), p. 40.
24. Stark, op. cit., p. 179.
25. Haarmann, op. cit., p. 88.
26. Schäfer's essays are most readily available in his collection *Das gespaltene Bewußtsein* (Frankfurt/M., 1984).
27. E. Schütz and Jochen Vogt, *Einführung in die deutsche Literatur des 20. Jahrhunderts*, vol. 2 (Opladen, 1977), pp. 17f.
28. H. R. Klieneberger, *The Christian Writers of the Inner Emigration* (The Hague, 1968); R. Grimm, 'Im Dickicht der inneren Emigration', in H. Denkler and K. Prümm (ed.), *Deutsche Literatur im Dritten Reich* (Stuttgart, 1976), pp. 406–27.
29. Schäfer, op. cit., pp. 23f.

THREE

Blut und Boden Fiction and the Tradition of Popular Reading Culture in Germany

EDA SAGARRA

The term *Blut und Boden* (blood and soil) was coined by R. Walther Darré, who combined in his person the offices of head of the *Rasse- und Siedlungsamt* of the SS (1931), Reich minister for food and agriculture (1933) and, from 1934, *Reichsbauernführer.* His *Neuadel aus Blut und Boden*[1] (1930) was both a political manifesto and an effective form of popularizing an already extant racialist literary genre, the *völkisch* peasant epic or drama. (The ugly abbreviation *Blubo* serves as an ironic commentary on the National Socialists' predilection for abbreviation, a process which at once distorts language and dehumanizes those involved.)

An important propagandist function of blood and soil literature in the Third Reich was to counter that 'most serious consequence of the industrialization of Germany', 'the weakening of the peasantry as a class'.[2] Such literature glorifies the German race, by contrast with, and generally at the cost of, other neighbouring races and peoples. In it the peasant farmer is seen to exemplify the German race. To him are attributed qualities of physique, of martial and moral character, which are represented as justifying the right of his people – *Volk* – to lay claim to and settle on lands beyond the political frontiers of Germany; for, as Hitler wrote in *Mein Kampf*, 'Die Natur kennt keine politischen Grenzen' ('In nature there *are* no political frontiers').[3] To the German is attributed a love of the land, a feeling for nature, which no other people is seen to possess in like degree. This, matched with his 'superior culture', will enable the German peasant to revitalize his race and secure the heritage of the German people. As the anonymous author of 'Der politische Bauernroman' in *Bücherkunde* (1935) put it: the peasant was called upon to bring about 'die blut- und rassenmäßige Wiedergeburt unseres Volkes', to be 'mit seiner Familie, seiner Sippe Blutquell des Volkes [and thus assure] daß unser Volk aus der Heimatscholle des Leibes Notdurft und Nahrung erhalten kann' ('the re-birth of our people in blood and race . . . with his family, his tribe, the blood source of the nation . . . that our people may draw their bodily needs and nourishment from their own native soil').[4] The peasant's valorous defence of his *Heimatscholle* (native soil) and the future conquest of neighbouring lands in the new *Heimat* by an army of peasant warriors would, National Socialist propaganda proclaimed, secure Germany her food supplies and the necessary *Lebensraum* in Eastern Europe. Nebulous abstractions, such as 'need' (*Not*), 'need for living space' (*Raumnot*), 'historic mission' or 'ineluctible destiny', abound in *Blut und Boden* fiction as in National Socialist propaganda.

A function of this literature in the Third Reich was to prepare public opinion for the future conquest of *Lebensraum*, one which Darré, for example, planned and pursued systematically.[5] Such propaganda could, however, already draw on a well-established body of literature, of peasant, regional (*Heimat*) or colonial novels. Many of the novels were set wholly or in part in colonies overseas, such as Gustav Frenssen's much-read *Peter Moors Fahrt nach dem Südwesten* – dating back to pre-war days (1906) – or one of the bestsellers of the 1930s, Hans Grimm's *Volk ohne Raum* of 1926. Colonial novels had enjoyed a wide vogue in Germany in the age of Wilhelmine social imperialism and bourgeois *Sammlungspolitik*, and their appeal was paradoxically renewed after the loss of Germany's colonies in the 1920s, as the immediate success of Grimm's 1200-page novel of 1926 indicated.[6] However, after 1933 such colonial models were given little official encouragement. According to guidelines issued by Goebbels in 1933: 'die ganze Kolonialpropaganda [sei] heute keine vordringliche Lebensfrage unseres Volkes' ('colonial propaganda is today no longer a vital, urgent issue for our people').[7] Hitler himself had declared in *Mein Kampf*:

> Die Erwerbung von neuem Grund und Boden zur Ansiedelung der überlaufenden Volkszahl besitzt unendlich

> viel (sic) Vorzüge, besonders wenn man nicht die Gegenwart, sondern die Zukunft ins Auge faßt. . . . Allerdings eine solche Bodenpolitik kann nicht etwa in Kamerun ihre Erfüllung finden, sondern heute fast ausschließlich nur mehr in Europa. (The acquisition of new soil and lands to settle the teeming masses of our people has immeasurable advantages, above all in the context, not of the present, but of the future. . . . However, today the implementation of such a geopolicy will be located not in the Cameroons but virtually exclusively in Europe.)[8]

The axiomatic 'Vergrößerung unseres Lebensraums im Osten', located evidently in 'Rußland . . . und die ihm untertanen Randstaaten' ('expansion of our living space in the East . . . Russia and its satellite states')[9] was accorded pride of place in Nazi ideology, and the settlements of the *Auslandsdeutschen* (German settlers abroad) in the Carpathians, in Hungary or on the Volga, became favoured settings of blood and soil epics written in the Third Reich, as for example in the work of the *Südetendeutsche* Wilhelm Pleyer, or of the *Gauleiter* of the Banat, Karl von Möller.

The particularized local setting is a general feature of *Blut und Boden* writing, as it had been of the *Heimatroman* or *Bauernroman* of the Wilhelmine era; both are set either in the time of writing or at alleged 'historic' moments in the history of the German race and its 'destiny'. Among the preferred landscapes rural Westphalia, Austria, Silesia or Schleswig figure prominently. The epics purport to portray the problems and opportunities of the day, but in fact promote a view of society which is both utopian and orientated towards the past, to an 'age of former glory', an 'idyll that was'. The narrative passages contain references to discrete and identifiable *Heimat* landscapes and their inhabitants, while evoking a society without significant class or property distinctions; if social conflicts play a role, as they frequently did in the *Bauernroman*, they are resolved in blood and soil epics within the compass of the story.[10] The narrative strategy is to project this *heile Welt*, this anachronistic rediscovery of the past, into the future, and to cause the reader to identify it as the characteristic form of society under the aegis of the German state, or, more specifically, as the work of the Führer and the Nazi state. The millenary element commonly associated with fascism and evoked by its ideologies is always present in some form in *Blut und Boden* literature, understood as a kind of 'special grace' conferred on those in whose veins German blood flows.

After the seizure of power by the National Socialists in 1933 authors of *völkisch* literature, such as Stehr, Bartels, Grimm and Frenssen, were given prominence in the purged Academy of the Arts, although a number of the most prominent, including Adolf Bartels and Grimm, did not voluntarily join the Party. On the day of the promulgation of the Enabling Law, Hitler himself outlined the role to be played by artists and writers in the new dispensation:

> Die Welt bürgerlicher Beschaulichkeit ist in raschem Schwinden begriffen. Der Heroismus erhebt sich leidenschaftlich als kommender Gestalter und Führer der Völkerschicksale. Es ist die Aufgabe der Kunst, Ausdruck dieses bestimmenden Zeitgeistes zu sein... Blut und Rasse *werden wieder* zur Quelle der künstlerischen Intuition. (The world of bourgeois passivity is disappearing rapidly. Passionately the Heroic rises up as the future moulder of and leader of the destinies of nations. It is the task of Art to lend expression to this all-pervading Spirit of the Age... *Yet again* blood and race are to be the wellspring of artistic intuition.) (My italics.)[11]

Established *völkisch* writers were quick to obey the call; less well-known figures, such as Friese or Berens-Totenohl rose to prominence and enjoyed not only the patronage of the regime but also, very largely because of diminished competition from exiled or purged authors, of the reading public also. The sales figures after 1933 of selected authors give an idea of the significance of official patronage; the number of copies printed of Grimm's *Volk ohne Raum* rose from 65,000 in 1931 to 250,000 in 1935, reaching 460,000 in 1939; Frenssen's *Jörn Uhl* (1901), the story of a Schleswig peasant, from 315,000 in 1929 to 416,000 in 1935; his *Peter Moor* from 215,000 in 1931 to 238,000 in 1935; Stehr's *Der Heiligenhof* (1918) from 20,000 in 1926 to 159,000, also in 1935. By comparison, other successful Nazi works such as Pleyer's *Der Puchner* (1934) rose to 10,000 in 1935, while Johst's drama *Schlageter*, originally published in 1933, reached 35,000 in 1935 and Erwin Guido Kolbenheyer's *Paracelsus* trilogy (1917–26) reached 30,000 in the same year.[12]

Academic critics turned their attention enthusiastically to the blood and soil theme. The prestigious German literary historical periodical, *Euphorion*, changed its name to *Dichtung und Volkstum* in 1934; in the following years to 1945 its pages abound with analyses of blood and soil literature and its alleged literary predecessors.[13] Scarcely two months after Hitler's speech of 23 March 1933, in a lecture given in May 1933, Paul Kluckhohn, professor of German at Tübingen university and co-editor of the *Deutsche Vierteljahresschrift für Literaturwissenschaft und Geistesgeschichte*, called on writers to create works which would illuminate

> den Zusammenhang der Gegenwart mit der Vergangenheit... Der Mensch fühlt *jetzt wieder* den Zusammenhang mit seinen Vorfahren, mit seiner Umwelt, nicht im Sinne des unfrei machenden Milieus nach naturalistischer Theorie, sondern im Sinne eines naturgegebenen Zusammengehörens mit der Landschaft, in der er aufwächst, mit der Ordnung der Dinge, die ihn umgeben (the bond of the present with the past.... Now *once again* man senses the bond with his ancestors, with his environment, not, as Naturalist theories would have it, in the sense of man in bondage to his milieu, but rather in the sense of a Nature-given belonging to the landscape in which he has grown up, forming part of the order of things which encompass him.) (My italics.)[14]

Common to both writers and academic advocates of *Blut und Boden* literature was the view that their concern was to 're-discover' man's lost identity and his roots in the past, and in the course of this discovery to identify the spiritual ancestors of the National Socialist regime.

In common with all revolutionary regimes, the Nazi state was at pains to establish its legitimacy by asserting its place in a recognized historical and cultural tradition. German historiography in the nineteenth century had increasingly favoured a teleological interpretation of history, focusing on 'great men' as architects of national unity and greatness. Besides the obvious case of Bismarck as *Reichsgründer*, one could cite the manner in which Frederick the Great of Prussia, to whom every form of German nationalism was abhorrent, was stylized in historiography and literature as the 'Architect of the Fatherland'.[15] It was thus relatively easy for historians in the Nazi era to cast Hitler in the mould of the great men who had gone before him and present him in terms of some kind of apotheosis of German historical destiny.

At first sight it might seem as if the variety and sophistication of German literature since the eighteenth century lent itself much less readily to such a process of ideological manipulation by Nazi propaganda. However, on closer examination we see that it is easy, from the standpoint of the late twentieth century, to exaggerate the effort or compromise of conscience that was needed to 'purge' the German literary canon and school and university textbooks in order to establish the Nazi cultural legitimacy. Certainly the expurgation of Jewish authors from literary histories was blatant, and many other well-known names fell a victim to the campaign against what was styled 'alien' (*artfremd*) literature, initiated immediately after the seizure of power. But it is a striking fact of literary life in late nineteenth- and early twentieth-century Germany that, even in the face of the explosion of German letters associated with the names of Kafka, the brothers Mann, Rilke, Hofmannsthal or Brecht, of Döblin, Benn, Musil or Broch, a large proportion of the so-called *Bildungsbürgertum*, the educated élite, still displayed a marked tendency to disparage modern literature, indeed to use the term 'modern' as one of abuse or even ethical condemnation. Moreover, the middle classes generally continued to favour the kind of literature which the Nazis themselves were to promote: nationalist epics, village tales, or historical novels documenting Germany's mighty past. In other words, that kind of legitimacy which the cultural propagandists of the Third Reich sought for blood and soil literature did actually exist.

Furthermore, it is also easy to overlook the fact that the kind of consensus that now exists in educated circles and in the schools and universities both in Germany and abroad, as to what constitutes Germany's 'classical' or 'major' authors, did not exist to the same extent in the 1920s, nor indeed for fifty years before that. An examination of the publishing records for Germany over the seventy years between about 1860 and 1930, as well as of the school and university literary textbooks, conveys a notion of the 'nation's classics' different from current views of what was so regarded. Works of prose fiction which projected, on the one hand, a social utopia or, on the other, a heroic view of German history and culture, such as the novels of Auerbach, Immermann's *Die Epigonen*, the *Oberhof* section of *Münchhausen*, or the works of

Freytag, Dahn or Wildenbruch, had a sustained popular appeal. This is reflected in the steady stream of new editions, of abbreviated versions for use in schools or – in the late nineteenth century, manuals for teaching shorthand.[16] Despite the chauvinism of many of the Freytag or Wildenbruch texts, editors of 'German classics' for use in German departments abroad, favoured the same type of novel as did the German reading public, as is evidenced by the English Catalogue for the period 1860 to 1914 and even beyond.[17]

In the present context the commercial success of Freytag's *Soll und Haben* – in Franz Mehring's often quoted words – 'der meistgelesene aller deutschen Romane des neunzehnten Jahrhunderts' ('the most read of all German novels of the nineteenth century') merits particular attention, both for the sheer volume of editions and, above all, for the sustained character of its appeal. At no time between 1855 and 1933 did more than two or three years elapse between editions.[18] As is well known, the novel helped form German middle-class racialist prejudice against the Jews in their midst, and confirmed prejudices also existent against neighbouring races, particularly the Poles.[19] What is generally overlooked is the manner in which the novel provides role models for the authors of later *Heimat* and *Blut und Boden* novels. Thus in Book Three the hero, Anton Wohlfart, goes with his young associate Karl Sturm to work on an estate owned by the aristocratic von Rothsattels in Poland, and here contrasts the 'culture' and virtue of the scattered German peasant settlers with the brutalized and ignorant Poles. The extended rhetorical passage at the beginning of Chapter Four, Book Three reads like a text from the 1930s:

> Glücklich der Fuß, welcher über weite Flächen des eigenen Grundes schreitet; glücklich das Haupt, welches die Kraft der grünenden Natur einem verständigen Willen zu unterwerfen weiß! Alles, was den Menschen stark, gesund und gut macht, das ist dem Landwirt zuteil geworden. Sein Leben ist ein unaufhörlicher Kampf, ein endloser Sieg. Ihm stählt die reine Gottesluft die Muskeln des Leibes, ihm zwingt die alte Ordnung der Natur auch die Gedanken zu geordnetem Lauf. Er ist der Priester, welcher Beständigkeit, Zucht und Sitte, die ersten Tugenden eines Volkes, zu hüten hat... Und dreimal glücklich der Herr eines Grundes, auf dem durch mehrere Menschenalter ein

> starker Kampf gegen die rohen Launen der Natur geführt ist. (Blessed the foot which traverses its own broad expanse of land; blessed the head which can subject the might of verdant Nature to its wise willpower! Everything that makes a man strong, healthy and good has been given to the farmer. His life is an unending struggle, a victory without end. God's pure air steels the muscles of his body, Nature's ancient order directs his thoughts in orderly sequence. He is the priest, he is the custodian of constancy, of morality, of custom, these first virtues of a people. . . . And thrice blessed is the master of that land on which the mighty struggle against the rough moods of Nature has been fought out over many generations.)[20]

And Anton combines in his character of *exemplum* of the vigorous German race the martial virtues of a leader figure, pitted against the low cunning of semi-savages.

In *Soll und Haben* Freytag was attempting – successfully – to provide an alternative role for the German bourgeoisie in the aftermath of the failed revolution of 1848, which he, after initial enthusiasm, had come to regard with such scepticism. The section on the German settlers in Poland occupies fully one-third of the 700-page book, and it ends with the marriage of the hero's friend to his former sweetheart and the promise of 'eine Schar kraftvoller Knaben' ('a company of strapping lads') to people the rich lands of the East. *Soll und Haben* may lack the deliberate mythification of the peasant warrior and the self-conscious racism characteristic of blood and soil epics; in all other respects it anticipates both theme and values of the genre.[21] In his other, continually reprinted cultural historical writings, particularly *Die Ahnen* (1872–80), Freytag contributed to a further tradition of chauvinistic literature on which National Socialist literature would draw, and which spawned many imitators. These writings, with their intrinsic sense of the racial superiority of the Germans, in fact belong in the wider context of late nineteenth-century chauvinism and imperialism, which manifested itself in British jingoism and in France in the response to General Boulanger in the late 1880s as well as in the more notorious Dreyfus affair. The catalogues of German publishing in the post-1871 period, and more particularly in the reign of Wilhelm II, contain innumerable series of 'German' treasuries of poetry, prose fiction, biography, autobiography, of 'great Germans of the past', 'great Germans of our time', 'great German women'.[22] In the majority of these the stereotyping of hero and heroine are not intrinsically different from those of *völkisch* literature.

Another aspect of Freytag's work linked him at once with the popular village tale and with the ideal peasant communities of blood and soil imagination: this was the social utopia, generally featured in the 'happy endings' of *Dorfdichtung*, such as Immermann, Auerbach or Rosegger popularized. The anachronism of their prescriptive view of society was in every case a response to genuine and deeply felt social problems – in the case of the mid-nineteenth-century village tale to the massive increase both in rural population and rural pauperization and to a series of natural disasters in the shape of bad harvests and cattle plague; in the case of the *Heimat* and *Bauernroman* to the impact of the cyclical crisis in agriculture which hit Germany in the 1870s and affected agrarian regions of Germany for decades, most virulently the under-capitalized farmer. And similarly, blood and soil literature must be seen against the prolonged agrarian depression as part of a recognized tradition. Robert Musil recognized this when he wrote in 1926, the year in which *Volk ohne Raum* appeared, that the *völkisch* novel of the 1920s was 'zwar ein abgeartetes, aber ein legitimes Kind der deutschen Literatur zwischen 1890 und 1910' ('an abnormal but still legitimate child of German literature between 1890 and 1910').[23] (Though this was an overly conservative estimate.) The sustained popularity of such essentially escapist literature among middle-class urban or small-town readers is an eloquent example of their anti-modernism. Renate von Heydebrand's analysis of the character of late nineteenth-century German nationalist literature written specifically for a bourgeois reading public is in fact an acute characterization of the whole tradition which ultimately gave birth to the blood and soil epic:

> Die Unwahrheit des gedanklichen Grundgehalts – immer gemessen am Anspruch dieser Kunst, zeitgenössische Realität in ihrer auch ethisch verbindlichen Substanz (zu sein). . . . Diese Entzeitlichung aber, geboren aus der Angst vor eben diesen Wandlungen, ist das formbestimmende Merkmal aller dieser Dichtungen. (The untruthfulness of the basic intellectual position in terms of the claims of such

art to depict contemporary reality in its ethical substance. . . The temporal dislocation, born of the fear of those very changes, is a salient feature of all these literary works.)[24]

The regional component in this literary tradition, stretching from the peasant epic to *Blut und Boden* fiction, proved to be a powerful popularizer even to readers quite unfamiliar with the landscape and area described. In the Third Reich, people were encouraged, even urged, to identify closely with their own native region. At the same time they found themselves under pressure to associate themselves with the domestic and international successes wrought by a highly centralized, co-ordinated (*gleichgeschaltet*) nation state. Many came to believe in the process that the Third Reich had in fact achieved the reconciliation of the historic tension in Germany's history between particularism on the one hand and the desire for national unity on the other. Goebbels's propaganda was about the identification of the 'whole man' and the 'whole' community with the new state and regime. An important aspect of cultural propaganda, therefore, was to provide models for individual and group identification with smaller local units, which collectively made up the whole, that is, the ancestral landscape as a symbol of the great German *Heimat*, or with the 'village community' as the nucleus of the wider 'national community', in the same way as the Nazi *Blockwart* could feel himself to be an image in miniature of the whole 'caring' party structure. *Blut und Boden* fiction provides countless examples of such models. Many of the classics, such as Stehr's *Der Heiligenhof* or Grimm's *Volk ohne Raum*, open with a rhetorical evocation of an anthropomorphic landscape, such as the lower Rhine, Westphalia, the dykes of East Frisia. Man identifies with that landscape, forms part of it. Much of fascism's appeal lay in its claim to recapture the 'whole man', who was atomized and alienated by modern mechanized and industrialized society, to persuade him that he formed an organic part of a community based on 'soul'.

An important source of popular appeal, as in much escapist literature, lay in the text's ability to create a sense of identification between reader and narrator. The blood and soil epic appears to permit the reader to experience the same sense of 'wholeness of being', of re-discovery of the 'meaning of the world' and his or her own place 'in history' and 'in the community'. As Helmut Vallery puts it:

> Der durch das religiöse Vokabular vermittelte Anschein von Wissen um letzte Wahrheit und Sinnhaftigkeit findet seinen Niederschlag auch in der Schreibweise. Sie ist rigoros auf Identifikation und unkritische Übernahme zugeschnitten, dabei durchgängig auf den Eindruck von Authentizität bedacht. Hinter dem Zeitroman steht, wie mit Regelmässigkeit versichert wird, das tatsächliche Erleben des Erzählers – Brüche in der Erzählweise, wie sie die große Literatur des 20. Jahrhunderts entwickelt hat, werden vermieden. (The impression conveyed by the religious vocabulary of being in possession of ultimate truth and meaning is expressed in the manner of writing. Such narrative technique demands absolute identification and uncritical acceptance on the part of the reader, while a sense of complete authenticity is postulated. The novel of the age, as the reader is continually assured, is based on the actual experience of the writer: breaks in the narrative, characteristic of the great literature of the twentieth century, are avoided.)[25]

Thus Andreas in Stehr's *Der Heiligenhof*, once a passionate and violent man, on whose house a curse lies, is healed through contact with the Westphalian soil he tills and the love of his wife, Johanna, who frequently, as the descriptive passages suggest, actually blends with the natural scene. Andreas becomes in turn the healer of his community, on whom all depend and to whom all look. In Friese's novels (*Der ewige Acker*, 1930, etc.) the imminent destruction of the village community by profiteers – a common theme in the late nineteenth-century *Bauernroman* – is prevented by the heroic acts of a member of the village; in the same way the hero of *Volk ohne Raum*, Cornelius Friebott, ultimately gives his life in the crusade to direct his people towards a new simple life in the lands of eastern Europe. The heroes of such fiction are 'begnadete Führergestalten, die aus ihrer übermenschlichen Persönlichkeit heraus Völker und Reiche neu gestalten, Biologisierungen und Hypostasierungen von "Zeit" und "Schicksal"' ('charismatic leader figures who, through their superhuman personality, mould peoples and empires and who represent in biological form, in themselves, "time" and "fate"').[26]

Despite the focus on masculinity, blood and soil fiction was evidently enjoyed by a large female reading public and popular authors in the genre included a woman writer, Josefa Berens-Totenohl (b. 1891). For the socially conservative German women readers and for Nazi propaganda purposes, one of the attractions of such literature was the idealized role it appeared to afford its heroines. In the stereotyping of women figures, which owed much to nineteenth-century fictional role models, the woman appears variously as girlish and submissive, a kind of child bride, or as mother or sister figure, caring, healing, even saintly. The 'compensation' to women for their biologically determined and strictly circumscribed role lay in the alleged 'spiritual' influence which the 'true' woman exercises over men, especially 'her' man. Johanna in *Der Heiligenhof* is the spiritual healer of her demonic husband Andreas, and is presented as a kind of secular saviour, described in pseudomystical terms. *Blut und Boden* literature makes wide use of the topos of woman as being at one with creation, 'a new Eve', while man remains a Faustian figure. Woman is shown as being capable of immense suffering and endurance, but she suffers passively, while man struggles with his nature and his fate. 'Ein Weib,' writes Stehr, 'weiß nichts von den grauen Tieren der Luft, mit denen ein Mann ringen muß, wenn er auf dem Wege bleiben will, auf den ihn ein hohes Erwarten gestellt hat. Wonach er in Unrast immer langen muß, das trägt sie als unerworbene Sicherheit in der Seele.' ('A woman . . . knows nought of the grey beasts of the atmosphere with which a man must struggle if he is to remain on the path on which a high expectation has placed him. What he must needs restlessly strive after, she carries in her soul as a given certainty.')[27] A woman can thus never achieve the status of tragic figure; tragedy is reserved for the 'active part', for man alone.

The early historiography of National Socialism tended to stress its 'uniqueness', its character as an 'aberration' in German history. The work of historians and literary historians in the more recent past has demonstrated the tradition in which such manifestations belong. Thus in trying to account for the appeal of *Blut und Boden* literature, it is easy to overlook the fact that the function of such literature as serving *nationale Gesinnungsbildung*, the forming of nationalist attitudes from the classroom, through university and into adult life, was a well-established feature of late nineteenth-century German life. It was because Catholic Germans at the time of the founding of the Second Reich were considered, no doubt correctly, to possess too little sense of the 'nationalistic' aim of literature that the *Kulturkampf* legislation in 1873 made mandatory an examination in German national literature for Catholic priests who wished to give catechetics classes in Prussian schools. In Protestant Germany it was customary to associate the ceremony of confirmation – and indeed for Jewish boys the barmitzvah – both of which symbolized the passing from childhood to adulthood, with the gift of a work of German literature rather than with devotional works. The frequency with which the choice fell on Freytag's *Soll und Haben* is eloquent of the way in which the secularized Protestant and Jewish middle classes confused religious allegiance and national identity. However, von Heydebrand, in the work already alluded to, has shown that close parallels, particularly in terms of narrative strategy, actually exist between Catholic fiction of a conservative propagandist type in the period between the *Kulturkampf* and Weimar, and the *völkisch* literature of the same era.

This leads us on to the final question. Who were the hundreds of thousands of readers who read *Blut und Boden* literature? The answer, in general terms is: much the same people who voted for Hitler in one or all of the elections between September 1930 and November 1932, notably the old middle classes (*alter Mittelstand*), whose book culture was much more firmly established than the economic levels of many of their number might lead one to expect, and certainly more so than their equivalents in Britain or France. We have to see the appeal of the *Dorfdichtung* of the 1830s to 1850s to its middle-class readers against a background of anxious observance of the decay of those social groups on which their status and their economic existence rested, the artisans and small farmers. Similarly the success of the *Heimatroman* in the late nineteenth century is to be understood in the context of the great cyclical crisis of German agriculture dating from the 1870s and its consequences; in the same era the vogue for utopian nationalist epics distracted middle- and lower-middle-class readers from their own fears of the impact of industrial and financial capitalism, and of organized labour on their world. So too the success of blood and soil epics in the 1920s and 1930s can be interpreted as a kind of barometer of middle-class anxiety and the literature itself as a form of cypher through which escape from a harsh economic, social or political reality was made to seem possible.

The English reader of the Victorian novel will find in it an acute understanding of the English character and also of the workings of English political and social institutions. The same is true for France of the reader of Balzac or Stendhal. Not so for Germany. Although I have argued elsewhere that there is a great deal of implied social criticism in the major works of nineteenth-century German fiction,[28] the body of the fiction that people liked to read in Germany from the age of the industrial revolution up to the Second World War tended to be strong in ideology but weak or even wholly lacking in social analysis. The problems treated there, however obliquely, are nevertheless serious ones. As Brecht said of blood and soil literature, although the Nazis might treat these issues 'ungeheuerlich falsch',[29] the problems themselves were genuine ones and were the source of deep concern to those who thought themselves affected – by the decline of farming, the spread of industrial capitalism, the erosion of the countryside, the destruction of private property, particularly that of the 'small man'.

To the middle-class reader in the 1920s and 1930s, used to seeing society in fiction presented in terms of social health or social pathology, it was thoroughly acceptable to have the catastrophe of war, inflation, unemployment and the threat to livelihood and status interpreted for him in literature in terms of 'disease' or 'blight', personified in Jewish speculators, Bolshevist agitators, the teeming Slav millions or whatever, undermining the health of the 'true' community.[30] And *Blut und Boden* fiction, for all its aberrant character, does belong, not in the central tradition of great German literature, but in the central tradition of middle-class German reading habits for almost a century preceding the Third Reich.

Notes

1. R. Walther Darré, *Neuadel aus Blut und Boden* (1930); *Landvolk in Not und seine Rettung durch Adolf Hitler*, 2nd edn (1932); *Das Bauerntum als Lebensquell der Nordischen Rasse*, 2nd edn (1933); *Um Blut und Boden. Reden und Aufsätze* (1940) (all Munich).
2. *Mein Kampf* (Munich, 1936) (2 vols. in one), p. 255.
3. ibid., p. 147.
4. *Die Bücherkunde*, 2 (Bayreuth, 1935), p. 290, quoted in Helmut Vallery, 'Völkisch-nationalsozialistische Erzählliteratur', in H. A. Glaser (ed.), *Deutsche Literatur. Eine Sozialgeschichte*, vol. 9 (Hamburg, 1983), p. 148; cf. also Friedrich Friese's affirmation of

Darré's description of cultivating the land as 'eine Aufgabe am Geschlecht' in 'Von der bäuerlichen Ehre', *Dichtung und Volkstum*, 42 (1942), p. 22.

5. Peter Zimmermann, 'Kampf um den Lebensraum. Ein Mythos der Kolonial- und der Blut- und Boden-Literatur', in Horst Denkler and Karl Prümm (ed.), *Die deutsche Literatur im Dritten Reich. Themen, Traditionen, Wirkungen* (Stuttgart, 1976), p. 171.
6. For a general discussion of colonial literature in Germany, cf. Hugh Ridley, *Images of Imperial Rule* (London, 1983).
7. Quoted in Zimmermann, op. cit., p. 170.
8. *Mein Kampf*, pp. 151f.
9. ibid., p. 742.
10. This was, for example, a key theme in Wilhelm von Polenz, *Der Büttnerbauer* (1895) or in the stories of Peter Rosegger, and one which Hans Grimm also featured in *Volk ohne Raum*.
11. Quoted in Ralf Schnell in 'Die Zerstörung der deutschen Historie. Versuch über die Ideologiegeschichte faschistischer Ästhetik', in *Literaturwissenschaft und Sozialwissenschaften 10. Kunst und Kultur im deutschen Faschismus*, Schnell et al. (ed.) (Stuttgart, 1978), p. 48.
12. All information in this article on size and number of editions is taken from the relevant volumes of W. Heinsius, *Allgemeines Deutsches Bücherlexikon*, vols. 13–19 (Leipzig, 1864ff.), *Hinrichs Funfjahrs-Katalog*, vols. 9–13 (Leipzig, 1896ff.), and *Deutsches Bücherverzeichnis*, vols. 1, 4, 7, 8, 12, 13 and 17 (Leipzig, 1916ff.).
13. cf. the vogue for selected 'authors of peasant life', e.g. Stehr (1935, vol. 36), Immermann/Gotthelf (1939, vol. 38) and Friese (1936, vol. 37; 1941, vol. 41; and 1942, vol. 42).
14. Schnell, op. cit., pp. 48f.
15. Eda Sagarra, 'The image of Frederick II of Prussia in the Century before Unification', *European Studies Review*, 4 (1974), pp. 23–32.
16. Evidence of the sustained popularity of Auerbach's *Barfüssele* and Immermann's *Der Oberhof*, generally published separately from the early 1860s, is to be found in Hinrichs et al. (cf. note 12), 1858–1935.

Year	vol.	*Barfüssele* as separate publication	All works incl. *Barfüssele*	Immermann *Der Oberhof* as separate publication	All works incl. *Der Oberhof*
1858–59	13	–	1	–	1
1863–67	14	1	16	1	3
1869–75	15	4	20	6	13
1877–79	16	–	16	2	8
1880–84	17	?	13	3	20
1885–88	18	1	2	1	7

Year	vol.	*Barfüssele* as separate publication	All works incl. *Barfüssele*	Immermann *Der Oberhof* as separate publication	All works incl. *Der Oberhof*
1889–91	19	1	4	3	4
1892–95	9	–	5	5	6
1896–1900	10	1	5	4	6
1901–05	11	1	3	7	12
1906–09	12	2	7	2	7
1910–12	13	3	10		
1911–14	1	11	68	7	11
1915–20	4	2	13	6	10
1921–25	7	5	13 vol. 8	12	21
1926–30	12	7	22 vol. 13	9	13
1931–35	17	1	6	1	4

Barfüssele went into its 46th edition on the eve of the First World War (1912). Both were published as textbooks for use in school and *Der Oberhof* was published in shorthand for teaching purposes (as was frequently *Soll und Haben*).

17. Auerbach's *Barfüssele* was published in 14 editions in England, 1863–1905, and Immermann's *Der Oberhof* in 3, though Heine remained the most popular author apart from Goethe; Freytag's *Soll und Haben* appeared in three separate editions within two years of its publication; two further editions followed in 1873 and 1893; in all, 23 separate publications appeared in England between 1855 and 1921, including the *Bilder* (with 'Der Staat Friedrichs des Großen' and 'Die Erhebung Preußens' featuring prominently) and *Die Ahnen*. Moreover, other nationalist writers, such as Wildenbruch and Frenssen, found a public in English: *Jörn Uhl* (1901), for example, was published in English translation in 1905 and 1923, while *Peter Moors Fahrt nach dem Südwesten* (1906) appeared in 1908 and again in 1914 and 1915; cf. *The English Catalogue of Books* (London, 1873–1935).
18. Every volume of Heinsius, Hinrichs, etc. (cf. note 12) from 1855 to 1935 contains reference to at least one and usually several editions of the novel. Volume 12 of *Deutsches Bücherverzeichnis* devotes three and a half pages (1159–62) to editions of the Freytag works in print, and five to Goethe, two to Schiller, one and a half to Lessing.
19. e.g. E. Kohn-Bramstedt, *Aristocracy and the middle classes in Germany. Social types in German literature 1830–1900* (London, 1937); Roy Pascal, *The German Novel: Studies* (Manchester, 1956); and Eda Sagarra, 'The function of stereotypes in Gustav Freytag's

Soll und Haben', *The Writer as Witness: Literature as Historical Evidence*, Tom Dunne (ed.) (Cork, 1987).

20. *Soll und Haben* (Munich, 1978), pp. 397f.
21. ibid., p. 624: 'ich stehe jetzt hier als einer von den Eroberern, welche für freie Arbeit und menschliche Kultur einer schwächern Rasse die Herrschaft über diesen Boden abgenommen haben. Wir und die Slawen, es ist ein alter Kampf. Und mit Stolz empfinden wir, auf unserer Seite ist die Bildung, die Arbeitslust, der Kredit.'
22. cf., for example, entry in Hinrichs, *Fünfjahrs-Katalog*, vols. 10, pp. 256f.; 11, pp. 281f.; 12, pp. 263ff.
23. Robert Musil, *Prosa. Drama. Späte Briefe* (Hamburg, 1957), p. 611; quoted in Vondung, op. cit., p. 52.
24. Renate von Heydebrand, *Literatur in der Provinz Westfalen 1815–1945. Ein Literaturhistorischer Modell-Entwurf* (Geschichtliche Arbeiten zur Westfälischen Landesforschung, Geistesgeschichtliche Gruppe, Band 2; Veröffentlichungen der Historischen Kommission für Westfalen XXII B (Münster, 1983), p. 89. Compare also F. Sengle, 'Wunschbild Land und Schreckbild Stadt. Zu einem zentralen Thema der deutschen Literatur', *Studium generale,* 16 (1963), p. 619: 'Zum Wesen des Mythos gehört es, daß einem Phantasieprodukte unmittelbarer Realitätscharakter verliehen wird.'
25. Vallery, op. cit., p. 151.
26. ibid., p. 150.
27. Hermann Stehr, *Der Heiligenhof* (Leipzig, 1926), p. 43.
28. Eda Sagarra, *Tradition and Revolution* (London, 1971) (German trans., Munich, 1972).
29. Bertolt Brecht, *Gesammelte Werke* in 20 Bänden, Suhrkamp Verlag with Elisabeth Hauptmann (ed.) (Frankfurt, 1973), vol. 20, p. 222.
30. cf. Peter Zimmermann, *Der Bauernroman. Antifeudalismus, Konservatismus, Faschismus* (Stuttgart, 1975), pp. 151ff.

FOUR

The Predicament of the Weimar Republic

EBERHARD JÄCKEL

The failure of the democratic Weimar Republic and the conditions that made the rise to power of Hitler possible have traditionally been ascribed to Germany's defeat in the First World War and, in particular, to the Versailles Treaty which followed it. While this interpretation is not entirely wrong, it misses the central point. My thesis is that the principal predicament of the Weimar Republic was not defeat or the difficulties which its governments faced in the post-war years, but the social and political structure of German society. Since this structure and the predicament which resulted from it had their origins in the nineteenth century it is necessary to look first at the structure of the Wilhelmine Reich.

German society was then divided roughly into two conflicting classes which can, with some over-simplification, be described as the monarchists and the democrats. By monarchists, I mean the ruling class in the German Empire of 1871, comprising several different elements, rather than the adherents of a particular form of state. Politically the monarchist class was represented by the conservatives, the old Prussian nobility, and to a large extent, the landed aristocracy. It was organized in the Conservative and the National Liberal parties. Socially the Conservative Party represented the nobility, followed by officers, the bureaucracy and other groups; the National Liberal Party, the second largest in the Empire, represented the upper levels of the bourgeoisie. These two groups had fought each other in the revolution of 1848 and again in the Prussian constitutional conflict between 1862 and 1866, before Bismarck's victory over the Austrians at Sadowa. Subsequently they had united and together they effectively controlled the state.

The monarchists were opposed by another group which in the beginning was not very significant but which grew in importance from 1871 onwards; for convenience this group will be called the democrats. Politically, it was represented in or by three different political parties: first of all by the Social Democrats or SPD, the party of the working class; secondly, by the Catholic Centre Party, where the common tie was religion; and finally by a third party, the Left-Wing Liberals, as I will call them. The Liberals had been split by Bismarck in 1866, when one faction, the National Liberals (mentioned above), had gone over to the ruling classes, had been absorbed by them and shared control of the state power, while another faction had remained in opposition.

These three 'democratic' groups had been engaged by Bismarck in three consecutive struggles. First he fought the Liberals during the revolution of 1848–9, and again, even more forcefully, in the so-called constitutional conflict after he had become Prussian prime minister in 1862. This was followed by the *Kulturkampf*, a fight against political Catholicism and against the Centre Party. When that conflict was over Bismarck opened the third domestic battle, this time against the working class and the socialists, and enacted laws against the Social Democratic Party. By 1890 it had, however, become evident that his attempts to suppress these three groups had failed and that there remained a very strong opposition or coalition of parties hostile to the Bismarckian system.

In 1871 the ruling classes, the monarchists, won a majority of 60.3 per cent of the votes while the opposition won less than a third. The monarchists' support declined and the democrats grew at their expense until, by 1884, for the first time, they won a sizeable majority of votes. From 1890 onwards they constantly had a majority of seats in the Reichstag. The monarchists could still remain in power because, even though Germany had a constitution with universal male suffrage, the chancellor was not required to have the support of a majority in parliament. Had he been required to have that support, as is the normal case in a democracy, the rule of the monarchists would have ended in 1890. The monarchists, although they were a declining class and a minority both in parliament and in the population, remained in control of the state.

They were confronted by the rising class of the democrats, who were soon to have a two-thirds majority and who demanded either that they have a share of power, or else possess it totally. It was foreseeable that sooner or later the democrats would reach this goal, and the decisive question, crucial in the history of Germany as of many other countries, was how this transition of power would be achieved. There is an almost comparable situation, for example, in France before 1789 where an aristocratic minority faced a rich, strong and well-developed bourgeoisie which wanted a share in ruling the state; when the revolution came the minority was completely displaced. After 1890 it was quite obvious to many contemporaries that the decisive question would be how the transfer of power would come about. The various possible answers to this question were widely discussed. One answer was constitutional reform, or what was called parliamentarization. This would require the Reich chancellor to have a majority in the Reichstag, and once such a constitutional reform had been pushed through the question would be solved. If and when the government was required to have a majority in parliament, the democrats would form a government, but the monarchists were, of course, not prepared to retire without resistance. Another answer to the question of how this transition of power would come about was revolution, revolution which was advocated (at least verbally) by a large number of the Social Democrats. And a third answer, which was increasingly discussed in the first years of the twentieth century, was war. War was dreaded by some monarchists but desired by others.

In the event the constitutional reform came in October 1918, in the wake of defeat but while the Kaiser was still on the throne and before the outbreak of the revolution of November 1918. When the constitution was changed so that the government was required to have a majority in the Reichstag, the democrats automatically came to power. Three parties, the SPD, the Centre and the German Democratic Party now joined in a coalition which became known as the Weimar Coalition because the National Assembly met in Weimar rather than in revolutionary Berlin. They established a new government and adopted a new constitution. In some respects little had changed, since the democratic parties had formed a parliamentary majority for many years. In the last pre-war elections in 1912, the monarchists had won only 26.3 per cent of the vote and their share fell slightly between then and 1919. This was largely due to the difficulties faced by the conservative People's Party. Between 1912 and 1919 the democrats' share of the vote rose from 63.5 per cent to 76.1 per cent.

Historians often succumb to the temptation of seeing the First World War as marking a clean break; they place a full stop after the Empire and begin a new paragraph with the Weimar Republic. Such an approach overlooks the strong elements of continuity between the two systems. The transition of power from the declining monarchist class to the rising class of the democrats took place in 1918, but the change proved to be of short duration. In June 1920, in the first normal national elections after the war, the democrats lost their majority of the votes for the first time since 1884 or 1890, dropping to 43.6 per cent. It was a strange development. The German democrats had had a majority since the last quarter of the nineteenth century, but the very year after they finally came to power they lost that position and in subsequent elections never regained it. The election of 1920 was crucial.

If the monarchists had then been returned to power Germany would have had almost the same government as it had before the war, and it would have appeared that the wheel had turned full circle and things had returned to normal. This did not happen – the monarchists never did win a majority of votes or seats. So whereas up to 1920 one group had always been in the majority, after 1920 none of the leading political groups held this position. One can provide a long list of explanations as to why the democrats lost their long-held support in 1920. One principal reason was a split within the working class. The Social Democratic Party had divided, with first the Independent Socialists and then the Communist Party breaking away from the bulk of their colleagues. If the votes cast for the Independent Socialists and the Communists, 20 per cent of the total, had been added to the democratic votes, they would have been exactly as strong as they had been in 1912.

The problem now was that neither of the two leading classes in Germany fighting for state power had a majority after 1920, and it was this deadlock which made the political struggle in the Weimar Republic so severe. Both groups tried to return to power, the monarchists trying to regain the position which they had before 1918 and the democrats trying to regain that which they had before 1920. In this situation the position of the president of the Republic was of extreme importance because he had a number of prerogatives which enabled him not only to appoint chancellors but also to pass emergency decrees. The first president after the abdication of the Kaiser in 1918 had been Friedrich Ebert, a Social Democrat. He died in February 1925. In the first ballot for the ensuing presidential election an absolute majority was required, whereas on the second ballot a relative majority was sufficient. For the first ballot almost all the German parties presented a candidate, but in the second ballot the two main groups each ran a single champion. The monarchists put forward Field Marshal von Hindenburg, who in every sense of the word had been a leader of the monarchists; together with Ludendorff he had been practically dictator of Germany during the last years of the war. The democrats merged to nominate one candidate, Wilhelm Marx, one of the leaders of the Catholic Centre Party. The fight was very close. In the end Hindenburg won 14,655,060 votes and Marx 13,751,000; had Marx received 1 million more votes he would have been elected president. On the second ballot all the other parties had withdrawn their candidates except for the Communists; they insisted on running Ernst Thälmann, who gained just under 2 million votes. Had most of these been added to Marx's total the democrats would have won the 1925 presidential elections.

After the victory of their candidate the monarchists, although well aware that they had no chance of coming to power as a result of their support in the country, hoped to regain their lost influence through the exercise of the president's powers. Ideally they would have liked to restore the Kaiser, but precise forms of government were relatively unimportant to them. In the short run they hoped to establish a different sort of republic from that which had operated since 1919, and to secure their position of state power without having to win a majority. They could do so, as they realized soon after 1925, by using the combination of different prerogatives or articles in the constitution of the Weimar Republic. According to Article 48, the president could take any steps necessary to restore law and order should they be considerably disturbed or endangered. And the president alone decided when exactly that state of emergency was reached and what measures could be taken. The constitution had originally called for a law to provide detailed regulations for carrying out Article 48, but such a law was never passed and Hindenburg resisted its passage because he knew very well that his prerogatives would be diminished. The president's power under Article 48 was restricted, however, by the stipulation that he, the president, had to inform the Reichstag immediately of any such emergency measures taken and that the Reichstag itself could then annul those measures by a simple majority vote. Thus the president's great emergency powers could be nullified if and when the majority of the members of parliament so wished. In his first three or four years as president, Hindenburg ruled more or less according to the constitution.

In the 1928 elections the democrats scored a limited victory and returned to power. For the last time until 1969 a Social Democrat became chancellor in Germany. But in 1930, finally, Hindenburg made a definite attempt to change the constitution and to bring the monarchists back to power. Once again it must be emphasized that this did not mean a recall of William II from his exile in the Netherlands; that was a separate matter. The principal question was which of the two parties or groupings would exercise power, would be able to decide on the most important national questions. Hindenburg was free to appoint a chancellor of his own choice, and in 1930 he nominated Heinrich Brüning, a politician from the Centre Party but one who was sympathetic towards the monarchists and who even wanted to help restore the monarchy. Brüning did not command a majority in the Reichstag but it was not intended that he would govern in this way. In the event of a bill being rejected by the Reichstag Hindenburg would enact the same bill as a decree under Article 48. That is what he did soon after he had appointed Brüning. The Reichstag was able by a simple majority vote to nullify the president's decree, and that happened to Brüning's cabinet soon after his appointment in July 1930. But in that case the president had yet another weapon in reserve. According to Article 25 he could dissolve the Reichstag. Within sixty days of a dissolution a general election had to be held, and Hindenburg first dissolved the Reichstag in July 1930, then made full use of this period of sixty days that followed. During this time his chancellor could continue to govern without parliamentary interference as no Reichstag sessions were held after the dissolution.

By the time these elections were held in September 1930, a new party had arisen which in the beginning had nothing to do with this struggle between the two leading classes: Hitler's National Socialists. In the elections of September 1930 they scored their first victory, increasing their percentage of votes from 2.6 to 18.3 and their number of seats from 12 to 107. After that Brüning could not hope to have a majority in parliament, but he was tolerated for some time by the Social Democrats who abstained from nullifying the decrees that were passed by Hindenburg. The president and his circle continued with their policy of conservative restoration and after some time dismissed Brüning and appointed another conservative chancellor, Franz von Papen, in 1932. Again, the Reichstag was dissolved. That gave Papen the chance of governing freely until the next elections. Then, in July 1932, the Nazi Party became the strongest party in parliament and gained 37.3 per cent of the votes. That was, by the way, the highest vote that Hitler ever gained in free elections; he never won an overall majority.

The policy of conservative restoration pursued by Hindenburg, under Brüning and Papen, had opened the way to a third political party, the Nazis, who within two years became the strongest party in the state. That made it more and more difficult for Hindenburg and his chancellors to rule. For example, when the Reichstag elected in July 1932 convened in the following month, it passed a vote of no confidence in Papen's government by the enormous majority of 512 to 42 with 5 abstentions. Out of 600 members of the Reichstag less than 50 voted in favour of Hindenburg's candidate. There was no other means of escaping from that permanent cabinet crisis except to dissolve the Reichstag, and this was done again in November 1932. The votes for the Nazis dropped slightly from 37.3 per cent to 33.1 per cent but they remained the strongest party.

Hindenburg was most reluctant to appoint Hitler. The president was not in favour of Nazism or of Hitler personally, but none of the leading classes or groups in German society commanded a majority and he had to find a way out of the political crisis. That is why, after Papen had to be dismissed and the third of Hindenburg's chancellors, General von Schleicher, had been appointed, Papen tried to construct a new coalition government which would include Hitler. He made an attempt at what he called fencing Hitler in, forcing him to accept the responsibility of power and form a government in which the Nazis would be outnumbered and, he hoped, outmanœuvred by the monarchists. This finally happened in January 1933 when Hindenburg appointed Hitler. Such a development held considerable advantages for Hindenburg. Hitler had, as we have seen, only a third of the seats in parliament, but together with his conservative partners he was short of an overall majority by only 45 votes, and this was a much broader parliamentary basis for governing than either Papen or Schleicher had enjoyed. That was the reason why Hindenburg appointed Hitler chancellor in 1933.[1]

Note

1. The thesis of this chapter has been explained more fully in my books *Hitler in History* (London, 1984) and *Hitlers Herrschaft* (Stuttgart, 1986).

FIVE

The Weimar Republic between the Second and the Third Reich: Continuity and Discontinuity in the German Question, 1919–33

IMANUEL GEISS

One of the great problems which has tormented the German mind ever since 1945 is 'Why Hitler'? This question has found its heart-searching expression in much German historical scholarship since the war, institutionalized in the Munich Institut für Zeitgeschichte and the splendid work which it has done for more than thirty-five years. A more subtle consequence has been the search for the relationship between continuity and discontinuity in recent German history, roughly in the period from Bismarck to Hitler.[1] Since 1960 this has been provoked by the new round of debate over the First World War and Germany's role in its origins, a debate sparked off by Fritz Fischer's *Griff nach der Weltmacht*[2] and the ensuing 'Fischer Controversy'.[3]

In the course of German history[4] from the Second to the Third Reich, World War I and the Weimar Republic constituted the historical links between them. The First World War was the supreme universal factor that made for disruption or discontinuity everywhere, and the Weimar Republic was only the German means of dealing with the new post-war situation. All elements of continuity in recent German history, therefore, have to pass, as it were, through World War I and the Weimar Republic.

Because of the enormity of the events associated with Nazism and the Third Reich, this could not be an ordinary historical problem capable of being discussed in a purely academic or detached way. Inevitably, moral and ideological overtones crept into the debates. This is indeed one of the great 'peculiarities of German history' in

Blackbourne and Eley's phrase. As usual, there were positive and negative effects: the question of 'German war guilt' in 1914,[5] the (absurd) charge that there was or is a constantly wicked or aggressive German national character which has caused all the trouble, or that the Germans had not changed enough in, for example, the Revolution of November 1918 and, consequently, in the Weimar Republic. Yet surely, after so many years of self-critical introspection, the time has come for Germans to move on to the next stage of synthesis with wider historical horizons, if only to catch up with recent achievements outside Germany. The passage of time, a new globalization of world history,[6] new research on the wider historical background to the origins of World War I (in recent years increasingly taking place outside Germany), and the new perspectives offered by the manifold challenges of our present, should now render it possible to approach the whole complex with a fresh mind. However, it is important to avoid two basic traps which have marred much recent discussion, including my own contributions to research and debate:[7] too narrow a focus on Germany's part in World Wars I and II, and too narrow a concept of continuity, particularly when this term is loaded with a conscious or subconscious tinge of moralizing. Both dangers can only be avoided by rigorous intellectual self-discipline (including self-criticism) and by the widening of historical perspectives to truly global horizons. The whole point is missed or even abused, however, if universality becomes no more than a new cloak for national partisanship.[8]

Historical explanation has to go back a long way beyond 1890 or even 1871.[9] Instead, World War I has really to be treated as a supreme event with shattering consequences, an event which requires a truly global approach for its proper explanation.[10] In 1914 the European state system exploded from within, from its German centre. The consequences of this development led, amongst other things, to an extreme widening of the political spectrum both to the left (communism) and to the right (fascism and Nazism). This in turn resulted in polarization and an increase in tensions and violent conflicts which tore the Weimar Republic apart and weakened many other contemporary societies in Europe.

Another key category which helps us to achieve a degree of objectivity is that of 'historical mechanisms'. In particular, power and the pursuit of power[11] are not exclusive monopolies of Germany and the Germans. Instead, power, the pursuit of power and their consequences are all universal. In every instance where they are mentioned here in the context of German history, they are only meant as German illustrations of phenomena which are universal in time and space. Only their specifically German variations, with a few unique German features such as Germany's central position in Europe, make for those extraordinary complications of German history which appear to defy all rational explanation. In order to make sense of recent German history a quasi-scientific, even mechanistic approach must be adopted, if only to cut out all emotions and moralizing judgements. This is why 'historical mechanisms' is one of the key concepts in this study.

Correspondingly, in such a broad historical sweep there is no longer room for tacking any moral value judgements on to the word 'continuity'. It simply serves here as an essential category for a better understanding of the perennial tensions in history between change and the preservation of identity. Continuity is not the same as identity, sameness, but it implies modification of a given historical subject and even implies changes, more or less radical, in form and partly also in substance. In such a wider definition, continuity is to be found in all world history and to mention it here might be considered an empty, commonplace statement. But it is fascinating to see how it operates in the German context. As a tool for historical analysis, it can make for a better understanding of the tension between change and non-change, both in general and in our particular case for German history between the two world wars.

If we take continuity as the most universal or general starting point, it makes many otherwise inexplicable factors fall into their places and form rational patterns. These seem irrational only because so many factors are involved which make them almost hopelessly complicated. One reason, again a universal one, is that our history textbooks emphasize dramatic changes, breaks and discontinuities. Continuities usually emerge much later, often after decades or centuries, and are therefore much more difficult to observe, analyse and appreciate.

In the German case, we have obvious elements of discontinuity with the rapid change of political regimes in Germany in the first half of the twentieth century, from Imperial Germany through revolution, the Weimar Republic and the Third Reich to the Federal Republic and the German Democratic Republic (GDR). These are condensed into the household dates of 1918, 1933 and

1945–9 and everything they stand for: the collapse of the monarchy and the November Revolution of 1918, the stormy birth of the Weimar Republic in early 1919, and its pseudo-constitutional death in early 1933 which opened the flood of violence of the Third Reich, first at home and subsequently abroad.

Because the Weimar Republic lasted at most only fourteen years there are also, of course, strong elements of personal continuities, even identities, linking the two world wars. Hitler, the corporal of World War I, became Germany's Führer in World War II, and the junior officers of 1914–18 became the generals and field marshals of 1939–45. There is also a dialectical continuity, as in the members of the Prussian aristocratic élite associated with 20 July 1944, the most serious effort to overthrow Hitler from within.

However, as historical distance increases through the passage of the years, more fundamental elements of continuity are coming increasingly to the fore. Behind the turbulent changes of façades we can see at work historical mechanisms which make for an astonishing degree of continuity or continuities. At present in the two German states we even have a split of historical continuities, with the GDR officially claiming to represent the best of German historical and cultural traditions, leaving to the Federal Republic only the odious aspects of German traditions. (Objectively, it is rather the other way round; in fact, the GDR is carrying on some of the worst traditions or continuities from Germany's recent past – totalitarian rule, manipulation of people and truth, censorship, indoctrination, the militarization of society and the fact that it is a police – or, rather, secret police – state. The novelty is that it does so as a communist state.)

By the same token, many elements of continuity from Imperial Germany to Nazi Germany are emerging, and inevitably they do so via the Weimar Republic because of its interim situation between the Second and the Third Reich. There is, however, no historical guilt by association implied. We all know the vast array of continuities, sometimes even of identities that have stifled the development of the Weimar Republic. The bureaucracy, the army, industry, organized agriculture, the churches, judges and most of the academic establishment were all shaken or at most reformed but were not thoroughly changed by the November Revolution. The widespread claim that the failure of a genuine social or socialist revolution in 1918–19 led straight to the rise of Nazism is, however, at best a historical speculation which leads at worst to a new ideological bias. Similarly, an excessive concentration on Germany's part in unleashing World War I has outlived its usefulness. Such an approach has a necessarily narrow focus on German history between 1871 or 1898 to 1914–18. Inevitably it blurs or even obscures other important factors outside Germany as well as aspects of the German past before the establishment of the Reich in 1871 or Bismarck's coming to power as Prussian prime minister in 1862.[12] It was in these debates, however, that the concept of continuity in recent German history was first thrown up tentatively,[13] and was later discussed in more detail.[14]

Notwithstanding the great intellectual stimuli and political values of German research and discussions in the quarter century since Fischer's *Griff nach der Weltmacht*, their overwhelmingly German terms of reference and the unavoidable moral burden of history imposed by Nazism and World War II are producing a kind of intra-German statement that makes it even more urgent now to move on to more European or even worldwide historical perspectives. Today they alone appear adequate to the global challenges of our present. Such a new approach requires the elimination of any kind of moralizing, whether intended or not, even at the risk of being charged with amoral cynicism. This risk is particularly great in the case of German historians.

The supreme element of continuity in the problems discussed in this essay might be the permanence of the German Question. This concept could provide intellectual coherence to a vast field of historical knowledge, it could help to broaden the view of German history and make an objective approach easier. Literature on the German Question is at present growing rapidly.[15] In the absence of any universally accepted or recognized definition of what is the German Question, a private definition must do provisionally. It can take an interrogative form:

'Are the Germans to have a national state of their own, as is the case with most other nations or nationalities?'

'If so, within which frontiers?'

'With which internal structure (centralised or federal)?'

'With what consequences for themselves, their immediate neighbours, for Europe and the world at large?'

By raising a roster of counter-questions this definition of the German Question offers several advantages. It makes possible a flexible analysis of what would otherwise be confusingly complex material taken from German as well as from European history. It allows us to parallel the German Question with other national questions, at least in Europe, because the same criteria can also be applied to the national questions of the Poles, Slavs, Italians, Czechs, Hungarians, Romanians or Irish (to confine ourselves to nineteenth-century Europe).

The German Question is no longer obsessively isolated, but remains squarely within the context of European history, directly linked to all the other national questions of the Continent. This, however, made the German Question particularly complicated and explosive: Poles, South Slavs and others could fulfil their rising national aspirations and give comprehensive answers to their national questions only at the expense of Germans, because they were all incorporated into a German state, Austria and/or Prussia. Indeed, the more extensively their aspirations were formulated, the more they clashed with the extensive demands of the Germans, in particular when it came to drawing new national borders. Thus, conflicts became inevitable.

Most national questions in Europe began when the particular nation or nationality had either lost its own political state, whether this state had been sovereign or autonomous (the Poles in 1795, the Irish in 1800, the Germans in 1806), or else started to fight for one, as in the case of the South Slavs with the Serbian uprising against the Ottoman Empire in 1804. Thus, the German Question was formally opened in 1806, with the end of the First German Empire, the medieval Holy Roman Empire of the German nation. However weak the Old Empire had been in its last centuries, it had provided at least a minimum of common political institutions and some collective, quasi-national identification for most Germans. After its demise the question arose automatically of how the Germans were to be organized politically in future. With it, inexorably, the power question (*Machtfrage*) cropped up again for the Germans, who were then at the height of their cosmopolitanism: was Germany to be a power vacuum or a power centre?

Throughout their history Germany and the Germans have moved backwards and forwards between the extremes of power vacuum and power centre. Such oscillations between the two poles are perfectly normal. But perhaps nowhere in world history were the changes between power vacuum and power centre so frequent, extreme and violent, or nowhere had they had more devastating consequences for the world, as in the case of Germany during the past two centuries. This has nothing to do with the alleged wickedness or inherent political stupidity of the Germans, but with universal historical mechanisms and the particular complications of German history.

The *Machtfrage*, the question of power, has been the hard core of the German Question ever since 1806. To understand it involves examining not only geography and numbers (the quantitative factor) but also what could be called the qualitative factor, the impact of economic and social developments or structures. These, however, are much more complex and subtle, and they defy any rough-and-ready analysis; that is why they will be dealt with here only after an examination of the simpler, more straightforward factors, the geographical and quantitative ones.

The combination of Germany's geographical position in Europe and her large population make for one basic difficulty in the German Question. Since German expansion to the East beyond the river Elbe began in the Middle Ages, the territories populated or claimed by Germans were so extensive that the unification of all or most of Germany into one state under a central government (whether federal or centralized) was bound to create a formidable power bloc in the middle of Europe. Since the Middle Ages the Germans have always been numerically the second largest nation in Europe, initially coming behind the French and then, since the nineteenth century, behind the Russians. National unity of all or most Germans would upset any European balance of power. This is what Clemenceau had in mind when he made his famous remark in 1919 which was so grossly misrepresented by German nationalists: that there were 20 million Germans too many in the heart of Europe to tolerate their political unity with equanimity.

Germany's central position in Europe raised another complication. There is no other nation in the world that has more neighbours than the Germans: Danes, Dutch, Belgians, Luxemburgers, French, Swiss, Austrians, Czechs and Poles, Russians or Lithuanians (depending on the historical period in question). If Old Austria is included as part of historic Germany, then the Italians, Hungarians, Slovenes, Serbs, Romanians and even Ukrainians were also, historically speaking, German neighbours. Even Sweden and England may be counted as indirect neighbours, across the

Baltic and the North Seas. Since neighbours, according to Machiavelli, very often are enemies, such a fragmented neighbourhood made for complicated patterns of conflicts between Germany and nearby states or nations, particularly after the rise of national movements.

The Germans started their historical career in a power vacuum because the Germanic (later the German) tribes were politically fragmented. Their unification after the foundation of the German Kingdom in 911–19 automatically made Germany the greatest power in Europe between Muslim Spain to the West and Byzantium to the East. It is a rare if not unique development in history when a nation, by the very act of its establishment, is pushed into the position of becoming the strongest power in its region. And with their victory over the Hungarians near Augsburg in 955 the Germans emerged automatically as the quasi-hegemonial power in Latin Europe. This process culminated in 962 with the resurrection of the Roman Empire, now under German leadership.[16]

Germany had become the power centre in Latin Europe but, also because of Europe's geographical figuration at the time, she had emerged at the periphery of the future European state system that was gradually arising from the chaos which had followed the downfall of the Western Roman Empire. Yet the struggle between emperor and pope, and the necessity for the emperor to go to Rome for coronation by the pope, which in its turn involved a series of military campaigns against parts of Italy, eroded the central power of the crown in its dual role as King of Germany and Roman Emperor. Ever since the conflict between the rival dynasties of Welfs and Staufers in 1198, Germany with her Roman Empire was declining and becoming a power vacuum. After the battle of Bouvines in 1214 she was overtaken by France as the leading European great power. The autonomy of ecclesiastical and secular principalities achieved between 1220 and 1231, the Reformation and the Thirty Years War all further increased Germany's political fragmentation. By the Peace of Westphalia in 1648 the sovereignty of her almost innumerable political units was recognized and guaranteed, giving the neighbouring powers a right of intervention sanctified by international law. Germany's role as the battlefield of European powers was maintained during the wars fought against French attempts at hegemony under Louis XIV, the revolutionary governments and Napoleon I. It was in reaction against the traumatic experience of the Thirty Years War that Brandenburg started its course of militarism and power politics.

With the end of the Old Empire and Prussia's crushing defeat, both of which took place in 1806, the question of what to do with the Germans had to be answered. German patriots like Freiherr vom Stein demanded a new German Reich after Napoleon's downfall, but Europe shrank back from such an idea at the Congress of Vienna; her statesmen could see the ramifications of the German Question and of the *Machtfrage* in the middle of Europe. German political unity would automatically create a formidable power centre which would seek to expand, as all power centres in history have done, and would strive for hegemony over Europe, again as all power centres have done in comparable circumstances. The upshot was the *Deutscher Bund*, a compromise and interim answer to the German Question: a loose confederation, without a common sovereign power, with only the barest minimum of common political institutions. Germany remained a power vacuum neatly balanced in itself by German dualism – paralysed on the one hand by the rivalry between Austria and Prussia which had endured since 1740, and on the other by the interests of the medium and smaller German states.

Meanwhile, Germany's role as a power vacuum had become indispensable for the European balance of power, since great states had arisen, following a common pattern in world history, at the peripheries of Europe. The continent of Europe, regarded as a single power centre, collectively dominated most of the world as a result of European expansion overseas. France and Britain to the West, and Russia to the East, sought to protect their expansion overseas and over Eurasia, respectively, by balancing a weak Central Europe (Germany, Italy and Poland) in their rear. They were unwilling to forgo the political and strategic advantages offered by Germany's continuing political fragmentation.

The Vienna Settlement was reversed by a set of complex developments, above all by the economic, social and political effects of the industrial revolution and of nationalism. The German aspects of these developments became the core of most subsequent problems, but they remained linked to the many non-German factors around Germany. The change from the German Confederation to any form of national state (whether republican and democratic, as pursued only by the extreme left in the Frankfurt Assembly of 1848–9, or as some kind of monarchy) would have involved a tremendous change in the European balance of power. It would amount to what Disraeli called the 'German Revolution' in his famous speech in the House of Commons, commenting on the founding of the Second German Reich and the defeat of France. Now, all great changes in history have always been accompanied or brought about by violence: civil wars, revolutions, international wars; the greater the change, the greater the violence involved. This is also true of Germany in the nineteenth century.

But the decisive dynamism probably came with what has been described above as the qualitative factor: Germany's spectacular growth. Within less than a century she became a first-class power centre in Europe, at first culturally and later also in economic, military and political terms. One of the positive, and in a sense dialectical, consequences of Germany's political fragmentation had been her cultural diversity and richness since the early eighteenth century. Between approximately 1770 and 1830 the nadir of Germany's political impotence coincided with a cultural awakening which was symbolized by the personality of Goethe and was centred on the duchy of Weimar. It provided an inspiration to subsequent generations, and it was partly because of the city's historic associations that the Constituent Assembly met in Weimar in 1919. This period of eighteenth-century enlightenment will be referred to as 'Weimar I'. Its main contribution to modern world civilization can be seen in thinking through the consequences of the emerging modern world of industrialism and political revolution, the tensions between its positive and negative aspects, between its constructive and potentially destructive possibilities.[17]

Yet the dazzling achievements of Classical and Romantic Germany in Weimar I in literature, philosophy and music were only the beginning. As a consequence of Prussian reforms after 1807, and of the industrial revolution spreading to Germany about the same time, Germany's cultural awakening was followed by educational, scholarly, scientific and technological explosions that soon propelled her into the cultural leadership of the world – a role she played until 1933 – and also into the position of the leading technical and industrial power on the European Continent.

The overall effect of these different expansions was tremendous: Germans, conscious of their increasing economic strength, now also pressed for corresponding political progress. German unity was logically the next step. There remained, however, the question which was first thrown up by the revolution of 1848: whether German unity ought to take a *grossdeutsch* or a *kleindeutsch* form; whether the new German state should include or exclude Austria. The dynamism generated by Germany's cultural, economic and technological advances became so overwhelming that, once favourable international conditions emerged, it pushed aside all 'artificial' barriers erected against German political unity by international law. In 1848–9 in particular, Russia had decided the issue by its hostility to any German great power emerging from the revolutionary fermentation from below, i.e. under liberal leadership.[18] After the Crimean War, both Russia and Britain, for different reasons, largely withdrew from the Continent into relative isolation, allowing Prussia to fill the traditional power vacuum in Central Europe. Bismarck exploited this unique opportunity; Prussia's quick and fairly easy victories over Denmark, Austria and France enabled him to establish Germany as the new super-power in the middle of the Continent. Unless opposed, she was bound to go on to seek hegemony over Europe.

As feared by statesmen in 1814–15, German unity revolutionized the balance of power in Europe, all the more so since industrialization had further increased Germany's power. As in 955–62, Germany in 1871 had become the strongest power centre in Europe. But meanwhile, by the very expansion of Latin Europe to Scandinavia, Poland and Hungary in the Middle Ages, and by the inclusion of Russia in the European system, a process which began with Peter the Great (1689–1725), Germany had moved to the geographical centre of Europe. This simple fact alone created another complication, with devastating repercussions for Europe and the world. While new power centres usually arise at the periphery of existing power centres, Germany's emergence as Europe's new super-power in the very *middle* of the European power centre was unique in world history. New power centres at the periphery could always safely expand further into the periphery. NB But Germany, through factors beyond her responsibility, was denied such 'normal' expansion, because there were hardly any power vacuums left, at least none in her immediate neighbourhood. After the period of Bismarck's Continental Policy (*Kontinentalpolitik*) she tried to expand overseas with her World Policy (*Weltpolitik*), as the German version of the universal imperialism, but inevitably ran into the resistance of all the established and emerging world powers – Britain, France, Russia, America and Japan.

The spectacular, almost sudden, rise of Germany from relative cultural, economic and political insignificance to the dazzling heights of a European super-power created one of the elemental continuities in recent German history. The intoxicating feeling of success pervaded all layers of German society in the Second German Empire. It did not simply disappear overnight just because of military defeat in late 1918; Germany had continued to grow economically, demographically and in military strength during the comparatively peaceful decades between 1871 and 1914. This background only added to German bitterness about the inexplicable rudeness and unfairness which, most Germans felt, the world had displayed towards them in the aftermath of the Great War.

Several *idées fixes* had taken strong root in the German mind: the growth from little Brandenburg via Prussia to the mighty German Empire of 1871 would go on, almost knowing no bounds; European hegemony, the status of a minor or junior world power, would be followed by that of a full-fledged world power in her own right; she would even exercise a kind of world domination such as had been enjoyed by the British Empire from 1815 to 1914. Germany's cultural, economic and technological leadership induced a superiority complex that was resented as German arrogance in the world at large. Germany, as a kind of collective superman, banked on her qualitative superiority over quantity in the race for world power, in the end blinding most Germans to the harsh realities in the world, including the rights and potentialities of other nations and powers. Furthermore, Germans had taken their national unification as a natural right, not seeing the complexities and dangers of Germany becoming a great power. Bismarck was one of the few who saw the potential problems in founding the Second German Empire, but he did so only after 1871 and he failed to educate his fellow Germans on that score. Instead, they naïvely thought, the world would tolerate Germany reaching out yet further and achieving the status of a great world power. They failed to realize that, if it was natural and normal that Germany wanted to achieve national unity as other nations had done, and that she would reach out for ever more power, then it would be equally natural and normal that the one supreme mechanism which Europe had exercised since the second half of the Middle Ages would make itself felt, this time against Germany. This mechanism was the European states' collective rejection of any of their number which sought Continental hegemony.

Germans, however, saw only envy and hatred on the part of less successful powers and nations against the rising German superstar, against Siegfried encircled from outside and treacherously slain from inside. The myths of encirclement and 'stab-in-the-back' became very powerful in the Weimar Republic, providing a negative link between Imperial and Nazi Germany. German refusal to apply the same categories of power politics or of the *Machtfrage* to her setback after 1918 only underlines the prevailing image of the Weimar Republic as a by-product of military defeat and 'international conspiracy', helped by 'traitors' from within. The Weimar Republic was seen as a hangover resulting from Germany having drunk from the sweet but heady wine of Imperial power and glory of the Reich.

With Germany's defeat in November 1918 the German Question, which seemed to have been answered for good in 1871, again became virulent. Yet the *kleindeutsch* or Lesser German solution, realized through Bismarck's Germany by excluding Austria from the Reich, implied, much against Bismarck's original wishes, a future pressure to move on towards Greater Germany as part of the normal expansion of any new power centre. Austria-Hungary would have been affected most of all, but so, at least marginally, would Russia with her minority of socially dominant Germans in the Baltic provinces.

One more step in the same direction was the dream of uniting all Germans into one powerful Empire, including the former *membra disiecta* of the Old Germano-Roman Empire to the West (Switzerland and the Netherlands), and the far-flung German minorities in the East and South-East. Such a programme, as formulated by the Pan-Germans (*Alldeutsche*), amounted to a declaration of war against the rest of Europe. On one central point the Pan-Germans were realistic: their programme could be fulfilled only through a great war, which they wished to come about, even if Imperial Germany were to lose it. They reckoned that, as a reaction against such a defeat, a militarist–dictatorial regime would rouse Germany's tremendous energies even more efficiently for a second round of war.[19]

That historical projection of the Pan-Germans proved correct and contributed to the rise of Nazism and Germany's second involvement in a world war. In spite of their position as a kind of respectable 'lunatic fringe' in the Kaiser's Germany, the Pan-Germans constituted a strong element of historical continuity from World War I to World War II. By 1939, while executing the original Pan-German programme, they had come to represent the new majority consensus in the Reich. They even comprised its relatively moderate wing when compared to the practices of National Socialism and Himmler's SS.

By the same token, the Greater German ideal was another powerful factor of continuity from the Second to the Third Reich. After 1871 Bismarck had used the appeal to the common historical background of his German Empire with Austria when pleading for the Dual Alliance in 1879. During World War I Germany systematically carried to its logical conclusion the pre-war trend of relegating declining Austria-Hungary almost to the status of a German satellite. In the shock of military defeat and revolution, Germans in the Reich and Austria, ever since the turn of the year 1918–19, were almost unanimous in demanding the merger of the German fragments of the Danube Monarchy with the Reich. They failed to appreciate the implications of *Machtfrage* for Europe: Germany, even after her defeat and the territorial losses that went with it, would have become again a super-power on the Continent. But German feelings kept running high against the Allies banning any *Anschluss* with Austria by the Treaties of Versailles and St Germain. This Greater German resentment also powerfully contributed to the political success of the ex-Austrian Hitler in Germany and to the widespread enthusiasm with which most Austrians greeted the *Anschluss* in 1938.

The almost unanimous naïveté with which Germans expected to bring about the Greater German solution around the turn of 1918–19, and the bitterness with which they reacted against the allies denying them their 'natural' birthright of national self-determination, points to another aspect of continuity: since 1871 the existence of the German Reich had become for most Germans a matter of course, dwarfing all political differences between right and left, or Catholic, Protestant, Jew and atheist. This was a perfectly normal reaction, but it had implications which escaped most Germans then (and probably escape them even now). The existence of a German

Reich in its modern version amounted to Germany being a first-class power centre. Apart from a few separatists, no one in 1918–19 wanted to dissolve the Reich or diminish its power, even on the left; the socialist SPD was proud to have saved the Reich in the storms of revolution and inflation between 1918 and 1923. The Communists would have liked to take over Germany as a whole and put it at the disposal of world revolution. Even in Lenin's mind this revolution should really have started not in backward agrarian Russia but in Germany, which led the world both industrially and in the strength of its socialist movement.

Indeed, Germany under the Weimar Republic remained a European great power, however shorn of some of the more prestigious outward symbols of great-power status such as a fully developed army, navy and air force, and colonies. In spite of her territorial losses, Germany's position as a great power was never endangered, if only because the allies had to find a precarious balance between weakening Germany as a threat to themselves and keeping her sufficiently strong to resist Communism and hold her own against Soviet Russia.[20]

Moreover, Germany had even become relatively stronger in Europe in other respects: as a result of the Russian Revolution and Versailles, Soviet Russia and America withdrew into relative isolation, to be followed by Britain. With the break-up of the Danube Monarchy and the territorial losses Russia had to suffer, Germany faced only a France, almost bled white in World War I, to the West, and a string of weak successor states to the East and South-East. Once Germany had recovered from the immediate shock of defeat and its aftermath (revolution, economic dislocation, inflation), she was bound to tower even more powerfully in the centre of Europe. Just as after World War II, Germany's economic recovery was indirectly spurred on by reparations in kind and by the dismantling of part of her industries, because she was thus forced into a wave of powerful modernization at the most advanced level, which even then was represented by the USA. The determination to make Germany again a fully recognized great power in Europe after World War I was another overwhelming factor of consensus and continuity in Germany, and it was one on which the Third Reich could build after 1933 to expand German power even more rapidly and efficiently than the Weimar Republic had done.

Another factor with telling effects on the Weimar Republic

remained the dual character of Germany's economic and social structures, the split between agriculture and industry. As in Bismarck's Empire, Weimar Germany remained predominantly industrial in the West and predominantly agrarian in the East, with the Elbe still remaining the dividing line. In the universal transition from agrarian to industrial society such a dichotomy is normal, and so are tensions arising from such a split. However, in the German case this universal mechanism produced between 1919 and 1933 more factors of continuity – some straight ones, others with a kind of dialectical twist introduced by the revolutions in Russia and Germany. But to appreciate them fully, one has to go back once more in time to mention at least one other powerful factor of German and European history.

About 1500 the river Elbe emerged, anew, as a structural divide in Europe; East of the Elbe, the 'new serfdom' developed, and became the social basis of absolute monarchy and autocracy in Prussia, Austria and Russia. West of the Elbe, however, the trend since the late Middle Ages – beginning in the Île-de-France about 1315 – was to emancipate serfs as free peasants. The last remainders of serfdom and feudalism were swept away by the great political revolutions after 1789. In the West more-or-less free peasants, together with burghers in the cities (free since about the year 1000), became the social basis of emerging national monarchies and later of the modern national state with parliamentary and democratic rule. With the rise of Britain and Russia as competing new great powers from the early eighteenth century onwards, differences polarized and escalated to an ideological level between the West (liberal, parliamentary, democratic, rationalist) and the East (autocratic and predominantly agrarian). The industrial revolution only exacerbated tensions by increasing the distance between the economic and social developments in East and West.

Germany, caught in the middle of growing polarization between East and West, had, correspondingly, greater and greater difficulty in finding her place in either camp. Culturally and intellectually, she clearly belonged to the West, even as far as her easternmost outposts of Königsberg and Vienna. But since the Great Nordic War of 1700–21, Russia, the ever-growing and expanding hegemonial power in the East, began to overshadow Germany politically. This tendency was more marked in some states than in others; clearer in Prussia and Saxony, for example, than in Austria.

As long as Germany had elastic but weak political structures such as the Old Empire or the *Deutscher Bund*, these tensions did not matter so much and their impact was also limited because they were still in their opening stages. The founding of a new German Empire, already at a higher and steadily expanding level of industrialization, suddenly made such tensions potentially dangerous because they were now penned into a powerful, yet rigid, political structure of 'national' character. From now on, Germany as a whole proved increasingly unable to opt clearly either for the West or the East; any clear-cut decision would have destroyed the precarious economic and social compromises between agriculture and industry which were centred roughly East and West of the Elbe. For the same reason the Second German Empire refused to come down either for the West or East in its foreign policy and decided to go it alone with her 'free hand' policy, especially in her phase of *Weltpolitik*. Two major results were the First World War, at least in the way in which it came about, and the ideology of the *deutscher Sonderweg*, or the German 'Special Path', which arose during World War I as an alternative to parliamentary democracy of the West and Russian autocracy of the East.[21]

Also after World War I the same structural problems returned to plague the Weimar Republic, both at home and abroad, albeit with many modifications imposed by the overall new situation for Germany after defeat and revolution in November 1918. But the ideology of the *deutscher Sonderweg* persisted, giving a positive form to the continuing inability to come down clearly either on the side of the West or of the East. German society was polarized by conflicting forces, particularly in the Berlin of Weimar II, where, in a similar manner to the pattern followed a century earlier in Weimar I, the constructive and destructive potentialities of the modern world found their articulation in the brilliant cultural life of the new Republic. Superficially, or only with reference to the domestic scene in Germany, party alignments flowing from the by-now traditional agriculture–industry dichotomy remained unchanged in the Weimar Republic. The right drew most of its electoral strength from rural areas; the left, including the workers' wing of the Catholic Centre Party, mostly from industrial and urban constituencies. Both farmers and farm labourers, together with the leaders of industry, sided with the right; industrial labour mostly with the left. Once important aspects of foreign policy or of the

Machtfrage in the European context are taken into consideration, however, the agrarian–industrial correlation within the national framework was drastically modified or even blurred by the rise of Soviet Russia and a strong Communist Party in Germany which waxed in strength at the expense of the SPD during the great Depression, from 1930 to 1933. Germany's traditional oscillation between East and West had reached a new dimension, since the October Revolution had dramatically reversed the social, political and ideological definition of the 'East'. The 'East' was no longer backward, agrarian, autocratic and undemocratic Czarist Russia, but the revolutionary Soviet Union, forging ahead towards modernization and industrialization, towards a new kind of democracy and proletarian internationalism.

This, at least, was the propaganda and mystique of revolutionary Communism, which then had a wide appeal in the West at large and particularly in Germany. But in Germany, separated from Soviet Russia only by Poland, the appeals of a pro-Russian party carried special weight; ever since the Great Nordic War Prussia and Saxony had been allied with Russia for most of the time. Because of Russia's enormous power, even Prussia was a kind of Russian satellite, having been saved *in extremis* three times by Russia, in 1762, 1807 and 1812–13. Also after 1871, Prussian conservatives remained the protagonists of a pro-Russian orientation, although their economic bread-and-butter interests already clashed with those of their Russian counterparts after Russia's policy of exporting grain to pay for part of her industrialization had fully come into its own.

Even after the October Revolution, a wing of mostly Prussian conservatives and German nationalists stuck to their pro-Russian line, by now shorn of all its ideological components. They became instrumental in establishing a foreign policy of the Weimar Republic that avoided a clear-cut and one-sided commitment for the West, their task facilitated by the allies' association with the repugnant Versailles *Diktat*. Instead, they set up a working relationship with the new Communist regime to play off the West against the East. Again, as in her period of *Weltpolitik*, Germany opted for a policy of a free hand between East and West. Its proponents could point to the Prussian tradition of 'friendship' with Russia before 1879 or 1890, while ignoring Prussia's subservience to Russia until 1871. Hitler, of course, could fall back on that tradition in the summer of 1939 for *his* period of collaboration with the Soviet Union until June 1941.

Yet the genuine and openly Russian party in the Weimar Republic was not the remnants of Old Prussian junker traditions on the right, but the new revolutionary party on the extreme left, the Communist KPD. After its failure to engender a Communist revolution in the first years of the Weimar Republic, and after the Stalinist takeover, the KPD became the tool of Soviet Russian foreign policy and propaganda, following obediently every twist in the line of Soviet or Comintern foreign policy.[22]

The hard core of the working relationship between the Soviet Union and Germany, under both the Weimar Republic and the Third Reich, was common enmity towards Poland. Here the ideological extremes of the political spectrum met in pragmatic *Real-* and *Machtpolitik* with rare harmony; ever since the partition of Poland, Russian *Westpolitik* and German *Ostpolitik* have seen eye to eye in their desire to eliminate Poland as a sovereign state and to keep her divided.[23] The much-quoted Russo-Prussian friendship was largely based on the destruction of Poland. Through the results of the First World War this acquired an additional ideological stimulus thanks to Poland's equally traditional orientation to the West, to France in particular. Thus, Prussia also ensured that the German and Polish Questions were fused to each other by a deadly mechanism: a positive answer to the German Question would be negative to the Poles; a positive answer to the Polish Question would be negative to the Germans.

The First World War had been, in Polish eyes, a war between the three partitioning powers which the Poles, after the failure of their national uprisings between 1794 and 1863, had been praying for before 1914 – 'O Lord, give us the Great War!'. The simultaneous collapse of all the three partitioning powers at the end of the war had made possible, in Komarnicki's phrase, the 'Rebirth of the Polish Republic', but only in a power vacuum which would not last for long. Poland's new borders hurt the national feelings of all her neighbours except Romania, and engaged her in wars with all those neighbours. Russians and Germans in particular, whatever their political regimes, joined in a common deadly resentment against territorial losses to a Polish state which they both despised and hated. By the same token, Germany's right and left met in their opposition to Polish nationalism; moderate Social Democrats such as Paul Loebe belonged to the organizers of the German *Volkstumskampf* in Silesia. German Communists had a particular ideological grudge against the Poles as instruments of Western imperialism and capitalism, the more so since at Warsaw, in August 1920, Poland had blocked the victorious Red Army's path to Germany and the triumph of World Revolution. The KPD denounced the Versailles Settlement in just as stridently chauvinist terms as the Nazis but, in contrast to the 'national socialism' of the Nazis, the Communists couched their protest in terms of 'proletarian internationalism'; Germany, the coming centre of world revolution, had to be strengthened, territorially and in other ways, while Poland and, for that matter, France had to be weakened correspondingly. The KPD in Upper Silesia identified itself wholeheartedly with the German cause against Polish nationalism, while the Polish Communists, mostly hailing from non-Polish nationalities, in particular the Jews, refrained from embracing the Polish national cause for the same ideological reasons.

During the advance of the Red Army through Poland in Summer 1920, towards its ultimate aim of Berlin, Germany literally held her breath, paralysed by conflicting political considerations. On the one hand, most Germans probably relished with *Schadenfreude* the thrashing which insolent Poles were receiving from the hands of revolutionary Russia. On the other hand, most were against Communism. After the Poles had beaten back the Red Army in the 'Miracle of the Vistula', the Weimar Republic coolly reaped the advantages from Poland's military efforts and exploited Poland's ensuing economic and political weakness for its own purposes. The Treaty of Rapallo in 1922 was the logical result. Its innocent public stipulations (mutual diplomatic recognition and the cancelling of financial claims) were offset by a secret protocol which established political and ultra-secret military collaboration between Germany and the Soviet Union. The anti-Polish component, in co-operation with Russia (whatever its political structure) can be seen as one of the most powerful factors of continuity in recent German history, secretly binding together right and left in both Russia and Germany. Hitler later used the same technique of dividing his treaty arrangement with the Soviet Union into an open Non-Aggression Pact and a secret protocol, once more directed mainly against Poland.

Beyond the Polish factor, Germany's shifting position towards

Poland and Russia, whether Czarist or Soviet, generally underscores her great difficulty in finding her place either in the West or in the East. Within Germany, the Weimar Republic had put down any attempts at Communist revolution, but gladly co-operated with the Soviet Union against Poland, since for Germans and Russians Poland was perhaps the most odious product of the odious Versailles Settlement. Moreover, Germany did recognize the new frontiers of Versailles in the West with the Locarno Treaties, but refused the same recognition to Poland and Czechoslovakia, thus hitting the West indirectly through its proxies.

As was the case with the Second Empire, Republican Germany proved unable, for the same structural reasons – the socio-economic rift along the Elbe – to come down clearly on the side of the West or the East. Again the policy of a 'free hand' was to strengthen Germany's bid for more power. But it only helped to prepare the way for the second German explosion into another world war.

Despite his initial tactical caution, imposed by Germany's relative military weakness in 1933, Hitler left no doubt in one respect: in contrast to the Weimar Republic, he wanted to restore his Third Reich to the status of a fully fledged great power. Within a few years, he made Germany once more a first-class power centre, strong enough to risk another 'bid for world power'. The Reich was grimly centralized and was made uniform by driving all political dissent into conformity, exile, concentration camps or underground. But Hitler also ended one great continuity from the past: culturally and intellectually, the Weimar Republic had succeeded in carrying on the great traditions of Weimar I. In spite of the initial moral isolation imposed by the allies immediately after the First World War, Germany, by and large, had preserved her leading position in the spheres of culture and scholarship. The very choice of Weimar as the seat of the National Assembly in February 1919 had a symbolic meaning: the new Republic adopted and exploited constructively a slogan of allied war propaganda that had distinguished between militarist Prussia, symbolized by Potsdam, and Germany's cultural traditions, symbolized by Weimar. The image stuck with the 'Weimar Republic', but its programmatic name acquired an awkward ambivalence of its own. For the dwindling band of republicans, Weimar was to demonstrate the clean break with the continuity of Prussian militarism and German power politics. For the right and the extreme left, Weimar became a symbol of weakness, at best a half-way house to their own respective ideal future – either Third Reich or Soviet Germany.

In that respect, there can be seen a different kind of continuity in the Weimar Republic, an effort to go back, at least in words, to positive and valuable traditions in the German past which were represented by Weimar I. It is certainly no coincidence that with the death of Weimar II, Germany also lost her cultural prominence in the world, when the Nazis drove the best part of Germany's cultural and intellectual potential into exile. Violent anti-semitism self-immolated Germany not only culturally and intellectually but, with the holocaust, morally as well.

Similarly, the well-known conflict in the Weimar Republic about her national colours – Black-Red-Gold *v.* Black-White-Red – demonstrates a corresponding rift in German society. Although Black-Red-Gold, the colours of the revolution of 1848 and of German liberalism, had ambiguities of its own in the *Machtfrage* for Germany, they pointed to less violent traditions than Black-White-Red, the tricolour of the Second German Empire. However, more massive and real continuities carried the day over less tangible, more spiritual continuities conjured up by Weimar I and the revolution of 1848. Even the official flag Black-Red-Gold was used only shamefacedly by the Weimar Republic, whereas Black-White-Red remained popular amongst the right and was even adopted officially as a second national flag in 1926, at a time when the monarchist Hindenburg was president and the German Nationalists were in the government.

The compromise over the national flag was indeed symbolic of the Weimar Republic as a whole; it was a weak, short-lived compromise between conflicting forces within German society which were pulling it in different directions. These pressures first tore apart the Weimar Republic and then, after the failure of a frantic effort to unite German society by force through the Nazi dictatorship in its bid for another round of German power, tore Germany apart as well. The Greater German Empire burst asunder in every possible direction. Rump Germany, not by historical coincidence, was divided roughly along the river Elbe, which from 1945 acquired a new significance as a structural divide, not only within Germany, but also for Europe and the world.

Through the various rifts and breaks, new kinds of continuities are cropping up again in Germany, in both West and East, once more in the context of the German Question. An adequate analysis of the developments, however, would at least take as much space as this historical sketch, focusing mainly on the Weimar Republic, between the Second and the Third Empires, between the First and the Second World Wars.

Notes

1. John C. G. Röhl (ed.), *From Bismarck to Hitler: the Problem of Continuity in German History* (New York, 1970).
2. Düsseldorf, 1961; the English edition, *Germany's Aims in the First World War* (London, 1967), was followed by his *War of Illusions: German Policies from 1911 to 1914* (London, 1975).
3. Fritz Fischer, *World Power or Decline: The Controversy Over Germany's Aims in the First World War* (New York, 1974); John A. Moses, *The Politics of Illusion: The Fischer Controversy in German Historiography* (London, 1975).
4. See A. J. P. Taylor, *The Course of German History* (London, 1945).
5. For the most recent reactions see Karl Dietrich Erdmann, *War Guilt 1914 Reconsidered: A Balance of New Research*, History Teachers' Association of NSW (Sydney, 1980) and Imanuel Geiss, 'Die manipulierte Kriegsschuldfrage. Deutsche Reichspolitik in der Julikrise 1914 und deutsche Kriegsziele im Spiegel des Schuldreferats, 1919–1931', in *Militärgeschichtliche Mitteilungen*, 4 (1984). For two recent studies on the effect of the *Kriegsschuldfrage* on German society, see Ulrich Heinemann, *Die verdrängte Niederlage. Politische Offentlichkeit und Kriegsschuldfrage in der Weimarer Republik* (Göttingen, 1983); Wolfgang Jäger, *Historische Forschung und politische Kultur in Deutschland. Die Debatte 1914–1980 über den Ausbruch des Ersten Weltkrieges* (Göttingen, 1984).
6. Above all pioneered by William H. McNeill, *The Rise of the West: A History of the Human Community* (Chicago, 1963); id., *A World History*, 3rd edn (New York/Oxford, 1978); also L. S. Stavrianos, *A Global History. The Human Heritage*, 3rd edn (Englewood Cliffs, 1983).
7. David Calleo, *The German Problem Considered: Germany and the World Order, 1870 to the Present* (Cambridge, 1978); Francis R. Bridge and Roger Bullen, *The Great Powers and the European State System 1815–1914* (London/New York, 1980); Paul Kennedy, *The Rise of the Anglo-German Antagonism 1860–1914* (London, 1980); Lancelot L. Farrar, *Arrogance and Anxiety: The Ambivalence of German Power 1848–1914* (Iowa City, 1981); Richard Langhorne, *The Collapse of the Concert of Europe: International Politics 1890–1914* (London, 1981); Arno J. Mayer, *The Persistence of the Ancien Régime: Europe to the Great War* (New York, 1981); Geoffrey Barraclough, *From Agadir to Armageddon: Anatomy of a Crisis*

(London, 1982); Richard Bosworth, *Italy and the Approach of the First World War* (London, 1983); John Keiger, *France and the Origins of the First World War* (London, 1983); D. C. B. Lieven, *Russia and the Origins of the First World War* (London, 1983); James Joll, *The Origins of the First World War* (London, 1984).

8. In that respect recent international research (see note 7) is providing a healthy stimulation for German historians to overcome their German limitations.
9. Erwin Hölzle, *Die Selbstentmachtung Europas. Das Experiment des Friedens vor und im Ersten Weltkrieg* (Göttingen, 1975).
10. e.g. Klaus Hildebrand, 'Julikrise 1914: Das europäische Sicherheitsdilemma. Betrachtungen über den Ausbruch des Ersten Weltkrieges', *Geschichte in Wissenschaft und Unterricht*, 7 (1985), pp. 469–502.
11. F. H. Hinsley, *Power and the Pursuit of Peace: Theory and Practice in the History of Relations Between States* (Cambridge, 1963).
12. Wilhelm Alff, *Materialien zum Kontinuitätsproblem der deutschen Geschichte* (Frankfurt/M., 1976).
13. Imanuel Geiss, *Julikrise und Kriegsausbruch 1914. Eine Dokumentensammlung*, 2 vols. (Hanover, 1963–4), vol. II, p. 753.
14. Fritz Fischer; see note 3. See also Gregor Schöllgen, '"Fischer-Kontroverse" und Kontinuitätsproblem. Deutsche Kriegsziele im Zeitalter der Weltkriege', *Ploetz Geschichte der Weltkriege. Mächte, Ereignisse, Entwicklungen 1900–1945*, Andreas Hillgruber and Jost Dülffer (ed.), (Würzburg, 1981), pp. 163ff.
15. Calleo (1978; see note 7); for a historical survey, see Wolf D. Gruner, *Die deutsche Frage. Ein Problem der europäischen Geschichte seit 1800* (Munich, 1985).
16. For a very instructive recent analysis, see K. J. Leyser, *Medieval Germany and its Neighbours 900–1250* (London, 1982).
17. Thomas Nipperdey, *Deutsche Geschichte 1800–1866. Bürgerwelt und starker Staat* (Munich, 1983), esp. ch. IV, pp. 451–594.
18. Werner E. Mosse, *The European Powers and the German Question, 1848–71, with special reference to England and Russia* (Cambridge, 1958).
19. Roger Chickering, *We Men Who Feel Most German: A Cultural Study of the Pan-German League 1886–1914* (London/New York, 1984).
20. A. J. Mayer, *Politics and Diplomacy of Peacemaking. Containment and Counterrevolution at Versailles, 1918–1919* (New York, 1968).
21. Bernd Faulenbach, *Ideologie des deutschen Weges. Die deutsche Geschichte in der Historiographie zwischen Kaiserreich und Nationalsozialismus* (Munich, 1980). For a controversial analysis of the *Sonderweg* problem, see David Blackbourne and Geoff Eley, *Mythen deutscher Geschichtsschreibung* (Berlin, 1980). In a stimulating and elegantly written lengthy introduction to an English edition of their book both authors have discussed the somewhat confused reception of their work in Germany. They tried to clear

up some misunderstandings arising from their criticism of the 'New Orthodoxy' of the social–economic history school of Hans-Ulrich Wehler, which they had intended to be a constructive one, broadly in agreement with the modern interpretation of recent German history and its various continuities, but disagreeing on specific points. In the face of the Nazi abnormities they tried to re-introduce some measure of normalcy into German history before 1933, without blurring the moral issues raised by Nazism. See D. Blackbourne and G. Eley, *The Peculiarities of German History* (London, 1984), Introduction, pp. 1–35.

22. Hermann Weber, *Die Wandlung des deutschen Kommunismus. Die Stalinisierung der KPD in der Weimarer Republik*, 2 vols. (Frankfurt/M., 1969).
23. Imanuel Geiss, 'German Ostpolitik and the Polish Question', *East European Quarterly*, 2 (1985), pp. 201–18.

SIX

Weimar and Versailles: German Foreign Policy, 1919–33

MICHAEL LAFFAN

The pattern of Weimar Germany's foreign policy differs markedly from that of her political and cultural life. The Republic's intellectual and artistic self-expression was characterized by conflict and polarization, novelty and change, diversity and experimentation. In its political history the relatively tranquil late 1920s were sandwiched between two periods of acute instability; revolution, violence and inflation scarred Weimar's early years, while unemployment, extremism and authoritarian government dominated its close. The average life of its twenty-one cabinets was a mere eight months.

German attitudes and policies towards the rest of Europe were, by contrast, both stable and predictable. Governments adopted different tactics, revealed different degrees of skill and achieved different measures of success, but from June 1919 to January 1933, and even beyond, they shared a common objective which transcended all others: to destroy the Treaty of Versailles.

The *Diktat* of 1919 astonished Germans by its harshness. The new democratic Republic was effectively to be demilitarized, its navy limited to 15,000 and its army to 100,000 men. It was to possess no tanks, warplanes or submarines and was to be allowed only six battleships. The general staff was to be dissolved and was not to be reconstituted in any form. Conscription was to be abolished, and the imposition of long-term military service (with a minimum commitment to ten years, and twenty-five years in the case of officers) was designed to prevent Germany from following Prussia's example between 1807 and 1813 by building up large reserves of trained soldiers. All her colonies were taken from her. In one of the treaty's most humiliating clauses Germany was forced to acknowledge responsibility for the war, and she was also obliged to sign a blank cheque promising to pay whatever reparations the allies should deem appropriate. Two years later these were fixed at £6,600,000,000.

Most importantly of all, Germany's frontiers were re-drawn and she was compelled to yield territory to several of her neighbours. Eupen-Malmédy was transferred to Belgium, North Schleswig to Denmark, Alsace-Lorraine to France, Memel to Lithuania, and West Prussia, Posen and part of Silesia to Poland. She would lose one-eighth of her area and 6 million of her population. The separation of East Prussia from the rest of the country and the surrender of ethnic Germans to the rule of the despised Poles were sources of particular bitterness. Woodrow Wilson's principles of self-determination were to be applied elsewhere in Europe, but despite the wish of most Austrians for their state's incorporation in a greater Germany such a union was expressly forbidden.

The German economy, already undermined by wartime debts and soon to be ravaged by inflation, was further weakened by the loss of much of the country's reserves of iron ore, coal and zinc in the territories transferred to Poland and France.

In some respects the Treaty of Versailles might be seen as giving little cause for complaint. Both sides won the Great War, Germany in the East in December 1917 and the allies in the West eleven months later. In comparison with the savage terms which Germany had recently imposed on her defeated enemies she was treated mildly when she was vanquished in turn. In the Treaty of Brest-Litovsk Russia had been deprived of Poland, the Baltic provinces, Finland, the Ukraine and other areas. She lost a quarter of her population, arable land and railway network, one-third of her manufacturing industry and two-thirds of iron reserves and coalfields. Soon afterwards, in the Treaty of Bucharest, the Germans showed exceptional foresight in securing control of Romania's oilfields for ninety years to come.

Such recent precedents were either ignored or dismissed as irrelevant. Germans chose to forget how they behaved towards their victims during the last months of the Empire and assumed that, as represented by their new democratic Republic, they would be able to share in the general benefits of Woodrow Wilson's Fourteen Points. They expected that America would be able to modify France's desire for revenge, and that in the brave new world which would follow the war to end wars bad old habits such as reparations and annexations would be discarded. Brockdorff-Rantzau, the Republic's first foreign minister, believed that Germany would be able to play an important role in European reconstruction. General Groener, Ludendorff's successor both as quartermaster-general and as the dominant figure in the army command, hoped that the allies would take Germany's interests into account, at the expense of Poland, in return for her co-operation in a campaign against Bolshevik Russia.[1]

As a result of such illusions all Germans were shocked by the terms presented to them at Versailles in May 1919; they believed that they had agreed to the armistice six months earlier under false pretences and that the allies had cheated them. Chancellor Scheidemann protested that 'the hand will wither which places us under this yoke'. (The peace terms also provoked some doubts and reservations elsewhere, particularly in Britain and her empire. Winston Churchill believed that the Germans would be traitors to their country if they signed the treaty,[2] and General Smuts wrote damningly to his wife, at home in South Africa, that 'we are treating the Germans as we would not treat a Kaffir nation'.[3])

In Germany conservatives and monarchists, comprising approximately half the population, were particularly vehement in their opposition; such elements wanted to restore not only the values and institutions of the Empire but also its power and territory. Their principal objective was to prevent or reverse losses in the East. Although Posen and the Corridor contained Polish majorities, they were none the less regarded as the core of Prussia and therefore, by extension, of Germany. Even while the peace conference was in session in Paris the chief of the army command and many of his most senior officers were prepared to resume the war, and thereby risk the occupation of Western Germany by the allies, in the hope of preventing the transfer of Prussian lands to Poland.[4]

In the end the military accepted the government's argument that signature of the treaty was unavoidable, but army officers and the German right in general continued to blame the Republic for the 'shameful peace' of June 1919. Democratic politicians, who had been carefully excluded from all power and responsibility until they inherited the consequences of the Empire's collapse, felt aggrieved that they, their beliefs and their political system should be damned by their enforced association with the treaty. They resented the injustice whereby they should be branded as the traitorous 'November criminals', while those who had led Germany into the war and had conducted her affairs until defeat was imminent should escape all responsibility and opprobrium for the peace which followed. They believed that the Republic could be vindicated and consolidated only by obliterating the disgrace which had fallen on it within a few weeks of its birth. They were anxious not to be outbid in patriotism by authoritarian and anti-democratic nationalists.

In one sense the democrats were even more revisionist than the right. The Bismarckian settlement of 1871 had rejected the Grossdeutschland of the 1848 Frankfurt Parliament and had excluded Austria from the new Second Reich. After the Empire's collapse many democrats sought a Greater German Republic in which the influence of militaristic Prussia would be diluted by the inclusion of Austria. While drafting the Weimar constitution Hugo Preuss was influenced by advice from the Austrian ambassador in Berlin, a proponent of Anschluss, in his choice of the irredentist Black-Red-Gold tricolour of 1848 as the flag of the new Republic.[5] Throughout the 1920s union with Austria tended to be an objective of the left rather than of the right. Though their methods might differ and their demands might be less strident, democrats were as eager to revise the Versailles Treaty as were monarchists and militarists. From 1919 onwards cabinet ministers, diplomats and generals saw Weimar's foreign policy as involving two main tasks. The first was to restore Germany's sovereignty and, as a natural consequence, regain her status as a great power. They wished to end such allied rights and German obligations as the occupation of the West bank of the Rhine and the demilitarization of the East bank, the inter-allied military control commission's inspection of armaments and installations, the payment of reparations and the supervision of German finances. This allied interference was not only humiliating to a former and future great power but it also restricted seriously Germany's room for manœuvre. She could not become once more the equal of Britain, France or Russia until she had removed such infringements on her sovereignty.

In the early 1920s the allies felt able to treat Germany in a similar manner to that in which Western powers had long behaved towards traditional victims such as Turkey and China: they bullied or threatened and she succumbed to their demands. Germany submitted to the reparations schedule of payments in 1921 when warned that the Ruhr would be occupied if she refused. The allies were not bluffing: the French had already seized Frankfurt and Darmstadt the previous year and in 1923 they finally moved into the Ruhr. France was able to use her army of occupation to assist Rhenish separatists who wished to break away from Berlin and establish an independent government under her protection.[6] Germany was even vulnerable to invasion by a second-rank power such as Poland whose army was twice the size of the Reichswehr. German governments were regarded as passive rather than active participants in international affairs. When Chancellor Cuno proposed a mutual guarantee pact of the sort which later formed the basis of the Locarno Treaty, the British foreign secretary felt that it was 'hardly for Germany to make any independent proposals' in the matter and dismissed the idea as a 'piece of impertinence'.[7] Nearly two years later Stresemann, faced with the prospect of Anglo-French negotiations which would exclude Germany, complained bitterly that 'here once again we are an object in the policies of others'.[8]

Only when the various limitations on her sovereignty had been removed could Germany expect to achieve her second major objective: territorial revision and the recovery of much of the land which had been taken from her. She was obliged to be selective in this process. Stresemann pointed out that grievances over Alsace-Lorraine, Eupen-Malmédy, Schleswig, the Corridor, Silesia, the Sudetenland, Austria and Memel created discord between Germany and all her neighbours; to attempt to restore the *status quo ante* 'would be a policy of war against the whole world'.[9] In some instances the losses were seen as unimportant and Germans were prepared to accept them. North Schleswig was not greatly missed, and Eupen-Malmédy with its 64,000 inhabitants posed few problems.[10] There was a widespread readiness to accept the loss of Alsace-Lorraine. Stresemann, for example, remarked that a plebiscite might prove embarrassing for Germany; the great majority of the population would not summon up the courage to vote against France and so, after fifty years of German rule, 90 per cent of the inhabitants would choose to remain French.[11] Many nationalists disagreed, however, and in cabinet meetings and elsewhere General von Seeckt insisted that Germany should not contemplate any such renunciation.[12]

Whatever might be the differences of opinion or emphasis concerning the return of territory in the West there was total unanimity in attitudes towards the East. From 1919 onwards Germany's principal enemy was Poland. Her losses in area and population were heaviest in the East, and the traditional Teutonic contempt for Poles made the cession of territory to them more humiliating than was, for example, the abandonment of Alsace-Lorraine to France.

The distaste felt by all Germans at the prospect of their fellow-countrymen being subjected to Polish rule was reinforced in governmental and military circles by strategic reasons for revising the post-war border. German territory was divided in two, important railway centres and coal resources were in foreign (and potential enemy) hands, and the frontier was a mere hundred miles from Berlin. The Eastern provinces taken from Germany between 1919 and 1921 must be restored.

In late 1924 Maltzan and Schubert, successive state secretaries in the foreign ministry, wrote to the German embassy in Moscow of the need to push Poland back to her ethnographic boundary.[13] The following year Stresemann informed the Crown Prince that one of the great tasks of German foreign policy was 'the readjustment of our Eastern frontiers; the recovery of Danzig, the Polish Corridor, and a correction of the frontier in Upper Silesia'.[14] Seeckt's claim that 'Poland's existence is unbearable. . . . It must disappear . . . Russia and Germany must re-establish the frontiers of 1914'[15] was one which he made frequently in conversations with Russians as well as with German ministers and generals. Even Joseph Wirth, the chancellor who embodied the short-lived fulfilment policy in the early 1920s, was recorded as insisting that Poland must be destroyed.[16]

The Poles had no illusions about German (or Russian) intentions. In January 1919, at the beginning of the Paris Peace Conference, their foreign minister described Germany as being like the God Janus: she had 'one face towards the West, where she had made peace, and the other face towards the East, where she was organizing for war',[17] and after Locarno the Polish ambassador to Germany forecast that the two countries would be at war within five to eight years.[18] Warsaw governments appreciated that Berlin would not relax its hostility until the 1919 frontier had been re-drawn.

Germany was disarmed and surrounded by enemies, and at least in the 1920s her loss of sovereignty and military power made treaty revision difficult or even impossible. But her short-term vulnerability could not conceal long-term strengths and opportunities, and in certain respects her position in 1919 was potentially more formidable than that which she had enjoyed in 1914. France had been exhausted and demoralized by the scale of her wartime losses. The dissolution of the Habsburg Empire created a vacuum in Central Europe which Germany was best equipped to fill. Russia was no longer hostile as she had been between 1891 and 1918, and she might even become a future ally against the successor states which separated her from Germany. Russo-British antagonism prevented any co-operation between the two which might contain German expansionism.[19] America's withdrawal into isolation removed the other great power which had contributed to her defeat.

France was acutely conscious of her weakness and she was anxious to perpetuate the improbable and unnatural result of the First World War by a rigid enforcement of the treaty terms. Clemenceau had failed in his efforts to detach the Rhineland from the Reich and transform it into a buffer or satellite state. His policy at the peace conference was similar to Stalin's after 1945, but Stalin was stronger, more ruthless and less dependent on his allies than Clemenceau had been, and he succeeded in establishing a separate state in the part of Germany nearest his own borders while the French were unable to achieve a similar objective after 1918. Conscious that she had lost the Russian alliance which had made victory possible, that America was unlikely to rescue her in the future and that Britain might prove unreliable, that while Germany had clearly lost the war she herself had not so clearly won it,[20] France tried to construct a new power bloc in Eastern Europe which would take the place of Czarist Russia. Following her alliance with Belgium in 1920 she negotiated treaties with Poland in 1921 and Czechoslovakia in 1924.

Although the British appreciated that the balance of power was still clearly in France's favour in the early 1920s, and although they were inclined to regard Germany with condescension and distaste (Lloyd George must have enjoyed describing one of her governments as 'very moderate, even timid'),[21] they shared French fears that she would regain her former predominance. In the mid-1920s Churchill was able to remark that without American or Russian support Britain, France and Belgium 'would be a combination which does not inspire much confidence' in a future war against Germany.[22] Some forecasts of future German designs were remarkably accurate in detail. The historical adviser of the Foreign Office speculated about

> What would happen if there were to be a new partition of Poland, or if the Czechoslovak state were to be so curtailed and dismembered that in fact it disappeared from the map of Europe? Imagine, for instance, that under some improbable condition, Austria rejoined Germany; that Germany, using the discontented minority in Bohemia, demanded a new frontier far over the mountains, including Carlsbad and Pilsen, and that at the same time, in alliance with Germany, the Hungarians recovered the Southern slopes of the Carpathians. This would be catastrophic, and even if we neglected to interfere to prevent it happening, we should be driven to interfere, probably too late.[23]

However, such fears were projected into the distant future, and in the immediate post-war years Britain's fear of Communism, suspicions of France and dependence on German trade all inclined her towards a policy of generosity and moderation. From 1919 onwards she practised an intermittent policy of appeasement.[24]

Successive governments in Berlin looked forward to a breach between Britain and France which they could then exploit. They were always disappointed. Lloyd George and other British leaders urged their French counterparts to be patient and flexible, but there were limits beyond which they felt unable to go in straining the alliance. In all the various reparations negotiations during the early 1920s the allies first compromised among themselves and worked out a joint policy before they encountered German delegations. Even in 1923, when Britain disapproved strongly of the Ruhr occupation, she refrained from taking measures which could have embarrassed the French and Belgian forces.

For several years after the Versailles Treaty reparations payments were the most important and controversial aspect of Germany's relations with the Western powers. Her governments tried to circumvent the allies' demands, believing correctly that the less they paid during the initial phase the less they would have to pay subsequently. Their evasion and procrastination ultimately provoked the French and Belgians into seizing the Ruhr and attempting to extract reparations in the form of coal. The eight-month confrontation which followed resulted in the utter collapse of the already-tottering German currency, the impoverishment of large sections of the middle-classes, and challenges to both the democratic system and national unity. Eventually Germany, the weaker protagonist, surrendered. But by ensuring that France received fewer reparations during the period of occupation than she had done before January 1923, by damaging the franc as well as destroying the mark, and by alarming Britain and the United States, she succeeded in provoking a general reassessment of the reparations question. France was too weak to exploit her triumph and the Anglo-Saxon powers used their financial strength to impose a solution more acceptable to themselves and to the defeated Germans than to the victorious French.

The resulting Danes Plan of 1924 both eased the burden of Germany's annual payments and also guaranteed her against any repetition of the Ruhr occupation; allied unanimity would be needed before such a step could be repeated. Britain could protect Germany more effectively in future, and Germany would be better placed to exploit allied divisions. The Reparations Commission's powers were reduced, and henceforth, in practice if not theory, reparations payments would be financed by American loans. Germany paid less in reparations between 1924 and 1930 than she received in foreign investments.[25]

Throughout the 1920s Germany was always vulnerable in her dealings with the Western powers. When she looked to the East she felt able to take the initiative, though even here her room for manœuvre was limited. Despite her designs on Polish territory there could be no question of her risking a war on two fronts as in 1914–18. Germany would have to display flexibility, seek friends and allies, and detach Poland from her French protector.

The first significant step in breaking out of allied encirclement was taken with the Rapallo Treaty in 1922. In this agreement Germany succeeded in normalizing her relations with Russia and restoring the long-standing community of interest which had preceded the breach of the 1890s. As before, this new friendship was based in large part on common hostility towards Polish nationalism and independence.[26] The speed with which Germany escaped from the isolation imposed on her by the Versailles Treaty, a mere three years, contrasted with the twenty years which the French Third Republic had needed to break out of its quarantine after the Treaty of Frankfurt in 1871. Rapallo was accompanied and even preceded by military contacts between the Reichswehr and the Red Army. German officers and pilots were trained in Russia, and airplanes, tanks, engines and shells destined for use by the Reichswehr were produced by German firms in Russian factories.

Ideally, Germany would have wished to maximize her freedom of movement by playing East and West against each other, but in the last resort the two sides were too unevenly matched for such an exercise to be feasible. The Weimar Republic was vulnerable to pressure from Britain and France but not from the Soviet Union. The Western powers dangled a large carrot and wielded a large stick, and the burden of occupation or reparations payments could be eased only by winning goodwill and concessions from Paris and London. While the Poles might be frightened by a Russo-German rapprochement, they would none the less feel relatively secure, and therefore intransigent, as long as they could count on French protection. The road to Warsaw, or at least to Posen and Danzig, ran through Paris.

Co-operation with Russia continued intermittently throughout the 1920s but it was marred by tension and distrust. Germany's experience of Communist revolts in 1919, 1921 and 1923 made her suspicious of her Eastern partner, while Russia feared that Germany might join Britain and France in an anti-Bolshevik crusade. Although the Russians were determined to win back the areas which had been taken from them between 1918 and 1921, the prospect of a shared frontier with Germany would not have been an unmixed blessing.[27] Despite their common interests and common enemy there was no alliance between the two powers and they did not reach agreement on a fourth partition of Poland until August 1939.

The limitations on Germany's freedom of action, her dependence on the West and her ability to loosen at least some of the bonds which tied her are all illustrated by the Locarno Treaty of 1925. At the beginning of that year Stresemann was faced with a double threat. Because Germany had not disarmed sufficiently, the allies refused to evacuate the Cologne occupation zone according to the timetable laid down by Versailles.[28] Stresemann interpreted this decision as the bankruptcy of his policy of conciliation.[29] At the same time he was dismayed by the prospect of an Anglo-French alliance which would perpetuate Germany's post-war isolation. To avert such a threat, and to win sufficient allied goodwill to ensure the evacuation of Cologne, he proposed an Anglo-Franco-German agreement which would effectively guarantee the territorial *status quo* in the West. He also indicated Germany's readiness to sign arbitration treaties with her neighbours. If France could be assured that she was safe from German attack she would be more likely to pursue a mild 'British' policy and less likely to link her own security with that of Poland.

Stresemann described his objectives, admittedly to critics whom he hoped to disarm, as ending the Anglo-French entente, shortening the Rhineland occupation, and opening the way for 'a development in the east which will bring us new boundaries there'.[30] The 1925 negotiations ended with the Locarno Treaty in which Germany confirmed both the territorial settlement in the West and the demilitarized status of the Rhineland. She agreed to join the League of Nations despite her knowledge that such a move would worsen her relations with Russia. In return she made substantial gains. She ended the threat of an Anglo-French alliance against her and ensured her formal equality with the Western powers. The Franco-Polish treaty was modified so that after Locarno France would be able to intervene in a German-Polish war and assist the Poles with impunity only if Germany were the aggressor in the conflict; any unprovoked French attack across the Rhine would oblige Britain and Italy to take action against France in defence of Germany. Such a development may have seemed highly improbable, but the two guarantor governments would be likely to restrain France in order to avoid the embarrassment of violating their treaty obligation to defend Germany against French aggression.[31]

As part of the informal consequences of the agreement Stresemann was able to secure the evacuation of Cologne. Perhaps of greatest importance for the future was the fact that, by voluntarily recognizing and reinforcing her borders with France and Belgium Germany implicitly weakened those with Poland. Henceforth there would be two classes of European frontiers: those in the East, guaranteed only by the Treaty of Versailles, and those in the West doubly guaranteed by Versailles and Locarno. The French tried to limit the damage done to their Eastern protégés by this distinction, but the Polish and Czechoslovak governments were dismayed by the new agreement. The Poles were even willing to co-operate with their other great enemy, the Soviet Union, in constructing a Baltic bloc which would help contain German revisionism, but nothing came of this idea.

Each of the protagonists interpreted the treaty differently; in the words of the French diplomat, René Massigli, there were three things which should not be confused with one another: the Locarno spirit, *l'esprit de Locarno* and *die Locarnogeist*.[32] Germany had extended her sovereignty and saw the new agreement as providing further opportunities for undermining the Versailles Treaty. She could continue to reassure French public opinion, calming fears of any new invasion such as those of 1870 and 1914, and thereby make it possible for French governments to modify their policy of strengthening Germany's Eastern neighbours. With patience she might be able to weaken the links between Paris and Warsaw. The French saw Locarno in a very different light. For them it was a consolidation of Versailles by which, at the expense of some allied concessions and modifications, Germany confirmed voluntarily the *Diktat* which she had been forced to sign six years earlier. While international relations were conducted more harmoniously after 1925 than they had been before, Franco-German differences remained insuperable.

For the rest of his life Stresemann tried to build on the achievements of Locarno, but progress was slow, and he was unable to maintain the momentum of 1924–5. German public opinion shared his frustration at what he saw as the paltry nature of the *Rückwirkungen*, the by-products of the treaty.

At Thoiry in 1926 tentative agreement was reached on a deal whereby Germany could buy her way out of some of the restrictions imposed by Versailles. In return for accelerated reparations payments which would reinforce the French franc, the Military Control Commission would be withdrawn and the whole of the Rhineland would be evacuated within a year. Partly owing to American opposition, British obstruction and French suspicions, nothing resulted from this scheme.[33]

After only five years in operation the Dawes Plan was modified in 1929. Under the new Young Plan the allies' right of intervention in the German economy was ended. Reparations payments would continue for another fifty-nine years, but the initial level of annuities, correctly assumed to be the sole aspect of reparations which would have any practical significance, would be diminished. Such long-term planning was soon overtaken by a sudden crisis, and the impact of the Great Depression ensured that Germany's payments ended in 1931 rather than 1988.

Not until 1927 did the Western powers agree to the final disbandment of the Control Commission or to any significant reduction in the number of troops in the Rhineland. The evacuation of the second and third occupation zones, Koblenz and Mainz, was delayed for years because France refused to abandon such a valuable form of security against future German aggression until she had acquired an adequate replacement. French governments, with their own public opinion to consider, were unable to make concessions of the sort which Stresemann needed to placate his domestic critics. A new defensive system, the Maginot Line, was approved in principle in 1927, but not until its construction was far advanced did France show herself flexible in her occupation policy. Only in the last months of his life could Stresemann achieve his final triumph and ensure that the French would evacuate Koblenz and Mainz in 1930. Germany would then be free of allied troops on her territory and would once more become mistress of her own fate. But as the Weimar Republic eased its way back towards sovereignty and respectability, as it became in some respects a partner and an equal of the Western powers, the German people's demands became steadily more insistent. They felt more self-confident and less vulnerable than before, they appreciated that the European balance of power had begun to tilt back in Germany's favour, and they expected that the 1919 settlement should be modified accordingly. Stresemann faced increasing pressure to win new foreign policy successes. He had to engage in exhausting battles, not only with his British and French counterparts but also with his own party, his coalition partners and the German electorate. Even the concessions he had been obliged to make at Locarno proved too much for the most right-wing members of the cabinet and they resigned in protest. At the end of his life he complained that his inability to extract concessions from the French was driving voters towards the Nationalist Party.[34]

German opinion, and in the early 1930s German governments as well, proved unappreciative of the gains which were made in dismantling the treaty. Ten months after Stresemann's death, as the Rhinelanders celebrated the departure of the last French troops, President Hindenburg and the government shared in a mood of triumphant nationalism. In their speeches they made no reference to Stresemann, whose determination and skill had achieved the allied withdrawal; he and his moderate policies were already forgotten. Instead they demanded further concessions from the allies. Although resentment at Versailles was only partly responsible for the revival of German nationalism in the late 1920s and early 1930s it fuelled this new mood and gave it a focus, a set of symbolic grievances. The departure of the occupying forces in July 1930 removed the last restraints on German impatience and frustration. Ten weeks later, in the September elections, the Nazis made their first major breakthrough by winning 18.3 per cent of the vote and becoming the second-largest party in the Reichstag.

This advance of the nationalist right revealed an important failure of German foreign policy as practised by democratic politicians such as Stresemann. They had hoped to use their achievements in undermining the Versailles system to vindicate the Republic and to rally support behind it, to reconcile and integrate monarchists and nationalists, to bind together coalition partners who disagreed on domestic matters but were prepared to co-operate in removing the impositions and limitations of the peace treaty.

Their strategy backfired. Even though many allied politicians and diplomats wished to strengthen democratic German governments against their anti-democratic enemies by applying a policy of judicious appeasement, the concessions which they offered were too few and came too late. Foreign policy successes proved inadequate to keep pace with the German electorate's rising expectations and did little or nothing to reinforce the Republic.

The Young Plan of 1929, although broadly advantageous to Germany, none the less provoked a bitter response from extreme nationalists. They launched a nationwide attack against the agreement, which they linked with the Versailles Treaty and the 'war-guilt lie', and it was in the course of this campaign that Hitler first achieved notoriety as the 'drummer' of the right.[35] In a referendum 5.8 million Germans voted against the plan.

Within a few months this nationalist revival was reinforced by the effects of the Great Depression. The government's unpopularity grew as its austerity measures appeared to worsen the crisis and add more millions to the total of unemployed. Brüning acquired the soubriquet of the 'hunger chancellor'. Public opinion swung towards the totalitarian parties of both right and left, to the rival extremes of the Nazis and the Communists, both of which could claim freedom from all responsibility for the slump and could promise radical alternatives to the government's policies and style.

Welcoming any distraction from internal problems, Brüning sought public support through a more aggressive foreign policy and diplomatic triumphs. At the same time he used Western powers' fears of Hitler to lure or blackmail concessions from them. In 1931 he and Curtius, his foreign minister, decided on a dramatic stroke. They abandoned Stresemann's caution and, in an obvious move towards both Anschluss with Austria and economic penetration of Central Europe, negotiated an Austro-German customs union. This attempt at unilateral revision of the Versailles Treaty provoked an immediate and drastic response. Despite France's defensive and almost defeatist 'Maginot mentality', her government was able to use its economic strength to hinder badly needed loans to Austria and thereby force the abandonment of the scheme. The ensuing financial crisis helped provoke a banking collapse in Germany. Brüning was humiliated, and his most important foreign policy initiative compounded rather than relieved his domestic problems.[36]

Brüning and his successors made gains in other areas but these did nothing to help preserve democratic or non-Nazi government. The allies agreed that the minimum term for military service could be reduced and that larger numbers could be trained in the army, but the Reichswehr's diminutive size remained a source of national resentment and shame. The Hoover Moratorium of June 1931, which brought an effective end to reparations payments, was an act of magnanimity or realism by the American government for which Brüning could claim no credit. At the Lausanne Conference of 1932 the Young Plan was abandoned and Germany's debts were reduced drastically, but by this time she was no longer paying reparations and her public had expected complete cancellation rather than mere reduction; the more limited achievement made little impact and provoked no gratitude. The government, von Papen's cabinet of barons, was so unpopular that no foreign triumph could have won it public support. In the event Germany never resumed reparations payments, but at a time of crisis and collapse this passed almost unnoticed. In December 1932 Britain and France formally accepted Germany's 'equality of rights in a system which would provide security for all nations'.[37] The beneficiary was not the new chancellor, von Schleicher, but Hitler, who succeeded him a month later.

In the early 1930s political stability and moderate governments were not strengthened by an aggressive foreign policy. The world crisis facilitated revision of the treaty but it also helped destroy mere revisionists and bring to power a man and a party whose ambitions were vastly more extensive. Stresemann and his successors had extracted important concessions from the Western allies between 1924 and 1932: evacuation, more reasonable reparations payments and eventually no payment at all, and the removal of some of the restrictions on the size and equipment of the Reichswehr; in effect they secured the virtual restoration of that sovereignty which had been violated in 1919. But Germany's desire for great-power status seemed little nearer achievement in 1933 than it had been five or even ten years earlier. France was in retreat from her role as policeman of Europe and enforcer of the treaty, but, as shown by her reaction to the project for a customs union with Austria, she remained unpredictable and occasionally formidable. Russia was unreliable as a potential ally. German governments had enjoyed only limited success in their efforts to differentiate between East and West and to isolate Poland from her protectors; they had no success whatever in regaining the lost provinces.[38]

Long before Hitler came to power it seemed as if Germany's foreign policy objectives could not be achieved without war. Other measures were preferred, and from time to time there was discussion of achieving territorial revision by peaceful means, particularly by exploiting Poland's economic weakness; 40 per cent of her trade was with Germany and less than 5 per cent of Germany's with her.[39]

In 1925, during one of Poland's economic crises, Stresemann wished to refuse German loans unless the Poles paid in the form of frontier adjustments.[40] Just as Berlin was vulnerable to economic or financial pressure from London and Paris, so, he hoped, Warsaw would be vulnerable to pressure from Berlin. At Thoiry Stresemann wanted to buy sovereignty; in the case of Poland he wanted to buy territory.

The Polish economy recovered, but the idea of using economic pressure to facilitate border changes persisted. Six years later von Bülow, state secretary in the foreign ministry, wrote that the proposed customs union with Austria would be the prelude to the incorporation of Czechoslovakia within Germany's economic bloc. She could then develop relations with the Baltic states so that Poland 'with her unstable economic structure would be surrounded and exposed to all kinds of dangers: we should have her in a vice which would perhaps in the short or long run make her willing to consider the idea of exchanging political concessions for tangible economic advantages.'[41]

But in general little hope was invested in such schemes, and Stresemann made clear his scepticism about the worth of economic pressure; a non-violent revision was possible only if the Polish economy disintegrated completely, but 'as long as the country retains any of its strength no Polish government will be in a position to reach a peaceful understanding with us on the frontier question'.[42]

Ultimately force would be needed, and among the policy-making élite there was a widespread view that war, or the threat of war, would be a legitimate means of conducting foreign policy. The resort to force was not desired or welcomed as it would later be by Hitler, but it was accepted as a risk which might, reluctantly, have to be taken as the final stage of revising the Versailles Treaty. No one envisaged a repetition of a two-front war such as that of 1914–18. What was contemplated was a seizure of territory while Poland was distracted either by conflict with Russia or by internal problems; alternatively Germany might inflict on Poland a neat surgical operation, an amputation, with the assistance or acquiescence of the Soviet Union and the passivity of the Western powers. (The campaign of September 1939, in its military and diplomatic aspects although not in the ensuing slaughter, followed a pattern broadly similar to some of the ideas which circulated in the late 1920s and early 1930s.)

This readiness by Weimar governments to risk war in order to overthrow the Versailles system might seem to imply a continuity with the bellicosity of the Wilhelmine Empire on the one hand and the expansionism of the Third Reich on the other. It might seem to reinforce that view of German history which sees a progression from the *Drang nach Osten* of the Teutonic Knights, through the aggressive wars of Frederick the Great and Bismarck, the *Weltmacht* policy of Wilhelm II, Bethmann Hollweg's September Programme of 1914, the Treaty of Brest-Litovsk, and Weimar's designs on Polish territory, to the end product of Hitler's New Order in the 1940s.

But the attitudes prevalent in the Weimar Republic were in no way unusual. Many other states had foreign policy objectives which could be secured only by victory on the battlefield.

Piedmont-Sardinia's aim of a united Northern Italy, France's desire for the recovery of Alsace-Lorraine, Serbia's designs on the South Slav areas of the Habsburg Empire, the Soviet Union's determination to regain the lands lost to Poland and Romania between 1918 and 1921 – all could be achieved only at the cost of war. Large states virtually never abandon territory except as the result of military defeat. Weimar Germany's revisionism conformed to a European rather than a German pattern.

Naturally some of its policies were shared with the Third Reich. Stresemann and Brüning, like Hitler, wanted to build up a powerful army and regain the Polish Corridor. Hitler was able to extend his predecessors' achievements in removing the limitations on Germany's sovereignty and in undermining the hated treaty. He could claim, and could convince many foreigners as well as Germans, that he was simply pursuing more vigorously the revisionist policy of previous governments; just as Brüning had accelerated Stresemann's pace, so in turn he accelerated Brüning's. The allied policy of appeasement, one purpose of which had been to strengthen democratic German governments, would ultimately be used to strengthen their totalitarian successor.

Despite the undoubted continuities and similarities, there was a vast difference between the political aims and methods of the Weimar Republic and those of the Third Reich. In January 1934, fearful that Pilsudski might launch a pre-emptive strike at Berlin, and feeling free to indulge his hatred of Communism, Hitler signed a non-aggression pact with Poland. This diplomatic revolution effectively reversed the guiding principle of the German foreign policy since 1919, as well as of Prussian and imperial policy before the 1890s. For the next five years the Berlin–Warsaw feud was buried, and relations with Russia soon deteriorated. In March 1935 Hitler announced the existence of a German air force and the expansion of the Wehrmacht to the level of 500,000 men. In March 1936 he violated the Treaties of Versailles and Locarno by remilitarizing the Rhineland.

Such measures were merely preliminary steps, an improvement of Germany's position so that Hitler could begin to implement his foreign policy in earnest. His objectives surpassed more restoration of the 1914 borders, and within weeks of his appointment as chancellor he told the Reichswehr generals that his aim was Lebensraum, the ruthless Germanization of Eastern Europe.[43] He intended to extend his rule across Poland and Russia as far as the Urals and to reduce the native Slav population to servitude. Objectives such as Anschluss with Austria or the recovery of Posen and the Corridor were no more than preliminary steps in this direction. Weimar's ends were his means.

The governments of the 1920s aimed at making Germany a great power comparable to, although stronger than, the other great powers. Hitler wanted Germany to be a great power unlike any other. In the last resort the Republic was prepared to contemplate war, but it believed that frontier revision would depend on Western and Russian toleration or support; the pattern of Prussia's expansion between 1866 and 1871 would be followed. Hitler was prepared to wage war on the rest of the world.

In their attitudes and values the politicians, diplomats and even generals of the Weimar Republic belonged partly to the pre-war world, partly to its post-war successor. The new world dissatisfied them in many of its details and they wished to modify it, to restore some of what was lost or overthrown in 1918–19. They had no wish to destroy it. Hitler by contrast, was determined to shatter both the remnants of the despised old world of 1914 and the hated new world of 1919. The creator of the new Third Reich had no interest in restoring the values or the frontiers of the old Second Reich.

Weimar Germany's foreign policy perished along with the Republic which it had failed to preserve or sustain.

Notes

1. Cabinet meeting, 24 April 1919, Hagen Schulze (ed.), *Akten der Reichskanzlei. Das Kabinett Scheidemann* (Boppard, 1971), p. 218. See also Klaus Schwabe, *Deutsche Revolution and Wilson-Frieden* (Düsseldorf, 1971), pp. 346–50; Ernst-Otto Schüddekopf, 'German Foreign Policy between Compiègne and Versailles', *Journal of Contemporary History*, 4 (1969), pp. 182–94.
2. Cabinet meeting, 14 April 1919, Thomas Jones, *Whitehall Diary I, 1916–1925* (Oxford, 1969), p. 85.
3. W. K. Hancock, *Smuts, the Sanguine Years, 1870–1919* (Cambridge, 1962), p. 524. Harold Nicolson complained bitterly that of the twenty-three different conditions in Wilson's Fourteen Points, only four were incorporated in the Versailles Treaty (*Peacemaking 1919* (London, 1933), pp. 43–4).
4. F. L. Carsten, *The Reichswehr and Politics, 1918–1933* (Oxford, 1966), pp. 38–42.

5. Stanley Suval, *The Anschluss Question in the Weimar Era* (Baltimore, 1974), p. 25.
6. See Ludwig Zimmermann, *Frankreichs Ruhrpolitik* (Zürich/Frankfurt, 1971) and Walter McDougall, *France's Rhineland Diplomacy, 1914–1924* (Princeton, 1978).
7. Curzon to Sir S. Head, 29 March 1923, *Documents on British Foreign Policy* vol. I, xxi (London, 1978), p. 181; Minute by Curzon, 5 January 1923, Public Record Office, London, FO 371/8696, C432/178/18.
8. Cabinet minutes, 20 December 1924, Günter Abramowski (ed.), *Akten der Reichskanzlei. Die Kabinette Marx I & II* (Boppard, 1973), vol. 2, p. 1235.
9. Article by Stresemann, 14 September 1925, Foreign Ministry, Bonn, Stresemann *Nachlass,* 29; Gustav Stresemann, *Diaries, Letters and Papers*, vol. II (London, 1937), p. 158.
10. Manfred Enssle, the leading authority on the subject, concludes that 'in itself Eupen-Malmédy was unimportant', and that Stresemann hoped to regain the area from Belgium as a 'legal precedent for future territorial revision in the East' (*Stresemann's Territorial Revisionism: Germany, Belgium and the Eupen-Malmédy Question, 1919–1929* (Wiesbaden, 1980), p. 192).
11. Memorandum by Stresemann, 1 July 1925, *Nachlass*, 26, *Diaries*, vol. II, pp. 112–13.
12. e.g. Cabinet minutes, 24 June 1925, Karl-Heinz Minuth (ed.), *Akten der Reichskanzlei: Die Kabinette Luther I & II* (Boppard, 1977), vol. 1, p. 366.
13. Josef Korbel, *Poland between East and West: Soviet and German Diplomacy toward Poland, 1919–1933* (Princeton, 1963), pp. 154, 159.
14. Stresemann to the Crown Prince, 7 September 1925, *Nachlass*, 29, *Diaries*, vol. II, p. 503.
15. Hans Meier-Welcker, *Seeckt* (Frankfurt, 1967), pp. 343–4.
16. Hans Helbig, *Die Träger der Rapallo-Politik* (Göttingen, 1958), p. 119; Carsten, *Reichswehr*, p. 139.
17. United States Department of State, *Papers relating to the Foreign Relations of the United States: The Paris Peace Conference*, vol. III (Washington, 1943), p. 775.
18. Memorandum by Olszowski, 1 December 1926, Harald von Riekhoff, *German–Polish Relations, 1918–1933* (Baltimore, 1971), p. 143.
19. Andreas Hillgruber sees the inter-war pattern as paralleling that of the decades after the Crimean War which Bismarck was able to exploit in his creation of a *kleindeutsch* Reich. He argues that circumstances between 1919 and 1939 provided Germany with her best-ever chance of dominating Mitteleuropa and that this aim was basically achieved before war began ('Revisionismus, Kontinuität und Wandel in der Aussenpolitik der Weimarer Republik', *Historische Zeitschrift*, 237 (1983), pp. 618–19).

20. Olaf Maxelon, *Stresemann and Frankseich* (Düsseldorf, 1972), p. 84. Denis Brogan makes a similar point: France 'was a victor, but she had in many ways the psychology of a defeated nation', *The Development of Modern France, 1870–1939* (London, 1940), p. 543.
21. Cabinet conclusions, 23 May 1923, PRO, Cab 23/30, Cab 29 (22) 1.
22. Churchill to Austen Chamberlain, 23 February 1925, PRO, FO 800/257.
23. Memorandum by James Headlam-Morley, 12 February 1925, PRO, FO 371/11064, W1252/9/98, p. 8.
24. Both the word and the policy were features of the 1920s as well as of the 1930s. In 1920, for example, Keynes defended his 'advocacy of appeasement and moderation' towards Germany (Etienne Mantoux, *The Carthaginian Peace* (Oxford, 1946), p. 13); in 1925 Balfour claimed that the British people and their post-war governments 'have always been anxious for appeasement' (Hansard 5S HL 62, col. 838, 24 November 1925). There are many other illustrations.
25. Etienne Weill-Raynal, *Les Réparations Allemandes et la France*, vol. III (Paris, 1947), p. 71; David Felix, *Walther Rathenau and the Weimar Republic: the Politics of Reparations* (Baltimore, 1972), p. 184; Sally Marks, 'The Myths of Reparations', *Central European History*, 17 (1978), p. 249.
26. On Rapallo, see Theodor Schieder, 'Die Entstehungsgeschichte des Rapallo-Vertrages', *Historische Zeitschrift*, 204 (1967) and Hartmut Pogge von Strandmann, 'Rapallo-Strategy in Preventive Diplomacy: New Sources and New Interpretations', in Volker R. Berghahn and Martin Kitchen (ed.), *Germany in the Age of Total War* (London, 1981).
27. André Malraux gives a later example of Russian fears. William Randolph Hearst interviewed Stalin in 1933 and asked how there could be a war between Germany and the Soviet Union when they had no common frontiers. Stalin replied simply 'they will have' (*Antimemoirs* (London, 1968), p. 91). Poland's existence might be offensive to Russia, but her role as a buffer could be useful.
28. Technically the French stance was fully justified. Article 429 of the treaty laid down that evacuation would take place 'if the conditions of the present Treaty are faithfully carried out by Germany', and it was obvious that the disarmament requirements had not been fulfilled.
29. Cabinet minutes, 29 December 1924, *Die Kabinette Marx*, vol. 2, p. 1256.
30. Henry Ashby Turner, *Stresemann and the Politics of the Weimar Republic* (Princeton, 1963), p. 189. The state secretary in the Wilhelmstrasse made it clear that Germany was not prepared expressly to renounce war against Poland (Schubert to Sthamer, 29 March 1925, Foreign Ministry, Bonn, *Büro des Reichsministers, Verhandlungen mit den Alliierten über einen Sicherheitspakt*, vol. III.

31. On Locarno, see Peter Krüger, *Die Aussenpolitik der Republic von Weimar* (Darmstadt, 1985), pp. 291–301; Wolfgang Ruge (ed.), *Locarno-Konferenz 1925. Eine Dokumentensammlung* (East Berlin, 1962); Henry Ashby Turner, 'Eine Rede Stresemanns über seine Locarnopolitik', *Vierteljahrshefte für Zeitgeschichte*, 15 (1967), pp. 412–36.
32. Hughe Knatchbull-Hugesson, *A Diplomat in Peace and War* (London, 1949), p. 53.
33. See Jon Jacobson and John T. Walker, 'The Impulse for a Franco-German Entente: the Origins of the Thoiry Conference, 1926', *Journal of Contemporary History*, 10 (1975), pp. 157–81.
34. Jon Jacobson, *Locarno Diplomacy: Germany and the West, 1925–1929* (Princeton, 1972), pp. 249–50.
35. See Joachim Fest, *Hitler* (London, 1973), pp. 260–4; Karl Bracher, *The German Dictatorship* (London, 1971), pp. 160–2.
36. Krüger, *Aussenpolitik*, pp. 530–5.
37. Edward W. Bennett, *German Rearmament and the West, 1932–1933* (Princeton, 1979), p. 267. However, as Sally Marks points out, the basic dilemma persisted: Germany demanded equality while France insisted upon security, but if Germany gained equality France would have no security since Germany was larger and fundamentally stronger (*The Illusion of Peace: International Relations in Europe, 1918–1933* (London, 1976), p. 128).
38. Gaines Post gives an extreme view: by the early 1930s 'Germany appeared to be half-sovereign, isolated between the West and Poland, vulnerable to invasion and unable to accompany all its policy objectives by peaceful means' (*The Civil–Military Fabric of Weimar Foreign Policy* (Princeton, 1973), p. 289).
39. Helmut Lippelt, '"Politische Sanierung": zur deutschen Politik gegenüber Polen, 1925–26', *Vierteljahrshefte für Zeitgeschichte*, 19 (1971), p. 332.
40. Post, *Civil–Military Fabric*, p. 38.
41. John Hiden, *Germany and Europe, 1919–1939* (London, 1977), p. 119.
42. Stresemann to London Embassy, 19 April 1926, *Akten zur Deutschen Aussenpolitik, 1918–1945*, series B, vol. II, part i (Göttingen, 1967), p. 363.
43. Klaus Hildebrand, *The Foreign Policy of the Third Reich* (London, 1973), p. 28.

SEVEN

The Breakthrough of the National Socialists as a Mass Movement in the Late Weimar Republic

HANS MOMMSEN

The parliamentary system of Weimar was weak and shattered from the start. Its very origins were not even the outcome of any decision or initiative by the parties of what later became the Weimar Coalition; parliamentarization was conceded by the German high command and the imperial government, it was not really extracted by its supporters in the political middle and on the left. In any case, since Wilhelm II did not resign in favour of his presumptive successor, the parliamentary republic appeared to be the only bearable compromise in Germany. Compared with the domestic developments in the Southern and Eastern European countries, the parliamentary system in Germany displays a respectable amount of formal stability. Taking into account the fact that the republican parties lost their majority as early as June 1920, its performance was not as negative as it appears in retrospect. The main question is not so much why parliamentarism eventually failed, but why it survived so long, in spite of unending internal crisis and disturbance. One may argue that its prolonged existence in Germany – except in Austria and Czechoslovakia it failed everywhere it was introduced through the Paris peace settlements – supported indirectly the National Socialist rise to power.

By the time Adolf Hitler took office as German chancellor the parliamentary democracy of Weimar had already ceased to exist, even though in a technical and formally juridical sense it survived the period of the presidential cabinets and even the Nazi regime. The only political alternative to the Nazi dictatorship consisted of some sort of an authoritarian regime relying mainly on the armed forces. It is quite illusory to believe that under the conditions of the early 1930s the road back to parliamentary government was still passable. The National Socialists knew how to exploit the weaknesses and misgivings of the parliamentary system very skilfully. They presented themselves as the only viable alternative to the decay and the rottenness of the democratic Republic, and many people's desperate hopes and expectations rested on their fateful promises. But it would be erroneous to assume that the Nazi seizure of power was inaugurated by what has been claimed by conservative writers as the outcome of mass democracy. Unquestionably, Hitler gained significant victories at the polls between 1929 and July 1932. But he was brought to power after the severe setback of the November elections in 1932 by the conservative-authoritarian notables who belonged to the entourage of the aged President von Hindenburg. They hoped and believed that the Nazi party would merely provide populist support for authoritarian rule, and they thought mistakenly that Hitler could effectively be tamed and framed in a conservatively blended coalition cabinet.

This has to be pointed out in order to prevent the misleading assumption that the emergence of the NSDAP (*Nationalsozialistische Deutsche Arbeiterpartei*) as a mass movement necessarily implies the irreversible rise of Hitler to power. Conversely, the inherent weaknesses of the movement and its fallacies are disclosed if one scrutinizes its rather shaky social and political foundations. In fact the Nazi party, although successfully absorbing the competing anti-semitic and *völkisch* groups, remained an insignificant splinter group up to 1928. The Reichstag election returns of May 1928 were deeply disappointing for the Nazi leadership. In spite of continuous and strenuous campaigning and organizational efforts the party faced a severe defeat at the polls by gaining not more than 2.6 per cent of the vote, thereby losing about 100,000 votes or 0.4 per cent since the elections of 1924. The numerical insignificance of the party in 1928 induced the Prussian republican government to lift the ban on public speeches delivered by Hitler. Nobody expected that the party would survive this lethal electoral blow. Above all, it had lost most of its former support within the urban districts. Part of this had been replaced by new rural voters, mainly from the Geest and the Hanover regions. This significant shift in the party's electorate foreshadowed further events.

The electoral returns in 1928 stood in clear contrast to the NSDAP's organizational growth. The membership figures increased from 27,000 in 1925 to roughly 108,000 in 1928. Four years later it had tripled; the party comprised about 329,000 members in 1932. Although this appears to be a respectable increase, the party was, in terms of membership, far from being a stable mass organization, at least compared with the Social Democrats whose membership at the same time ran up to 1.8 million. More revealing than the absolute growth in membership, however, is the extraordinarily high degree of intra-party fluctuation. The NSDAP claimed in January 1933 to comprise a membership of 1.45 millions, but the actual figure at that time did not exceed 849,000. Closer investigation shows that roughly two-thirds of the members entering the party since September 1930 had already left it in 1934. Furthermore, even during the period of rapid growth, not less than one-third of the party membership returned its badges while the drop-out rate in the preceding period was considerably higher.[1] This proves a considerable amount of organizational instability, in spite of Gregor Strasser's continuous efforts to stabilize the party's internal structure.

One could argue that a relatively low and shifting membership is significant for an expressedly anti-liberal party aiming at becoming a mass movement rather than increasing its parliamentary representation. While this is true, the fluctuation within the Nazi electorate tended to be considerable, especially after the spectacular breakthrough in the September elections of 1930 and up to the November ballot in 1932. Important social groups such as the farmers contributed to the party's success in September 1930, but were already withdrawing their support in 1932, while at the same time the party made significant inroads in other segments of the middle classes. Hence, the different social-protest potentials which generated the party's growth tended to provide only transitory support, although this voting pattern was partly covered up by the omnibus effects of great electoral landslides until July 1932. This meant that divergent social groups, shifting through the Weimar party spectrum as a whole, would only temporarily belong to the Nazi electorate.

In the light of the degree of membership and electorate fluctuation, the great many attempts to ascertain a specific class allegiance of Hitler's followers appear to be largely futile. In every phase of its development the NSDAP gained considerable support even from the industrial proletariat, but the workers' support in terms of membership as well as of voters was considerably lower than the relative support of the middle classes and the peasants. As Professor Tom Childers proves convincingly, the Nazis as a catch-all party of protest did not possess any sociologically stable constituency, at least up to 1930.[2] Until then, less than 20 per cent of the changes in the Nazi vote can be explained by structural variables. Not before 1932 did the NSDAP become, according to Childers's investigations, clearly identifiable by the traditional predictive indicators of German voting behaviour: class and religion. Even then these sociological correlations remain mainly negative, and simply show the relative absence of certain social groups such as workers or Catholic peasants. On the whole, the NSDAP appears to be a sociologically amorphous movement, although a strong correlation is discernible between members of the old middle classes who faced social decline, and Nazi voters. There is also a remarkable shift of the NSDAP's social composition after 1925 on account of its expansion into Northern and Western Germany, resulting in a considerable increase in its Protestant and agrarian elements. On the other hand, the widespread assumption that the NSDAP was particularly attractive to the socially ascending white-collar groups is not borne out by the available socio-statistical data for the period up to 1930.

This dynamic picture of the party's electoral support complements what we know about its organizational efforts. First of all, it is obvious that the party's internal consistency relied on the ability to engage members and sympathizers in continuous campaigning and advertising activities, thereby achieving secondary social integration. It was attractive above all to those groups whose social status was threatened by modernization and industrialization. Only through an uninterrupted political dynamic could the membership be held in line, in particular since the party's growth after 1930 did not lead to real political influence.

The political isolation of the NSDAP during the era of the presidential cabinets had ambivalent results. On the one hand, the party had to fear political responsibility which was not accompanied by real political power, power which would eventually be utilized for the destruction of opposition parties. Brüning's intention of burdening the NSDAP with political responsibility on the level of the state governments by supporting Centre–NSDAP coalitions was not totally wrong. In Braunschweig, after the Nazis entered a bourgeois coalition in 1931, their support decreased rapidly.[3]

Nevertheless it became more and more difficult to mobilize the voters by continuous election campaigns, as in 1932, without achieving any visible political result. The November elections and the intra-party conflict, reflected in the retreat of Gregor Strasser from his party positions, indicated the beginning of the internal dissolution of the Nazi mass movement. In his diary, Goebbels remarked desperately that, if the party would not achieve power in the very near future, it would die from its electoral victories.[4] The Nazi seizure of power, therefore, was not so much the result of an ingenious political strategy pursued by Hitler himself, who stubbornly refused to enter a right-wing bourgeois coalition government in which he was not able to set the terms, but of the inherent weakness of the dominant political and social élites of the late Weimar Republic and their inability to resist National Socialist pressure.

As Juan Linz pointed out, National Socialism, like the other fascist late-comers on the political scene, drew its strength from the political exploitation of widespread socio-economic resentments, stemming from the deeply rooted apprehensions of the ongoing process of modernization and urbanization.[5] As a protest movement, the NSDAP was eager to avoid premature political options. According to its specific fascist character, the party did not integrate its members and sympathizers by reliable commitments to clear-cut programmatical goals. During the crucial years its propaganda was extremely flexible and would stress incompatible political targets at different times as well as take account of regional peculiarities. Although Hitler saw the necessity of altering in favour of the farmers some sections of the party's programme which in principle he did not wish to alter or debate at all, and although the party leadership sought to reconcile its policies with the interests of German big-business circles, the NSDAP election campaigns deliberately avoided any clear option in favour of the liberal–capitalist economy versus pseudo-socialist stratagems. It is also not true that during the campaigns between 1930 and 1932 Nazi propaganda stressed racial anti-semitism. In fact, this topic was only of marginal weight even in Hitler's public speeches in the years before 1933, and anti-semitic issues were usually restricted to exploitation of widespread anti-capitalist resentment during the

Great Depression. In fact, the Nazis were well aware of the fact that racial anti-semitism did not pay off in the election campaigns.[6]

As a consequence of these findings, recent researchers coincide in the opinion that the extraordinary electoral successes of the Nazi party after 1929 are to be attributed to the fact that it did not possess any clear-cut programme and that the very few ideological traits separating the Nazis from competing right-wing parties had no real significance. The NSDAP's eventual success relied heavily on its skilfully designed strategy of presenting itself as an alternative to any other political movement or party and to avoid any involvement in the ugly manœuvrings symptomatic of the splintering of the Weimar party system. The party's support increased less because the average Nazi elector voted positively for specific aims proclaimed by the party's flexible propaganda than because of a loss of confidence in his former party allegiance. Basically there was no difference between the NSDAP's programmatic targets and those of the nationalist DNVP, except for the Nazis' far greater flexibility in exploiting actual political opportunities. They even defended the Prussian republican constitution after von Papen's *coup d'état* in July 1932. The fundamental differences were those of style, of impetus and of propagandistic techniques, including the systematic use of modern means of mass communication such as film and radio.

This picture of the inherent weaknesses of the NSDAP's internal structure, of its virtual instability, raises the question of how to explain the party's rise to the position of a veritable mass movement after the spring of 1929. Thomas Childers ascertained that the economic crises, first in 1923–4 and then between 1929 and 1933 provided the necessary catalyst for the socio-electoral dynamic of the Nazi success at the polls. This is certainly true for the period of the early thirties, although (except for the agrarian electorate) the social groups who would tend to vote in favour of the NSDAP were less affected by the crisis than was the working class. Furthermore, the slump speeded up the trend towards the progressive dissolution of the bourgeois parties, with the exception of the Centre Party, which proved to be remarkably stable up to the March elections in 1933. The process described by Eugene Larry Jones as the dying of the middle, however, preceded the Depression and, therefore, cannot be directly related to economic factors.[7]

The agrarian crisis, whose structural character and, after 1928, explosive repercussions are beyond question, can only partly explain the sudden growth of the National Socialist electorate. Hence the impact of the economic crisis on the quite exceptionally rapid change in the voters' allegiance in 1929 appears to have been limited, at least in so far as its direct influence on the Nazi vote is concerned, and the economic factor was seemingly restricted to an acceleration of already ongoing structural changes.

Peter Stachura, Jeremy Noakes and Jerzy Holzer followed Dietrich Orlow's lead in ascertaining that there was a qualitative shift within the party's propagandistic strategies under the impact of its significant defeat at the polls in 1928.[8] Although before 1927 there was no explicit strategy, as Orlow's assumption of the so-called 'urban plan' implies,[9] there is no doubt that up to that point the party gathered its support mainly among the urban population and was predominantly represented in the urban areas. Undoubtedly the party, above all the north-western wing, streamlined its organizational and propagandistic efforts with the principal aim of winning over parts of the working class. This seemed to be the precondition for achieving the mass support the party needed in its struggle to gain real power. The returns of the 1928 polls proved this endeavour to have been a complete failure. In fact, the party leadership did not hesitate to draw strategic conclusions from the unexpected wins in rural areas and small towns where virtually no party apparatus had existed at all. For example, the elimination in 1927 of point 17 in the party's programme (which concerned the confiscation of landed property) supports this strategical shift, as does the promulgation of a specific agrarian programme in 1930. However, this did not mean any renunciation of the still-cherished expectation of gaining mass support among the urban population, including broad segments of the working class.

The fundamental tactical change of the NSDAP towards becoming a middle-class movement, as Stachura maintains, did not mean the complete rejection of the urban plan, and it depended upon the political conditions and the mentality of the regional leaders whether a more left-wing or a straight anti-socialist agitation would be preferred. Furthermore, the down-grading of the pseudo-socialist elements in the Nazi propaganda must be perceived in conjunction with the changed coalition which by now was headed by the Social Democrat Hermann Müller. The imminent negotiations over the reparation problem necessarily induced Hitler to intensify the nationalist and revisionistic elements of the party propaganda.

Adaptability to given political circumstances was always the specific character of fascist movements, and sometimes Hitler was able to display his instinctive flexibility. Hence, the rational element in the party's move towards a pro-capitalist, middle-class-oriented and pro-agrarian line should not be overestimated.[10]

It was a common conviction of the Nazi leaders that the revolutionary change they were hoping for was to be achieved only through a takeover of the big cities, a move designed to counteract an expected Marxist upheaval. The NSDAP, therefore, did not rescind its former strategical device, although fully exploiting the windfall effects of its growing gains in rural districts and smaller communities. The Boxheim documents – the only available source relating to deliberate preparations for a takeover – reflect, however, the obstacles to the urban strategy which was fervently endorsed by Goebbels, the Gauleiter of Greater Berlin. Significantly, the first steps towards establishing a comprehensive agrarian organization, Walther Darré's creation of the *Agrarpolitischer Apparat*, was originally intended to be a means of preventing passive resistance by the farming population who might possibly obstruct the food allocation in the cities. Paradoxically, the agrarian apparatus provided one of the most effective propaganda tools for the party and secured much of the peasants' support in the 1930 election.[11]

In general the Nazis followed the path of success rather than laid its foundations. That suited Hitler's deliberate strategy of avoiding political options which might restrict his freedom of action. Furthermore, the party's campaign office showed sophistication in analysing local and regional election returns, and it responded with specific propaganda devices which recognized both electoral shortcomings and the necessity of appealing to groups of voters who had hitherto abstained.[12]

All this may explain to a certain extent the party's ability to overcome its relative political isolation and to narrow the gap between the electors' reluctance to vote for the Nazis and the party's increased membership up to 1928. But the fundamental change in the German electoral map which began early in 1929, and which was first reflected in the positive returns of the state elections early in that year, cannot be sufficiently concluded from the expressedly opportunistic features of Nazi electoral campaigning. In analysing this problem one has to be aware that voting patterns belong to the most stable elements of political behaviour, as a superficial glance at German electoral developments since the nineteenth century shows very clearly. Hence, this phenomenon must be perceived in conjunction with the severe crisis of the Weimar parliamentary system. The background of the NSDAP's breakthrough as a movement obviously consists in the shift occurring within the bourgeois party system which since 1928 was geared towards preventing further socialist inroads into the capitalist economy.[13]

In fact, since the formation of the Socialist-led government of the Great Coalition under the chancellorship of Hermann Müller, influential interest groups such as the Reich Association of German Industry and the Agrarian League dropped their former allegiance to parliamentary procedures and openly denounced the parliamentary system as being the very incarnation of socialist and trade union predominance. Ironically the strengthening of the SPD, by that time the only reliable defender of the Republic, resulted in a crucial weakening of the republican system. The so-called Ruhr iron strike, the lock-out in the North-Western Group of the German iron- and steel-producing industry, signifies this fundamental change in industrial relations. The explicit aim of the industrialists was not only to restrict state influence on collective bargaining, which they partly achieved, but also to eliminate the bargaining power of the Free and Christian trade unions. The failure of this operation reinforced their disappointment over the fact that the Prussian Diet, including the business-orientated German People's Party, voted in favour of the locked-out labour in the question of the payment of unemployment relief. These two developments resulted in the employers' decision to support by any means constitutional changes in favour of a semi-authoritarian system.[14]

In this respect, it was symptomatic that the bourgeois parties now resolved to fight against the Marxist parties which they identified (quite wrongly) with the abuses of the parliamentary system, and to look forward to constitutional changes of an authoritarian nature. Mussolini's system served largely as a model for them. However, this was certainly not their only motivation. The progressive political segmentation, resulting in an almost inconceivable splintering of the party system, contributed to the rising intra-party cleavages. These were particularly acute within the right-wing groups. The Nazis exploited this new development most effectively. Although the nationalist DNVP and the right wing of the DVP grew progressively more anti-parliamentary in their attitudes, they had for many years been involved in the parliamentary process. Hence, their shift towards a more or less outspoken anti-democratic stance did not exonerate them from the reproach of being responsible for the general political decay which – according to neo-conservative, nationalist and, above all, Nazi views – was largely due to the utterly suicidal adoption of Western constitutional models. Hence, in attacking parliamentarianism the NSDAP could claim more credibility than could Alfred Hugenberg, who eventually tried to copy the Nazi movement structures and its leadership principle. Similar attempts were made by Brüning for the Centre Party after his dismissal.[15]

Hitler's vitriolic attacks against the Weimar Republic and the party system fit neatly into this picture. The NSDAP could claim that it wanted to replace all existing parties and it was eager to present itself as an alternative to party government. When Hitler's Cabinet of National Concentration entered office, many observers regarded this as a reversion to party government on the part of the Nazis; their politics of radical and uncompromising opposition had secured much popular support, but this support had not lasted very long. The NSDAP exploited the organizational weakness of the right-wing parties on the local level and their decreasing control over interest and professional organizations of any kind. Furthermore, the party succeeded in getting the support of local notables, as for instance in Konstanz, where it managed to win over the city's mayor and thereby removed the barrier of social distrust which explained a certain reluctance on the part of the upper middle classes to support the party openly.

These unquestionable propagandistic advantages of the NSDAP, however, would not have paid off so much if the right-wing parties had not been willing to include the Nazi movement in what they called the 'national Germany'. Regional studies, above all those of Jeremy Noakes and Geoffrey Pridham, have shown that as early as 1928 the NSDAP participated in local bourgeois block governments which were primarily designed to isolate the Socialist and Communist parties.[16] This preceded the inclusion of the NSDAP in an alliance of the German Nationalist Party, the *Stahlhelm* or Steel Helmet, and other right-wing splinter groups in order to prompt the popular referendum against the Young Plan. Through the readiness of the German Nationalists to support the NSDAP, the party suddenly overcame its social isolation. It became respected even by representatives of the upper middle class whose prejudices against the National Socialists' rowdy public appearances and against their socialist bias had helped to maintain until then a hidden social barrier between the bourgeois and the National Socialist right. Furthermore, from now on the right-wing newspapers reported the Nazi party's activities. This was of considerable importance because the National Socialist press was restricted in the number of its newspapers as well as in their circulation. While entering right-wing alignments at all levels, the Nazi leadership did everything to avoid the impression that the party could be looked upon as being only an auxiliary annex to the German Nationalist Party. That was also true of Hitler's propagandistic strategies following the formation of the Harzburg Front.[17]

The changed domestic political climate support the NSDAP in its overall efforts to secure a base within the wide range of bourgeois interest groups, ranging from the Agrarian League and the German Nationalist White Collar Employees' Association down to local associations of a mainly apolitical nature. The policy of starting a systematic infiltration of what can be called the social substructure of the bourgeois middle and right-wing parties turned out to be one of the crucial keys to the overwhelming landslides in these years. Only the Catholic organizational network, which provided the background to the Centre Party's splendid performance during the decisive election campaign between 1930 and 1932, remained immune. By first replacing local notables in these bourgeois organizations, and then conquering massive influence within the central organizational bodies, the Nazis were able to secure the support of highly influential mass organizations, above all the Reich Agrarian League and the Rural People's movement.[18]

Hitler's reluctance to enter any coalition government had, independently of his personal motivations which appear to be extremely complex, gained much sympathy. But this impression could not last long, and the result of the November election in 1932 displays growing disillusionment among the Nazi constituency. Even before the election the Nazi leadership was aware that its voting potential was almost exhausted, and it is quite symptomatic that the regional election campaigning followed divergent and contradictory lines in order to attract certain professional and social groups who had hitherto not been affected by the Nazi agitation. Hence the Nazi Party drew its relative popularity not from having a clear-cut programme, but from the absence of one, and even its anti-semitic policy had only a limited influence.

It was not so much support from previous non-voters or even from new voters which contributed to the NSDAP expansion, but above all the breakdown of the DNVP and the liberal parties in the middle of the political spectrum. Peter Stachura and others have pointed out the general change in the bourgeois part of the Weimar party system in 1928, illustrated most notably by Lambach's opposition to Hugenberg and Westarp, the formation of Young Conservatives, the amalgamation of the Young German Order with the Democrats to form the German State Party, the change in the DNVP leadership and the replacement of Marx by Kaas in the Centre Party. The general shift to the right after 1928 and the increasing political polarization and the inconsistency of the presidential cabinets of Brüning, von Papen and von Schleicher helped to prepare the ground for the NSDAP's self-presentation as the fundamental political alternative to the existing political system. But it was not the breakthrough of the party as a mass movement, and not even the myth that this movement was unstoppable, but the endeavour on the part of von Schleicher, von Papen and the industrial and agrarian interest groups to integrate Hitler and his followers in a semi-authoritarian system which paved the road for Hitler's dictatorship.[19]

Notes

1. See Michael H. Kater, *The Nazi Party: A Social Profile of Members and Leaders, 1919–1945* (Cambridge, Mass., 1983); Hans Mommsen, 'Zur Verschränkung traditioneller und faschistischer Führungsgruppen in Deutschland beim Übergang von der Bewegungs- zur Systemphase', in Wolfgang Schieder (ed.), *Faschismus als soziale Bewegung*, 2nd edn (Göttingen, 1982).
2. Thomas Childers, 'The Social Bases of the National Socialist Vote', *Journal of Contemporary History*, vol. 11 (1976), pp. 17–42; and by the same author, *The Nazi Voter. The Social Foundation of Fascism in Germany, 1919–1933* (Chapel Hill/London, 1983); cf. Jürgen W. Falter, 'Die Wähler der NSDAP 1928–1933: Sozialstructur und parteipolitische Herkunft', in Wolfgang Michalka (ed.), *Die nationalsozialistische Machtergreifung* (Paderborn, 1984), pp. 47–59, and the quoted additional literature.

3. With respect to Brüning's strategy, cf. Hans Mommsen, 'Heinrich Brünings Politik als Reichskanzler: Das Scheitern eines politis hen Alleingangs', in Karl Holl (ed.), *Wirtschaftskrise und liberale Demokratie. Das Ende der Weimarer Republik und die gegenwärtige Situation* (Göttingen, 1978), pp. 16–45.
4. Joseph Goebbels, *Vom Kaiserhof zur Reichskanzlei* (Berlin, 1933), p. 87.
5. cf. Juan J. Linz, 'Some Notes Toward a Comparative Study of Fascism in Sociological Historical Perspective', in Walter Laqueur (ed.), *Fascism: A Readers' Guide*, 2nd edn (Harmondsworth, 1979), pp. 54ff.
6. cf. the analysis of Hitler's speeches during that period by D. Grieswelle, *Propaganda der Friedlosigkeit. Eine Studie zu Hitlers Rhetorik 1920–1930* (Stuttgart, 1972).
7. Eugene Larry Jones, '"The Dying Middle": Weimar Germany and the Fragmentation of Bourgeois Politics', *Central European History*, 5 (1972), pp. 23–54.
8. Peter D. Stachura, '"Der Fall Straßer": Gregor Straßer, Hitler and National Socialism', in Stachura (ed.), *The Shaping of the Nazi State* (London, 1979), pp. 88–130; Jeremy Noakes, *The Nazi Party in Lower Saxony* (Oxford, 1971), pp. 166ff.; Dietrich Orlow, *The History of the Nazi Party, 1919–1933*, vol. I (Pittsburgh, 1969), pp. 139ff.; Jerzy Holzer, *Parteien und Massen. Die politische Krise in Deutschland 1928–1930* (Wiesbaden, 1975).
9. Orlow, op. cit., pp. 126ff.
10. cf. Henry Ashby Turner, *German Big Business and the Rise of Hitler* (New York, 1985), pp. 181ff.
11. See Horst Gies, 'NSDAP und landwirtschaftliche Organisationen in der Endphase der Weimarer Republik', *Vierteljahrshefte für Zeitgeschichte*, 15 (1967), pp. 341–76.
12. See the forthcoming book by Thomas Childers on Nazi propaganda on the eve of the seizure of power.
13. See the survey on the election returns by Alfred Milatz, *Wähler und Wahlen in der Weimarer Republik* (Düsseldorf, 1969).
14. See Bernd Weisbrod, *Schwerindustrie in der Weimarer Republick zwischen Stabilisierung und Krise* (Wuppertal, 1978), pp. 415ff.
15. cf. Rudolf Morsey, *Der Untergang des politischen Katholizismus. Die Zentrumspartei zwischen christlichem Selbstverständnis und 'Nationaler Erhebung' 1933* (Stuttgart/Zürich, 1977).
16. See, besides the analysis of Noakes, op. cit., Geoffrey Pridham, *Hitler's Rise to Power: the history of the NSDAP in Bavaria 1923–1933* (London, 1973).
17. cf. Gerhard Stoltenberg, *Politische Strömungen im schlewsig-holsteinischen Landvolk 1919–1933* (Düsseldorf, 1962).
18. See especially Pridham, op. cit.
19. See my following chapter on 'The Failure of the Weimar Republic'.

EIGHT

The Failure of the Weimar Republic and the Rise of Hitler

HANS MOMMSEN

More than half a century after Hitler's appointment as Reich chancellor on 30 January 1933 the crucial causes of this event are still the subject of controversy. Official speakers of the Federal government still tend to interpret the failure of Weimar democracy as a result of increasing radicalism of the political left and the political right which eventually strangled the Republic under the pressure of the world economic crisis. Even outstanding historians are inclined to ignore or to underrate the role of the conservative élites and the bourgeois right-wingers in paving the way for Hitler's seizure of power. At the same time, the Weimar republicans are usually blamed for a lack of co-operative spirit and for not having defended the parliamentary system with more energy. The system itself is regarded as having been inherently unstable. Within the historiographical discourse the argument prevails that the decay of the Republic could have been prevented if the political parties had acted according to their constitutional role instead of pursuing particular party interests. A few years ago, a well-received collection of articles coined the term of a 'self-surrender' of Weimar democracy.[1]

Any analysis of the chain of events leading to the dissolution of the Weimar Republic has to distinguish between those factors which were responsible for the weakening of the parliamentary system as such and those which explain the rise of the NSDAP as a mass movement after the autumn of 1929. It is essential to appreciate that the growth of the Nazi movement to become a self-styled people's party was not the reason for the deepening structural crisis of Weimar parliamentarism, but rather its consequence. The democratic system was virtually destroyed before Hitler could claim to replace it by an alleged fundamentally new political order. Moreover, the call for a national dictatorship was anything but an invention by the National Socialists. It was raised by a great many right-wing politicians and nationalist intellectuals long before Hitler could claim that dictatorship for himself. Hence it is utterly misleading to claim that the National Socialist attack on the Republic was the main reason for its destruction.

First of all one has to be aware that the structural crisis of the parliamentary system was not confined to the Central Powers, but that almost all of those political systems which were installed after the end of World War I proved to be feeble from the start and ineffective in the long run. The parliamentary principle survived on the Continent only in a few states which were deeply influenced by the British parliamentary tradition, above all in the Scandinavian and the Benelux countries. From a merely technical viewpoint, French parliamentarism remained intact until the German assault in June 1940; the sharp political tensions within the political system of France, however, were already visible in 1936, and this explains her reluctance to respond to the imminent German aggression with means other than those of conciliatory appeasement. After the destruction of the newly introduced parliamentary systems in Poland and the South-East European countries, leaving aside the fascist takeover in Italy, there occurred a general decay which coincided with the evaporation of the informal French hegemony under the impact of the slump. The destruction of the Austrian Republic was the first, the dissolution of Czechoslovakia and the end of its parliamentary tradition the last visible defeat of the French constitutionalist influence. From this viewpoint the relative stability of parliamentarism there and in Germany during the 1920s needs to be explained.[2]

Under the impact of the Great Depression the overwhelming majority of contemporary political observers in Germany were convinced that the parliamentary system was no longer viable and had to be replaced by a more stable form of government. Any evaluation of the crisis of the Weimar Republic must be placed into this context. Consequently, the crucial question is not why the Weimar democracy failed but why it technically survived until 1931–2. Obviously, external conditions were responsible for the fact that the Weimar constitution remained valid although not effective through the whole period, in spite of the fact that the republicans lost their majority as early as the Reichstag elections of June 1920. Rosenau's theory of penetrated systems provides the clue to understanding this phenomenon.[3] As long as foreign political interests blocked the road to an unconcealed change of the constitutional system, a constellation prevailed which was called by Otto Bauer the equilibrium of the class powers.[4] This pattern changed definitely in 1932 when the financial predominance of Britain and France was shattered under the impact of the Great Depression.

An evaluation of the domestic factors leading to the dissolution of the Republic should not overrate the shortcomings of the Weimar constitution, especially in respect of its plebiscitarian elements. Not article 48 itself, but its abuse (beginning in the crisis of 1923) led to a virtual neutralization of the parliament. Although the system of proportional representation supported the fragmentation of the party system, the proportion of the votes given to splinter parties never exceeded roughly 15 per cent, and the endemic coalition crisis at the national level existed long before the expansion of interest parties during the hyperinflation. It is also difficult to maintain that the Reich government depended too much on changing parliamentary majorities. In fact, first in 1920, and then again during the bourgeois block period, the government acted relatively independently of its parliamentary basis.

One of the main shortcomings of the Republic consisted in the high degree of interest fragmentation within the bourgeois and socialist parties which compelled them to stress ideological issues, among them anti-semitism and nationalism, in order to attain intra-party integration. This proved to be an inheritance from the Wilhelmine period. The impact of the interest groups was considerably strengthened through the announcement in 1914 of the *Burgfriede*, during the war. In Weimar the interest groups, particularly big business and agriculture, exerted direct pressure on the bourgeois middle and right-wing parties and claimed also personal concessions where the composition of the leadership and of the Reichstag delegation were concerned. But as early as the stabilization period they did not hesitate to put pressure on the administration itself. In addition, the emergence of an increasing group of mere interest parties accelerated the continuous erosion of the liberal middle-class representation. It was symptomatic that the Reich Agrarian League presented itself as a parliamentary group in spite of the close ties it had with the German Nationalist Party.[5] The Social Democrats' room for manœuvre was also limited by the increasing influence of the Free Trade Unions which filled up to a third of their Reichstag seats.

Apart from the growing impact of interest fragmentation within and outside the party system, parliamentary representation was further weakened by the network of extra-parliamentary associations and circles. Some of these intervened directly in party politics. The Steel Helmet, the most influential war veterans' organization which found its republican counterpart in the democratic *Reichbanner* and Communist paramilitary associations, acted in the presidential elections of April 1932 as an independent political group. The Young German Order merged with the German Democratic Party in 1930 and formed the German State Party in order to achieve a reunification of the middle groups. This proved to be an abortive attempt to prevent the definitive dissolution of the bourgeois middle.[6] As well as mass organizations like the Reich Agrarian League, and the German National Association of Commercial Employees which exerted a strong influence on the bourgeois middle and right wing of the party spectrum, the role of the so-called 'ring-movement' cannot be overrated. The extended network of openly anti-parliamentary clubs, circles and semi-public societies comprised almost all members of the bourgeois and conservative functional and political élites. The establishment of specific publishing houses, such as the Hanseatische Verlagsanstalt which had close links with the German Nationalist Employees, provided the mainly neo-conservative writers of the ring-movement with an important public platform. All these circles, deriving from anti-bolshevik activities during the period of the November revolution, maintained close personal links with the interest groups of the bourgeois right-wing parties, especially with the Reich Agrarian League and the Reich Association of German Industry. Particularly after 1928, as a result of its experience of the Ruhr iron conflict, heavy industry did not hesitate to reactivate the anti-parliamentary potential of the neo-conservative ring-movement.[7]

The escalating influence of anti-parliamentary and anti-socialist propaganda, through neo-conservative and nationalistic writers like Oswald Spengler, Moeller van den Bruck, Edgar Jung, Ernst von Salomon, Ernst Jünger and many others, provided the intellectual climate for the destruction of the parliamentary system.[8] At the same time the terrorist activities of the Free Corps undermined the authority of the government. But not until the pressure groups of heavy industry and big agriculture decided to withdraw from the parliamentary system and replace it with a mixture of authoritarian and corporatist elements could the widespread anti-parliamentary agitation of neo-conservative and national-conservative groups gain momentum. In fact, it was interest cleavages, particularly in the field of social security and welfare, that led to the ultimate destruction of the parliamentary system. It is true that a silent majority regarded democracy as an imported product implanted in Germany under allied pressure in 1919. In their eyes it did not fit the allegedly specific German state tradition which relied on the principle of self-administration, rather than on parliamentary representation. But the early assaults on the Republic by extremist splinter groups such as the Free Corps movement in 1920 and the NSDAP and its national-conservative allies in November 1923 failed because any change of the constitution implied an open conflict within the Western-powers which big business wanted to avoid. Hence, the direct attack on the constitutional system was postponed until the late twenties.

During the immediate post-war and the inflation period capitalist interest groups secured their position by a partial alignment with the trade unions and by securing compensation for their concessions to organized labour through direct and indirect government subsidies. In addition, industry succeeded in exploiting the tax differentials produced by the galloping inflation to gain considerable profits and get rid of its pre-war and wartime debts. The unwanted side-effect of this strategy consisted of a significant economic deprivation of parts of the middle classes, especially artisans and peasants with small- and medium-sized holdings; these groups, burdened by the system of price controls and food rationing, were the economic losers. This effect contributed inevitably to the rise of the *völkisch* and right-wing opposition and to the weakening of the republican middle parties.[9]

After the ratification of the Dawes Plan in 1924, which turned out to be only a preliminary settlement of the reparation question, the employers at the Ruhr and the Reich Association of German Industry fell under the control of steel and iron producers and changed their political strategy; they started a wide-ranging campaign against the trade unions and the system of state arbitration in collective bargaining. The latter had been reintroduced, after its origins in the demobilization period, in order to protect the new currency stability. Most symptomatically, it became a permanent institution, especially in the realm of heavy industry, and thereby replaced the responsibility of capital and labour in the field of collective bargaining. According to the employers' beliefs the reconstruction of the German economy, additionally impeded by reparation payments, depended on the return to pre-war working hours and a considerable reduction of both the wage level and the costs of social welfare. The trade unions, seriously affected by the inflation crisis and simultaneously under pressure from the Communist movement, had to rely on the system of state arbitration which they accepted reluctantly although it fell far short of their original euphoric expectations.

It was not the bargaining power of the unions, but the employers' illusory expectation that they might be able to reconquer their former position in the world market, that induced them to put all efforts into rationalization and to take refuge in an artificial price dumping for exports at the expense of domestic consumption. The erroneous assumption that they could solve the crisis in production costs by expanding capacity in the steel and coal industry intensified social tensions. The employers felt compelled to reduce their increased labour costs almost at any price in order to tackle their international competitors, especially after the fatal loss of the Lorraine steel plants. Hence, heavy industry in the Ruhr was resolved to gain a free hand in fixing wage levels, even if that meant the virtual destruction of the unions. The Ruhr iron lock-out in 1928 reflected a turn towards an offensive entrepreneurial strategy which directed its attack against organized labour, the social welfare state and labour's representatives within the parliamentary system.[10]

The year 1928 signalled the turning point of Weimar democracy, although its erosion was under way for some time and had been actively pursued since 1924 through the bourgeois block governments. The formation of the Great Coalition under the Social Democrat Hermann Müller as chancellor was just a preliminary intermission in the progressive realignment of political forces against the Republic. The Great Coalition came into being because the German Nationalist People's Party (DNVP) refused responsibility for the imminent reparation negotiations which eventually resulted in the Young Plan of 1929–30. Although the rupture of the bourgeois block coalition occurred over the Reich school law and, therefore, over the denominational conflict between the Catholic Centre Party on the one hand and the Protestant German Nationalists and Stresemann's German People's Party (DVP) on the other, the reparation issue stood in the background. Contemporary observers, among them Hans Zehrer, the influential editor of the periodical *Die Tat*, predicted correctly that the Great Coalition would break down as soon as the reparation issue had been settled. Because of delays in the reparations negotiations due to international factors, what was internally the weakest cabinet of the Weimar Republic proved to be the one which remained longest in office.

Against the background of a parliamentary constellation in which the German People's Party was resolved to break the coalition immediately after the reparation settlement, the events of March 1930 leading to the fall of Hermann Müller have to be regarded in a less dramatic light than historians have usually seen them. Undoubtedly the resignation of Müller without waging an open parliamentary battle turned out to be a severe tactical blunder. Through their manœuvrings the Social Democrats (SPD) drew the suspicion on themselves that they or the unions had used the unemployment insurance issue as a pretext to return to their accustomed role of opposition. Actually, it was the German People's Party, freed by Stresemann's recent death from his resistance to any such move, which overthrew the coalition as a result of the prevailing pressure by heavy industry. Because of the stiffening protest by the People's Party, Hermann Müller had been compelled to cancel the original plan to provide proportional cuts in civil servants' salaries in order to cover the growing deficit of the unemployment insurance.

Although the Great Coalition might have survived another couple of months if the Social Democrats had acquiesced in the Brüning compromise, the basic decision to replace parliamentary government by a right-wing cabinet based on the presidential prerogative of article 48 had already been made. This was the result of the negotiations between General von Schleicher and representatives of the bourgeois right-wing parties, including Heinrich Brüning, the leader of the Centre Party's Reichstag delegation and intimate follower of Monsignor Kaas who represented the right-wing interests in the Centre Party. While Brüning still hoped to postpone the transition to right-wing government until the autumn of 1930, he was well aware of the fact that his appointment as chancellor rested on a gentleman's agreement to exclude organized labour from the political process. For the time being, however, he needed the parliamentary support of the SPD in foreign affairs because he did not expect to achieve a definite solution of the reparation issue before the US presidential elections in 1932.

After he took office, Brüning was confronted with exactly the same parliamentary alignment that had resulted in the overthrow of the Müller government.[11] Like his predecessor, Brüning took refuge in a cut in the salaries of civil servants to cover the growing deficit. He failed to win the parliamentary support of the German People's Party, which withdrew its minister of finance, Moldenhauer. In order to stabilize the shattered alliance with the bourgeois right, Brüning took the risk of breaking with the SPD and the parliamentary toleration offered by Rudolf Breitscheid. Instead of that, he inserted an additional poll tax in the budget proposals, although the SPD made it unmistakably clear that the so-called citizens' tax was completely unacceptable for the Socialist Reichstag delegation. In fact, the citizens' tax was designed to compel the municipalities to reduce their expenditure on social relief, that is, on those social benefits which were provided after the unemployed no longer received payment of unemployment insurance or of the *Krisenfürsorge*, the transitional payments from government funds for the unemployed. The new tax did not have any repercussions on the Reich budget. It was just a political concession to the employers in order to gain the political support of the People's Party.

The transition to rule by article 48, and the fatal decision to dissolve the Reichstag and schedule elections for September 1930, did not result from the necessity to fight against the consequences of the economic crisis. It resulted rather from an attempted parliamentary deal which failed because of the stubbornness of the intransigent Alfred Hugenberg; he insisted on the replacement of the Social Democratic coalition government in Prussia and a definitive end to reparation payments, but Brüning was not yet ready to concede these demands.

Already in June 1930 the outcome of the ensuing elections was clearly predictable. In a series of land and municipal elections the sudden rise of the Nazi vote was obvious. It was illusory to believe that relevant groups of the DNVP would break with Hugenberg and follow the People's Conservatives who had constituted a party of their own. They did not secure any significant press support, while Hugenberg put the full potential of the press trust he controlled in support of the DNVP, although, as the September elections proved, with limited success.

Undoubtedly, the severe repercussions of the economic crisis contributed to the increasing instability of the political system. Mass unemployment and mass misery intensified the climate of desperation, hopelessness and protest. Mass unemployment intensified the split in the German labour movement. In particular, young workers would not gain any contact with organized labour and would sympathize either with National Socialism or Communism. The tension between employed and unemployed was reflected in the relations between the SPD and the Communists (KPD). The Social Democratic leadership never effectively tried to lure back those workers who had defected to the KPD, which was predominantly a party of unemployed workers. Psychologically, those former Social Democrats were regarded as renegades who would never return to the democratic labour movement. Significantly, the SPD's election campaign was aimed at those workers who supported the Centre Party. Simultaneously, the weak attempts to achieve the support of agrarian workers and small peasants failed due to the half-heartedness of the official SPD agrarian policy.

At the same time, the trade union movement lost almost all its bargaining power under the condition of mass unemployment. Even the strategy of preserving the principle of collective bargaining and of tariff treaties proved to be futile under the actual political and social conditions. The weapon of strikes was no longer usable, and any labour conflict would only play into the hands of the Communists and, in some instances, into those of the National Socialist factory cells (NSBO). The trade unions could only hope to preserve the legal framework of collective bargaining, although this was also endangered through von Papen's far-reaching concessions to the employers. There were no means of stopping the actual decline of the real wages apart from the fact that net earnings had fallen well below the negotiated rates. Organized labour, therefore, was already on the defensive when Hitler became a real political danger after the September elections.

The weakening of labour through the economic depression continued a process of its gradual exclusion from the political system which had started early in the bourgeois block period. Except for Prussia, where Otto Braun could stabilize the position of the SPD by relying on the support of the relatively progressive Prussian Centre Party, the Social Democrats were almost everywhere politically isolated. The replacement of the legal Prussian cabinet by the commissionary government under Franz von Papen in July 1932 was the final step in a continuous erosion of the Social Democratic position in Prussia, and the commissionary government itself came as less of a surprise than did the way in which von Papen treated the former Prussian ministers. The democrats had already lost the battle in the April elections of 1932, and Otto Braun did not conceal his deep political resignation.[12]

The widespread assumption that during the first Brüning cabinet the democratic parties did not use their limited influence to stop further radicalization is ill-founded. Brüning himself put brakes on the clear-cut intention of the state governments to prohibit the SA, suppress the terrorist actions of the paramilitary units of the NSDAP, and forestall the latter's successful attempts to undermine the civil service and the police forces. The chancellor prevented measures at a time when they could have had at least partial results. The prohibition of the SA in June 1932 by General Groener, then Reich minister of the interior, came too late and met with the open protest of his adviser von Schleicher because it conflicted with the army leadership's wish to preserve the healthy human material of the SA as fighters for a future German rearmament. Brüning maintained regular and secret contacts with Hitler, not so much because of the pressure exerted by the entourage of the Reich president, but out of the tactical desire to lure the National Socialists into bourgeois coalitions on the state level in order to dissipate their political energies.[13]

The gradual domestic political change and decay after 1928 occurred not least because of the changed perspective of the Reichswehr leadership. As long as disarmament (in practice, rearmament) was not given priority over the reparations question, the armed forces restricted themselves to illegal preparations for a future resurrection of German military power. This was done through co-operation with the Red Army and also with Spain and some other neutral countries. This perspective was altered qualitatively when the international disarmament question was pressed upon the European allies by the United States. Thus the military leadership became familiar with the prospect of returning to general conscription or at least the establishment of a numerically significant militia within the foreseeable future. This had a decisive impact on their attitude towards the right-wing paramilitary units, including the Stormtroopers.

At the same time, the Reichswehr leadership decided in principle that German rearmament could not be achieved on the basis of a political compromise with the Social Democrats, since they were regarded as predominantly pacifist. In particular Otto Braun, who had struggled for years to get rid of informal military rule, would have to be replaced. Hence von Schleicher entered the field of active coalition politics and put all his influence on President Hindenburg to form a right-wing nationalistic government which would exclude the SPD from power. Brüning adhered to his programme, and although he co-operated with the SPD for the time being he did so with the intention of eventually splitting the party into a moderate and a Marxist wing.

It is against this background that the ominous affair of the German Battle Cruiser A must be analysed. What is frequently looked upon as a violation of the principle of parliamentary government by the SPD Reichstag delegation in fact consisted of a well-concealed attempt by von Schleicher to exclude the military budget from the general budget negotiations and, thereby, to take it indirectly out of the competence of the Reichstag. The battle cruiser served as a smokescreen to hide this operation from the public, and in this deal von Schleicher gained the tacit support of the Social Democratic chancellor.[14] The far-reaching SPD concessions, however, did not prevent von Schleicher's successful *coup* in replacing Müller with a chancellor who had the specific confidence of the armed forces. In fact, Brüning never rejected any military demand in spite of the financial crisis. But when the disarmament talks in Lausanne were in sight, even Brüning was no longer an indispensable tool in fulfilling von Schleicher's targets.

Along with this, the general change of the international constellation has to be taken into account in order to explain the decision of June 1932 to replace Brüning with a personality who would act according to the intentions of the military leadership. The role of the military in the Weimar Republic is frequently depicted as the outcome of the personal aspirations of General von Schleicher and as a matter of intrigues by certain influential individuals. Although von Schleicher fits personally into such a frame of reference, he nevertheless represented the interests of the armed forces as a whole, and he was by no means isolated in the Ministry of Defence. Hence, the weight of the military interests in the process of the final destruction of the republican institutions appears to be far higher than a tacitly apologetic historiography has maintained.[15]

It was of crucial importance to avoid the risk of becoming engaged in an open military conflict through pursuing a revisionist policy which would exploit France's newly weakened international position. The financial crisis, although it struck her later than Britain or Germany, had destroyed France's hopes of replacing her economic preponderance with a new South-East European customs union which would exclude Germany. Although the German–Austrian customs union failed in spring 1931, it was the first open step towards a restored imperialist Germany, turning in the direction of South-East Europe. Brüning, however, was not the man who could satisfy the growing nationalist appetite of the German right, and he was unable to fulfil its domestic political targets, the elimination of socialist influence, the destruction of the remnants of the welfare state and the financial reconstruction of the East-Elbian agrarian estates. Hence, in the view of the political right-wingers, he became dispensable, as had been the case of his predecessor after the ratification of the Young Plan.

This article will not describe in detail the ensuing attempts at an undisguised authoritarian restoration. They were doomed to failure because they ignored the very conditions of modern industrialized society, and they pursued an illusory dream of returning to anti-urban and pre-industrial social structures. The combined pressure of heavy industry, the military leadership and big agrarian landlords resulted in the ultimate isolation of the Social Democrats and the replacement of the Prussian coalition government, but these moves failed in their purpose of winning over Hitler and the NSDAP to at least a limited degree of co-operation. The growth of the Communist protest movement in the November election of 1932 served as a pretext to keep in power a group of political gamblers who were reluctant to use the means of military dictatorship and who, instead of that, clung to the illusion that they could tame Hitler for their own ends. In fact, after July 1932 there existed only the choice between authoritarian and fascist dictatorship since the pre-conditions for a coalition between Otto Braun and the Reich chancellor had been deliberately dismantled. The success of the NSDAP at the polls in July 1932, however, had not changed its self-intended and hazardous political isolation, and in August President Hindenburg made it publicly clear that he rejected the proposition, supported also by the Centre Party, that he appoint the Bohemian corporal as Reich chancellor. The severe setback of the NSDAP in the November elections was not unexpected. It provoked a deep internal crisis within the party which eventually was overcome by the coalition negotiations in January 1933.[16]

Hitler had proved to be not invincible. In fact, his defeat at the polls late in 1932 – in Thuringia he lost about 40 per cent of his vote – made him more attractive in the eyes of his conservative opponents. The obstacles they had built up against his chancellorship fell one by one, not because Hitler had changed his mind and turned to a more moderate appearance, but because of the obvious setback of the NSDAP in the November election. Most symptomatically, the conservative right made the deal with Hitler exactly at the moment when they became aware that the alternative to the cabinet of 'National Germany' would be the restoration of parliamentary government, at least through a Centre/DVP/NSDAP majority. That was exactly what they had persistently tried to avoid. In order to overcome the reluctance of Hindenburg to entrust Hitler with the Reich chancellorship ex-chancellor von Papen claimed that the new government would have the character of a majority cabinet, although Hitler did not abstain from the precondition that the latter should be based on the presidential prerogative of article 48. Nevertheless, von Papen alluded to the impending participation of the Centre Party, in spite of Hitler's intention to avoid any participation by the Centre in the 'Coalition of National Concentration'. The president, reproached with violating the constitution, reluctantly gave way.

Thus the appointment of Hitler as chancellor was anything but a revolutionary step. It was an attempt to stabilize the rule of the representatives of those classes which aimed at the restoration of their former social privileges and were resolved to cancel the social compromise arrived at during the November revolution. The democratic groups – the Social Democrats and the remnants of Weimar liberalism, mainly represented by the liberal–Jewish newspapers in Berlin – were completely isolated after the fall of the Braun government. The responsibility for the later events lay with the conservative groups and organizations supporting the formation of a 'National Germany'.

The Communists had largely contributed to the destruction of republican authority. But their fatal political course cannot justify the politics of authoritarian experiments aimed at the isolation of organized labour and necessarily leading to the even more fatal alliance of the conservative classes with Hitler.

Notes

1. Karl Dietrich Erdmann and Hagen Schulze, *Weimar – Selbstpreisgabe einer Demokratie. Eine Bilanz heute* (Düsseldorf, 1980).
2. See Hans Mommsen, 'Die Krise der parlamentarischen Demokratie und die Durchsetzung autoritärer und faschistischer Regime in der Zwischenkriegszeit', *Geschichte Europas für den Unterricht der Europäer* (*Schriftenreihe des Georg-Eckert-Instituts*, vol. 27) (Braunschweig, 1983), pp. 144–65.
3. See James N. Rosenau, 'Pre-theories and Theories of Foreign Policy', in Barry Farell (ed.), *Approaches to Comparative and International Politics* (Evanston, 1966); cf. Werner Lin, 'Der amerikanische Einfluss auf die Weimarer Republik in Dawesplanphase: Elemente eines penetrierten Systems', *Das Parlament. Aus Politik und Zeitgeschichte*, vol. 45 (11 Nov. 1973).
4. See Otto Bauer, *Die österreichische Revolution* (Vienna, 1923).
5. See Dieter Gessner, *Agrardepression und Präsidialregierungen in Deutschland 1930–1933. Probleme des Agrarprotektionismus am Ende der Weimarer Republik* (Düsseldorf, 1977).
6. See Eugene Larry Jones, '"The Dying Middle": Weimar Germany and the Fragmentation of Bourgeois Politics', *Central European History*, vol. V (1972), pp. 23–54.
7. cf. Bernd Weisbrod, *Schwerindustrie in der Weimarer Republik zwischen Stabilisierung und Krise* (Wuppertal, 1978), pp. 472ff.
8. cf. Walter Struve, *Elites Against Democracy: Leadership Ideals in Bourgeois Political Thought in Germany, 1890–1933* (Princeton, 1973); Joachim Petzold, *Wegbereiter des deutschen Faschismus. Die Jungkonservativen in der Weimarer Republik* (Cologne, 1978).
9. See Gerald Feldman *et al.* (ed.), *Die deutsche Inflation. Eine Zwischenbilanz* (Berlin, 1982).
10. cf. Ernst Fraenkel, 'Der Ruhreisenstreit 1928–1929 in historisch-politischer Sicht', in F. A. Hermens and Th. Schieder (ed.), *Staat, Wirtschaft und Politik in der Weimarer Republik. Festschrift für Heinrich Brüning* (Berlin, 1967), pp. 97–117.
11. See Hans Mommsen, 'Staat und Bürokratie in der Ära Brüning', in G. Jasper (ed.), *Tradition und Reform in der deutschen Politik.*

Festschrift für Waldemar Besson (Berlin, 1976), pp. 96ff.

12. cf. Gerhard Schulz, '"Preußenschlag" oder Staatsstreich? Neues zum 20. Juli 1932', *Der Staat*, 17 (1978), pp. 553–61; Wolfgang Benz, *Staatsstreich gegen Preußen am 20. Juli 1932* (Düsseldorf, 1982).
13. cf. Gerhard Schulz in Ilse Maurer and Udo Wengst (ed.), *Staat und NSDAP 1930–1932. Quellen zur Ära Brüning* (Düsseldorf, 1977).
14. See Hans Mommsen, 'Die nationalsozialistische Machtergreigung und die deutsche Gesellschaft', in Wolfgang Michalka (ed.), *Die nationalsozialistische Machtergreifung* (Paderborn, 1984), pp. 29–46.
15. See Michael Geyer, *Deutsche Rüstungspolitik 1860–1980* (Frankfurt, 1984), pp. 133ff.
16. See my chapter on 'The Breakthrough of the National Socialists as a Mass Movement in the Late Weimar Republic' in this volume.

NINE

Policy and Performance in the German Economy, 1925–35: a Comment on the Borchardt Thesis

J. JOSEPH LEE

The debate launched by Knut Borchardt on the economic policy options available to decision-makers in late Weimar has proved one of the most fruitful in recent European historiography.[1] The essence of Borchardt's argument is that a rapid rise in real wages, exceeding productivity increases at home and wage rises abroad, seriously damaged the competitiveness of the German economy between 1925 and 1929.[2] The resulting pressure on profits reduced the investment capacity of German industry, which further suffered from high taxation required to finance the ambitious social welfare programmes introduced under revolutionary and trade union pressure.[3] The consequent low level of investment caused high rates of unemployment, between 8 and 10 per cent, even in the 'good' years of 1927 and 1928, *before* the onset of the great slump in 1929.[4] The bitter distributional conflict between capital and labour that had been partly postponed through inflation, and later through capital imports, now flared into the open.[5] As wage settlements had become a political issue under the compulsory arbitration schemes introduced since 1923, both sides were tempted to behave irresponsibly. The politicization of wage negotiations meant that trade unions and employers felt they had to acquire additional political influence, whether through parliamentary or extra-parliamentary channels.[6]

Borchardt sees no solution to the dilemma of the distributional conflict in the context of fixed exchange rates and the gold standard – or indeed of Weimar parliamentary democracy.[7] Any attempt to curb significantly the rate of wage increases, or to reduce welfare benefits, would have destabilized the Republic by rousing the resentment of the working classes on which the survival of the regime depended. The trade unions themselves enjoyed little room for manœuvre. Had they been prepared to contemplate slower short-term gains in the hope of more stable long-term benefits, they would have risked being outbid for worker loyalty by more extreme left-wingers, uninhibited by any solicitude for the stability of the state.[8] In Borchardt's model, everybody was trapped.[9] Economic paralysis had made Weimar virtually ungovernable by 1929.

The real problem of the slump in Germany, therefore, was its pre-history, from which fatal economic consequences inexorably followed, and which greatly restricted the alternatives available to those policy-makers unfortunate enough to find themselves confronting the crisis.[10] When the much excoriated Brüning became chancellor in March 1930 he inherited a poisoned chalice, however reluctant he would prove to let it pass from his lips. The constellation of political forces on which he depended precluded the possibility of Keynesian-type deficit spending to reflate the economy. Brüning simply did not have the choices in this respect that his critics have so facilely retrospectively alleged.[11] Even had he wanted to reflate, economic circumstances would have frustrated him. Borchardt therefore tends to dismiss much of the passionate discussion about Brüning's motives as essentially peripheral, if not irrelevant. For irrespective of the motives of the participants, economic imperatives permitted no alternatives. No economic policy could have significantly reversed the remorseless rise in unemployment until the purification process, which essentially meant lower wages and higher profits, had worked itself out.[12]

It is no wonder, in the light of this profoundly pessimistic diagnosis, that Borchardt posited a tragic inevitability about the decline of Weimar. Distributional conflict subverted economic efficiency, and the intimate, and ill-advised, involvement of the state in this distributional conflict ensured that animosities fostered in the field of industrial relations would poison political life.[13] It is no wonder that the Borchardt thesis has provoked lively, and sometimes anguished, controversy. His argument implies, for instance, that trade unions, traditionally viewed as defenders of Weimar democracy, should really count, however inadvertently, among its grave-diggers. The thesis has implications for contemporary German, and indeed European, politics. Many of the issues raised by Borchardt seem to be highly relevant to understanding the economic circumstances of the post-1973 period. He asks fundamental, and uncomfortable, questions about the relationship between the state and the economy in a highly developed capitalist society.[14]

The questions posed by Borchardt remain of enduring significance. They will long continue to fructify debate, and to deepen understanding of the nature of economy, society and state in Weimar Germany. The discussion has happily attracted participants of unusually high calibre, and Borchardt himself, one of the most powerful, original and incisive minds among living economic historians, has responded frequently to his critics. There can be no pretence of trying to resolve the contentious issues, or to survey an already extensive literature, in this paper. Indeed, Borchardt's footnotes, which amount to a virtual parallel text, would alone require detailed exegesis in a comprehensive critique.[15] Instead, this essay seeks to contribute to the debate by identifying some aspects of the discussion that require further clarification. While I hope that some of the specific points advanced may be found useful, I am mainly concerned at this stage with the methodology of the debate, and with the framework within which it can be most usefully conducted.

The Borchardt thesis has been both criticized and defended on the basis of elaborate and ingenious calculations of the relationship between wages and productivity. Different conclusions can be reached depending on whether estimates refer to annual productivity, hourly productivity, etc.[16] Wages do seem to have risen somewhat faster than productivity between 1925 and 1929. As wages were exceptionally low in 1924, however,[17] it seems doubtful if so much emphasis should be laid on wage movements over a short period which involved a substantial element of 'catching up'. Borchardt has noted that factor shares shifted significantly in labour's favour in the late Weimar period compared with 1850–1913 or 1950–77.[18] This did result in lower profit levels, though Holtfrerich maintains that this was due more to changes in the internal composition of the labour force than to wage pressure in the cruder sense.[19] Perhaps the safest conclusion to be drawn at present from the welter of conflicting claims about the relative movements of wages and productivity is that there were some grounds for concern about the potential impact on German competitiveness of rapidly rising wages, but that the movement did not in itself constitute a crisis. Wages cannot be treated in isolation from other costs, and the relative importance of wages, interest rates and international trade restrictions for German export performance remains to be systematically explored.[20] As the influence of the various factors probably varied considerably from sector to sector, from firm to firm within sectors, and even from product to product within firms,[21] this can be most fruitfully attempted through comparative business history, whose value has already been well demonstrated by Plumpe's contribution.[22]

If the argument on wages has been pursued at the macro-economic level to considerable purpose, relatively little attention has been devoted to competitiveness. The contention that the Weimar economy had brought itself to the brink of catastrophe through excessive wage increases contrasts oddly with its apparently impressive performance in increasing exports by 40 per cent between 1925 and 1929.[23] It must seem, at least at first sight, somewhat incongruous to concentrate on the manner in which allegedly excessive wage increases were undermining the competitiveness of the economy when 'between the stabilization of the currency, and the beginning of the Depression, Germany's position on world export markets did indeed improve significantly'.[24] Not only was 'the economic recovery of 1926 . . . led by a very strong export performance', but 'in the later 1920s, exports went on growing when there were clear signs of depression in the domestic economy'.[25] Fischer's conclusion that the external sector of the German economy came through the stagnation of world trade relatively well, especially as the export of finished goods exceeded the highest pre-war level in 1929–30[26] – as well as increasing their share of total exports[27] – and that the specific problems must therefore have lain more in the monetary than in the industrial sphere,[28] warns of the danger of becoming obsessed with the question of what was 'wrong' with the Weimar economy. It is true that exports constituted a lower proportion of national income than 'before 1914'.[29] The quota was lower than between 1910 and 1913, but virtually the same as between 1905 and 1909, and higher than between 1900 and 1904. For that matter, the ratio was lower between 1890 and 1904 than between 1880 and 1889, but this hardly leads us to dismiss the role of German exports in the 1890s or in the early twentieth century.[30] Germany remained an impressive export performer in the late 1920s, and while this display of competitiveness may have been achieved only at the expense of a profit squeeze, that remains to be demonstrated from detailed investigation at the company level.

In this respect, the quotation from Keynes that Borchardt uses in support of the contention that German wages were excessive[31] permits of an alternative interpretation. 'For after all,' Keynes asked,

> what is the reason why Germany's exports are no larger than they are at the moment? It is certainly not that her export industries cannot get the necessary labour, for there is a surplus of labour in all the leading export industries. Undoubtedly, the reason why she has no more exports is because her costs of production do not enable her manufacturers to compete in international markets on a larger scale. She can only export more if she cuts down her costs of production, and it is roughly true to say that she can only cut down her costs of production materially if her wages are reduced. Now, it has been calculated that in order to produce an adequate export surplus, she would have to increase her exports of finished goods by at least 40 per cent. By how much would she have to reduce her wages in order to produce this result? I do not know. But the amount of reduction of wages which would be necessary is the measure of the difficulty of the transfer problem.

At first sight, this extract appears to be pitched at an elementary level. Did Keynes ever write a more superfluous sentence than 'the reason why she has no more exports is because her costs of production do not enable her manufacturers to compete in international markets on a larger scale'? It is tautology. Keynes was not given to tautology. It therefore behoves us to look further. As his last sentence makes clear, the competitiveness Keynes has in mind is not normal commercial competitiveness, but a level of super-competitiveness sufficient to resolve 'the difficulty of the transfer problem'. There were, he felt, three ways in which Germany could move towards solving that problem. The first was to increase the *relative* efficiency of her production. As, however, she was already highly efficient, she could hardly be expected to increase her *relative* advantage any further.[32] A second possibility was that 'the rate of interest in Germany must be lower than elsewhere'.[33] He could see no prospect of this. Therefore, the only remaining way to improve German competitiveness was through reduced wages. Keynes did not argue here that German wages were uniquely responsible for the failure of German exports to increase sufficiently rapidly to cope with the transfer problem. On the contrary, he obviously felt there was more than one reason why German industry was not even more competitive than it already was. He was arguing along purely pragmatic and political lines. The only significant variable that might prove responsive to policy measures was wages. He recommended reducing wages not because they were necessarily relatively high, but because they were relatively vulnerable. He honestly admitted that he had no idea how far wages should fall; the key variable would be the elasticity of demand for German exports.[34] As he felt that elasticity was low, the reduction in wages would have to be 'substantial'.[35]

While the transfer problem would come to be solved in a different manner, Keynes's contention does illuminate some of the key issues involved in the wider discussion. It is legitimate, for instance, to enquire from proponents of the 'excessive wages' hypothesis just what relative reduction they feel was necessary to cure the 'sick' Weimar economy. Was it 5 per cent? 10 per cent? 20 per cent? etc. The answer, as Keynes observed, must depend in large measure on assessments of export elasticities, which require detailed research.[36] Borchardt himself, for instance, is inclined to be sceptical of the potential impact of a devaluation in 1931, as urged by many, partly on the grounds that elasticities were probably low.[37] On the other hand, he is inclined to maintain that elasticities were sufficiently high to have justified reduced wages (by how much?) a couple of years earlier.[38] It may be that elasticities had declined in the interim. But much more probing research is necessary in this area before advocates of any argument can advance their case with confidence.

A more detailed study of sectors and, where possible, of firms, should help clarify one further important variable, the quality of the German business mind in the later 1920s. Businessmen were naturally highly vocal about 'excessive' wages. Borchardt believes that the objective record confirms the direction of their complaints, however exaggerated they may have been on occasion. Harold James, though himself quite sympathetic to the general thrust of the

Borchardt thesis, does not hesitate to express scorn for the frequent fatuity of both business performance and business opinion.[39] Much of his evidence confirms Fischer's observation that businessmen lacked comparative perspective and that 'only seldom do they lift their eyes to look beyond their own branches and very short-term developments'.[40] Indeed, James would attribute considerable responsibility for lower Weimar growth to entrepreneurial deficiency.[41] He finds management responsible for serious misallocation of capital,[42] presumably an even more grievous error than usual at a time of severe capital scarcity. Even when businessmen believed what they were saying about wage and tax burdens, the quality of the evidence they adduced requires systematic scrutiny.[43]

In trenchantly exposing the wishful thinking lying behind many of the 'solutions' to the Slump retrospectively suggested by historians, Borchardt has rightly demanded more severe standards of realism from scholars in reconstructing the actual choices confronting the actors on the historical stage in the circumstances of the time. He has thus introduced a new level of rigour into the study of decision-making during the Slump. He is particularly scathing about the fashionable assumption that an increase in government expenditure (usually of an unspecified amount) could have 'solved' the economic crisis through deficit financing. Brüning's critics have regularly pointed to the 'alternative' schemes advanced by contemporaries, not only outsiders, but important officials like Schaeffer and Lautenbach. Borchardt has summarily dismissed all these 'alternatives' on a variety of grounds. It is not the least of his contributions that he has been able to demonstrate that neither Schaeffer nor Lautenbach were proto-Keynesian expansionists of an adventurous type, as had come to be widely believed.[44] No doubt more remains to be said on the motives and mentalities of these and other officials, but Borchardt has established the narrow limits within which even the more innovative 'official minds' were prepared to, or obliged to, operate. But that is a different question from the fundamental one at issue. Could expansionist schemes have worked had they been implemented?

Borchardt answers with a resounding no. All the schemes, he feels, were so small in scale, envisaging expenditure of about 2.0–2.5 billion Reichsmark, that they could have made little impact in countering the dramatic decline of about 30 billion Reichsmark in national income between 1929 and 1932.[45] Borchardt seems reluctant here to contemplate possible multiplier effects. He draws an analogy with allegedly ineffective expansionist expenditure in 1975.[46] The appropriateness of this analogy needs to be more convincingly demonstrated. Plumpe posits an expansion effect of about 3.0, which would certainly have had an impact on national income.[47] It may be admitted that the whole question of the multiplier in the German economy during the 1930s, both in the Slump itself and in the subsequent recovery, remains curiously under-researched. May not, however, the impact that expenditure of the magnitude envisaged in the alternative schemes of 1931 and 1932, and on projects of the type suggested in those schemes, had during the actual recovery in 1933 and 1934, tell us something about the potential impact of this expenditure a year or two earlier? Borchardt does not believe that deductions about possible paths to recovery in 1931 or 1932 can be drawn from the actual experience of recovery in 1933 and 1934. His reasoning here is central to his whole thesis. Circumstances, in his view, changed fundamentally between 1931–2 and 1932–3. In so far as state initiative was reponsible for the recovery, various Papen/Schleicher/Nazi plans worked reasonably effectively precisely because the crisis had purified the economy by cleaning out the dirt that had been clogging up the economic system.[48] The huge cost reductions now enabled an expansionary policy to be adopted with better prospects of success. In addition, international recovery was spreading in the autumn of 1932.[49] The growth dynamic had taken hold before Hitler came to power. Indeed, the Nazis were beneficiaries of the relative retardation of the rate of growth in Weimar. The German economy was lagging so far below its 'potential' that Hitler could reap the harvest not only of cyclical recovery, but of a shift to a new (and more 'natural') trajectory after fifteen years of sub-standard performance.[50]

How valid is this rejection of the argument that the circumstances of the recovery do provide a pointer to the potential of alternative policies during the Slump? It seems generally agreed that the Slump reached its nadir in the summer/autumn of 1932. But that is a quite different matter from saying that recovery had begun. The rise in national income in 1933 was less than the amount spent on work creation.[51] This implies that but for work-creation expenditure, which cannot conceivably have involved 'crowding out' at this stage, national income would have fallen further. The performance of private industrial enterprise remained lethargic during 1933. Net private industrial investment actually remained negative not only in 1933, but during 1934 as well.[52] It did not become positive, and then only marginally, until 1935.[53] The tax remissions with which the regime sought to stimulate industrial investment were mainly used, not for new investment, but to liquidate existing debts.[54] There is little in this record to suggest that recovery could have been based on industrial investment by traditional sources.

Nor does German recovery from the autumn of 1932 seem to owe much to international circumstances.[55] There was a momentary chronological coincidence – but only a coincidence, not a causal connection – between the apparent recoveries in Germany and in some other countries in the autumn of 1932. But the international economy remained stagnant in 1933. The value of German exports actually fell in that year, and remained low in 1934 and 1935.[56] In contrast to some earlier German experience, there would be no export-led recovery this time.

International comparisons point to the exceptional scale of the German recovery between 1933 and 1935, even before re-armament assumed a major role. America and Canada stuttered to very partial recoveries, far inferior to the German performance, between 1933 and 1935.[57] Table 1 records the employment performance of several European economies.[58]

Unemployment Rates

Country	**1932**	**1933**	**1934**	**1935**
Belgium	23.5	20.3	23.4	22.9
Denmark	31.7	28.8	22.1	19.7
Germany	30.1	26.3	14.9	11.6
Netherlands	25.3	26.9	28.0	31.7
Norway	30.8	33.4	30.7	25.3
Sweden	22.8	23.7	18.9	16.1
Switzerland	9.1	10.8	9.8	11.8
UK	22.5	21.3	17.7	16.4

In addition, unemployment levels were high and/or rising in Austria and France during these years also.[59] Thus, the apparent incipient international recovery in the autumn of 1932 made little or no impression on the unemployment levels of Austria, Belgium, France, the Netherlands, Norway, or Switzerland. Even the

British, Danish and Swedish rates of recovery fell well below the German. The sources of the German performance must be sought predominantly in the dynamics of the domestic rather than the international economy.

In assessing the comparative performance of the German labour market, variations on the supply side deserve some attention. Fluctuations in the number of births between 1910 and 1921 significantly affected the supply of new entrants to the labour force between 1925 and 1935. Calculations of changes in the net size of the potential labour force have to take account of a number of variables. For our present purposes, however, it suffices to note changes in the number of school-leavers. The number fell from 1.231 million in 1928 to a projected 606,000 in 1932, before rising to an estimated 1.246 million in 1934.[60] Assuming a normal participation rate of 80 per cent for males, and 60 per cent for females in the 14–18 age group,[61] it may be calculated that about 1.1 million fewer school-leavers came on to the job market between 1930 and 1932 than between 1927 and 1929. The recorded unemployment figure for 1932 would probably have been a million higher had the demographic dynamics not altered so abruptly and so favourably. The last year to have a relatively low number of school-leavers was 1933. As the products of the post-war baby boom reached working age, more than 800,000 'extra' school-leavers came on the job market in 1934 and 1935. The fact that employment increased by 5 million, while unemployment fell by only 4 million, between January 1933 and July 1935, may reflect under-recording of the unemployed in 1933,[62] but presumably also indicates an enhanced supply of school-leavers coming on to the market in 1934 and 1935. The slackening in the rate of absorption of unemployed in the summer of 1934 may be partly due to this rise of roughly 400,000 'extra' school-leavers coming on the labour market at that time. The 8 and 9 per cent unemployment levels of 1927 and 1928 occurred in a situation where the economy was having to cope with a rapidly expanding labour supply at a time of relative sluggishness of international trade. Likewise, the performance of the labour market in 1934 and 1935 looks even more impressive than at first sight, while its performance in 1930–2 now looks yet more forlorn than the official statistics suggest.[63]

The safest guide to the course of the German recovery lies in the sectoral employment figures. These document the crucial role of the construction sector in the initial stages. One calculation estimated the percentage increases in employment in the main sectors between February 1933 and February 1934 as follows:[64]

Building	276 per cent
Building materials	91
Timber industry	53
Machine building	34
Electricity	34
Metals	34
Iron and steel	20

There was nothing mysterious about this. The impact of the Slump on employment was uniquely severe in the construction sector, where unemployment could reach 90 per cent at times.[65] The employment of construction workers, whether on residential building or on varieties of public works, was central to all proposed recovery plans. Neither the first nor second Reinhardt plans required any new thinking, merely the will to invest further in this direction.[66]

The construction sector occupied a pivotal role in the employment history of Germany between 1925 and 1935 for two reasons. Firstly, it was a relatively big employer. The size of the workforce in the building industry (including those involved in producing building materials such as stones and clays) just about equalled that in the metal-based sector of the economy between 1925 and 1934.[67] Secondly, it was largely a public-sector industry. Public authorities, whether at local or national level, exerted decisive influence on investment decisions in construction. High interest rates and decimated purchasing power severely restricted residential building after the First World War. Whatever views may be held about the policy of controlled rents pursued by successive governments, it was public action to subsidize building that largely caused the trebling in housing output between 1924 and 1929.[68] Employment in the construction sector rose by 800,000 between 1924 and 1928, compared with an increase of 200,000 in the metal sector.[69] But it was also government action that brought this growth jarring to a halt during the Slump. Between 1929–30 and 1931–2, total public expenditure on house construction fell 60 per cent from more than 1.5 billion to little more than 600 million marks.[70]

The condition of the construction sector in 1930 clearly distinguishes the trajectory of the Great Slump from the crisis of 1925–6. Whereas building activity actually expanded in 1926, thanks to increased state support, the number of building permits fell 31 per cent in the first eight months of 1930 compared with the corresponding period of 1929.[71] Although residential building completions held up well in 1930, as earlier investment was brought to fruition, complaints began to reach the Finance Ministry from June 1930 about the impact of interest rates on building.[72] As early as September 1930, unemployment in the 'seasonal' group of industries, predominantly in the construction sector, was already touching 40 per cent.[73] Contemporaries who expected 1930 to repeat the experience of 1919, 1923 or 1925–6 – short sharp slumps followed by spectacular upward rebounds – overlooked the implication of the inexorable decline in building activity that would characterize 1931. It would have needed a recovery of the export sector dwarfing that of 1926–7 to have compensated for the inevitable decline in building. State policy sharply exacerbated, rather than ameliorated, an already difficult situation.

It would be an exaggeration, but scarcely a distortion, to suggest that the expansion of the construction sector prevented much higher unemployment levels between 1926 and 1929, that the Slump became so pervasive because of the extent of the decline in construction, and that the initial recovery in 1933 and 1934 was first and foremost a recovery of the construction sector. The sources of this recovery were, however, rather different from those of 1926–9. Residential building played a more central role in the earlier period, while 'public works' activity was relatively more important in the later period. However, residential building did recover strongly. The number of dwellings completed did not, it is true, quite reach the level of 1929, even by 1935. But 1929 had itself been a post-war record. More relevant was the scale of the recovery from the trough of 1932 to 1934, a bigger increase in residential output than that recorded over any other two-year period between 1919 and 1937.[74]

The obvious question, in the light of the central role of construction in the economy, and particularly in the labour market, is whether the impact of the Slump could have been significantly moderated had the state refrained from so precipitately reducing public expenditure in this area? Balderston has noted that a main reason for the relative severity of the Slump in Germany and in the

USA compared with Britain is that non-industrial investment fell so much more rapidly in the first two countries.[75] The point at issue is not whether a slump could have been prevented. In the prevailing international circumstances, there was little prospect of that. Borchardt is quite right to dismiss the lack of realism in suggestions that any policy measures in 1930–2 could have simultaneously defended Germany from the international slump and retrieved the difficult employment inheritance of the 1920s. The real question, unheroic but not unhistorical, is whether unemployment could have been kept in the region of 15–20 per cent until sustained recovery began. This might not have sufficed to have prevented the rise of Hitler. But it should at least have increased the options of the anti-Hitler forces. P. C. Witt suggests that a substantial amount of the 2 billion subventions paid to big agriculture and big industry in 1930–2 might have been more productively retained for the construction sector.[76] It may be premature to pronounce dogmatically on this issue. The Brüning government had to balance on a financial tightrope. But it appears that it may have had alternatives, however limited, even within the confines of the balanced budget, that might have yielded better economic results.

More solicitude for the construction sector might also have yielded better political results. The *Mittelstand* was particularly involved in the fortunes of building. The files are replete with complaints and petitions reflecting the feeling, as a correspondent informed the finance minister in June 1931, that 'The building industry determines the level of activity and earning opportunities for almost the whole Mittelstand . . .'.[77] Activity in few other sectors impinged so immediately on the affairs of those small businessmen and small rentiers who would find themselves driven to vote for Hitler.

This approach to the problem of alternatives, focusing not on how the crisis could be solved, but on how damage could be limited, concentrating on containment rather than victory, must seem subversive of the goal of 'purification' which Borchardt, like so many contemporary observers, holds to have been necessary. If our interpretation of the nature of the recovery be correct, however, it would raise queries about the appropriateness of the purification model. Although it had a long and respectable ancestry, the concept remains essentially unscientific, owing more to moralistic inspiration and medical analogy than to economic history. Redemption could be earned only through suffering!

As a concept, 'purification' is both crude and elusive, crude because time and again it can be reduced in practice to simple wage reductions, and elusive because it is impossible to identify its impact except retrospectively. As a policy prescription, it is impossible to know whether it is working or not. Gerhard Colm put the case fairly to Trendelenburg. The point of purification, he felt, was already well past in September 1931. Further deflationary measures could only inflict more damage on the economy. Credit expansion now contained 'the sole hope for a rapid improvement', and it could safely begin as the purification process was now complete. But he then acknowledged that many economists disagreed with his analysis, believing that recovery was not yet possible because costs must fall yet further to restore profit prospects.[78]

The responses of the policy-makers to short-term fluctuations reflected their uncertainty about the progress of purification. Many felt that incipient recovery had already begun during the early months of 1931.[79] They were dismayed when this 'recovery' came to an abrupt halt in April/May. But recovery could not set in, according to their model, until purification had been completed. Did this apparent recovery mean that purification was believed to have been achieved? How? Wage levels were remaining stubbornly high, taxes had not fallen from their allegedly crushing 1929 level, while profits were lower rather than higher. If the Weimar economy were as 'sick' as the purifiers believed, and if the concept of purification had any objective validity, there could be no serious prospect of real recovery in the spring of 1931. There had not yet been sufficient 'cleansing'. That such ardent hopes were nevertheless entertained by the purifiers reflects the analytical looseness of the concept.

The recovery experience itself poses further queries about the place of purification in the real world. For the purification treatment had surely been completed by 1933. Wages and prices were now sharply reduced. Interest rates had fallen. General tax levels did remain high, but various judicious tax remissions were introduced by the new regime. Profit prospects had presumably improved enormously. But the patient was making only a weak and hesitant recovery, and seemed poised for a relapse but for 'artificial' measures taken by the state. Those industrial sectors that seemed destined to profit most from purification contributed relatively little to recovery before 1935, and then began to feature prominently only as re-armament expenditure increased. The construction sector, on the other hand, despite its plethora of small firms and far-from-scientific businessmen, responded exceptionally vigorously to the changing situation. The nature of the recovery, it may be suggested, warns us that the concept of purification requires much further refining before it can become analytically useful for economic historians.

Borchardt has, it seems to me, established that the room for manœuvre of policy-makers in late Weimar was far more restricted than many have presumed. But it remains an open question if there still wasn't some, admittedly limited, possibility for policy-makers to influence the course of economic, and therefore potentially of political, developments even within the restrictive environment in which they found themselves obliged to operate. The condition of the German economy, it may be argued, was not quite so critical in 1929 as Borchardt contends, nor need the Slump have been quite so deep and protracted, nor were policy-makers entirely bereft of 'alternatives'.

This debate will continue. That it will do so mainly within the terms of reference established by Borchardt at the outset is eloquent tribute to the fertility of his approach. Borchardt's work has already helped 'to build bridges across the periods of Weimar history'.[80] It is now time to begin building bridges across countries. Much of the discussion is, of course, already implicitly comparative. But one is struck by the almost incidental nature of many of the comparative statements, in contrast to the rigour of the discussion on Germany. What are the implications, for instance, for Borchardt's thesis of the observation by Harold James that 'The rise in the share of national income taken by labour and its effects on the economy were not purely German but rather general European phenomena.'?[81] James believes that the social cohesion of Britain enabled it to contemplate the measures necessary to tackle the Slump, contrary to the case in Germany.[82] Nevertheless, had Britain suffered as severely from the Slump as Germany, James feels that British democracy would have found the burden 'intolerable'.[83] Borchardt, noting that the economic condition of England was, if anything, even worse than that of his 'sick' Germany in the 1920s, identifies the role of the state in labour relations as a key variable.[84] Hildebrand seeks the cause of the contrasting responses of Britain and Germany to allegedly similar economic problems in the different parliamentary traditions of the two societies.[85] This is surely a research subject that demands a disciplined, systematic, wide-ranging comparative approach. The Borchardt debate has greatly raised the quality of thinking about the German inter-war economy. It has refined the questions, and sharpened insights. The participants in this debate about Germany have much to contribute to discussion concerning global aspects of the slump. They can too, no doubt, glean insights relevant to Germany from the study of the situation in other countries. The work of Klein, Weber and Jonung, to name but three, contains much to stimulate students of the German Slump.[86]

Such a collective project would have to deal with numerous questions ignored in this paper. Several important economic variables have been excluded from consideration, to say nothing of the relationship between economics and politics, which remains ultimately the central question in the debate, essential though it is to clarify the economic variables as a preliminary to locating the political decisions in their correct context. The conceptualization of such a comparative project itself offers a major challenge, but hardly one beyond the capacity of participants who have ensured that the Borchardt debate has already made so important a contribution to historical scholarship.[87]

Notes

1. Borchardt's two seminal papers were 'Zwangslagen und Handlungsspielraume in der grossen Wirtschaftskrise der frühen dreissiger Jahre: Zur Revision des überlieferten Geschichtsbildes', *Jahrbuch der Bayerischen Akademie der Wissenschaften* (1979), pp. 85–132, and 'Wirtschaftliche Ursachen des Scheiterns der Weimarer Republik', in K. D. Erdmann and H. Schulze (ed.), *Weimar, Selbstpreisgabe einer Demokratie. Eine Bilanz heute* (Düsseldorf, 1980), pp. 211–49. Both papers have been frequently reprinted, most conveniently in a collection of Borchardt's essays entitled *Wachstum, Krisen, Handlungsspielraume der Wirtschaftspolitik. Studien zur Wirtschaftsgeschichte des 19. und 20. Jahrhunderts* (Göttingen, 1982). All subsequent references to these articles relate, unless otherwise stated, to this collection, under the initials 'Z' and 'WU' respectively.
2. 'Z', pp. 176–7; 'WU', p. 198.
3. 'WU', p. 196.

4. 'Z', p. 178; 'WU', p. 196.
5. 'WU', p. 189.
6. 'WU', p. 205.
7. 'WU', p. 201.
8. 'Z', p. 181; 'WU', p. 204.
9. Borchardt, 'Zum Scheitern eines produktiven Diskurses über das Scheitern der Weimarer Republik. Replik auf Claus-Dieter Krohns Discussionsbemerkungen', in *Geschichte und Gesellschaft* (*GG*), 9 (1983), p. 137; 'WU', p. 205.
10. 'Z', p. 182.
11. Borchardt, 'Noch einmal. Alternativen zu Brünings Wirtschaftspolitik', *Historische Zeitschrift* (*HZ*), 237 (1983), pp. 74–5.
12. ibid., p. 72.
13. 'WU', pp. 187, 189–90.
14. For succinct summaries of the issues and the impact, see H. James, 'The problem of continuity in German history: the inter-war years', *Historical Journal (HJ)*, 27, 2 (1984), pp. 518–19, and H. A. Winkler, 'Vorbemerkung', *GG*, 11, 3 (1985), pp. 273–4.
15. The footnotes to 'Z' exceed the length of the text in pages, not to mention words!
16. C.-L. Holtfrerich, 'Zu hohe Lohne in der Weimarer Republik? Bemerkungen zur Borchardt-These', *GG*, 10 (1983), pp. 122–41; C. S. Maier, 'Die Nicht-determiniertheit ökonomischer Modelle. Überlegungen zu Knut Borchardts These von der "kranken Wirtschaft" der Weimarer Republik', *GG*, 11, 3 (1985), pp. 275–94; J. von Kruedener, 'Die Überforderung der Weimarer Republik als Sozialstaat', *GG*, 11, 3 (1985), pp. 358–76.
17. Maier, op. cit., pp. 24–5; T. Balderston, 'Links between inflation and depression: German capital and labour markets, 1924–31', in G. D. Feldman (ed.), *Die Nachwirkungen der Inflation auf die deutsche Geschichte 1924–1933* (Munich, 1985), p. 173.
18. 'WU', p. 198; 'Z', p. 281, n. 72.
19. Holtfrerich, op. cit., pp. 136ff. It may also be noted that while the wage–income ratio rose sharply in German industry in the late 1920s, in absolute terms it remained below US and UK levels (E. H. Phelps-Brown and M. Browne, *A century of pay* (London, 1968), pp. 232, 249). See also Maier, op. cit., pp. 283–4.
20. Holtfrerich, op. cit., pp. 134–5; Maier, op. cit., pp. 286–7.
21. W. Fischer, 'Die Weimarer Republik unter den weltwirtschaftlichen Bedingungen der Zwischenkriegszeit', in H. Mommsen, D. Petzina, B. Weisbrod (ed.), *Industrielles System und politische Entwicklung in der Weimarer Republik* (Düsselforf, 1974), p. 33.
22. G. Plumpe, 'Wirtschaftspolitik in der Weltwirtschaftkrise. Realität und alternativen', *GG*, 11, 3 (1985), pp. 115ff.
23. *Statistisches Jahrbuch*, 1934, p. 196.
24. H. James, *The German slump: politics and economics 1924–1936* (Oxford, 1986), p. 120.

25. ibid., p. 121.
26. Fischer, op. cit., p. 43.
27. W. G. Hoffmann (with F. Grumbach and H. Hesse), *Das Wachstum der deutschen Wirtschaft seit der Mitte des 19. Jahrhunderts* (Berlin, 1965), p. 153.
28. Fischer, op. cit., p. 44.
29. 'WU', p. 197.
30. Hoffmann et al., op. cit., p. 151.
31. 'WU', p. 198.
32. J. M. Keynes, 'The German transfer problem', *Economic Journal*, 39 (March 1929), p. 4.
33. ibid., loc. cit.
34. ibid., p. 6.
35. ibid., loc. cit.
36. For interesting, if controversial, calculations, see J. Schiemann, *Die deutsche Währung in der Weltwirtschaftskrise. Währungspolitik und Abwertungskontroverse unter den Bedingungen der Reparationen* (Bern, 1980).
37. Borchardt, 'Z', *Jahrbuch der Bayerischen Akademie der Wissenschaften*, p. 124, n. 55.
38. Borchardt, 'Zum Scheitern eines produktiven Diskurses über das Scheitern der Weimarer Republik. Replik auf Claus-Dieter Krohns Discussionsbemerkunge', *GG*, 9 (1983), p. 315.
39. James, *The German slump*, pp. 172, 209, 220–1.
40. Fischer, op. cit., p. 34.
41. James, *The German slump*, ch. IV.
42. ibid., p. 149.
43. For comments on the quality of business perceptions of the burden of taxation, see P. C. Witt, 'Die Auswirkungen der Inflation auf die Finanzpolitik des Deutschen Reiches 1924–1935', in G. D. Feldman (ed.), *Die Nachwirkungen der Inflation auf die deutsche Geschichte* (Munich, 1985), pp. 69, 73.
44. K. Borchardt, 'Noch einmal. Alternativen zu Brünings Wirtschaftspolitik', *HZ*, 237 (1983), pp. 78ff.; K. Borchardt, 'Zur Aufarbeitung der Vor- und Frühgeschichte des Keynesianismus in Deutschland. Zugleich ein Beitrag zur Position von W. Lautenbach', *Jahrbücher für Nationalökonomie und Statistik* (*JNS*), 197 (1982), pp. 359–70.
45. 'Z', pp. 174 and 279, n. 62.
46. 'Z', p. 174.
47. G. Plumpe, 'Wirtschaftspolitik in der Weltwirtschaftkrise. Realität und alternativen', *GG*, 11, 3 (1985), p. 354.
48. 'Z', p. 182; p. 271, n. 30; p. 279, n. 63.
49. 'Z', p. 267, n. 8.
50. K. Borchardt, 'Trend, Zyklus, Strukturbrüche, Zufaelle. Was bestimmt die deutsche Wirtschaftsgeschichte des 20. Jahrhunderts?', in Borchardt, *Wachstum, Krisen, Handlungsspielraume der Wirtschaftspolitik. Studien zur Wirtschaftsgeschichte des 19. und 20.*

Jahrhunderts (Göttingen, 1982), p. 108.
51. R. J. Overy, *The Nazi economic recovery 1932–1938* (London, 1982), pp. 35, 40–1.
52. ibid.
53. ibid.
54. ibid.
55. F. W. Henning, *Das industrialisierte Deutschland 1914 bis 1978* (Paderborn, 1979), p. 164.
56. *Statistisches Jahrbuch*, 1936, p. 218.
57. J. Potter, *The American economy between the World Wars* (London, 1974), p. 137; D. A. Wolfe, 'The rise and demise of the Keynesian era in Canada: economic policy, 1930–1982', in M. S. Cross and G. S. Kealey (ed.), *Modern Canada* (Toronto, 1984), p. 50.
58. B. R. Mitchell, *European historical statistics 1750–1970* (London, 1975), pp. 169–71.
59. ibid., p. 169.
60. H. J. Platzer, 'Die Steigerung der Erwerbsziffer in Deutschland', *JNS*, 135 (1931), p. 360.
61. ibid., pp. 337, 340.
62. C. W. Guillebaud, *The economic recovery of Germany* (Cambridge, 1939), pp. 45–6; James, *The German slump*, p. 371.
63. Systematic integration of demographic variables into economic analysis may temper some of the more unfavourable verdicts on the performance of the Weimar economy.
64. *Vierteljahreshefte zur Konjunkturforschung*, 23 April 1934.
65. *Statistisches Jahrbuch*, 1933, p. 310; *Bundesarchiv, Koblenz* (BAK), R43 I/2045, 2 May 1932, Stegerwald to Brüning, p. 5.
66. On the success of the early pre-Nazi initiatives, see BAK, R43 I/2046, 23 December 1932, Syrup to von Krosigk, p. 3.
67. Hoffmann et al., op. cit., pp. 68–9.
68. D. P. Silverman, 'A pledge unredeemed: the housing crisis in Weimar Germany', *Central European History*, III, I (1970), p. 120.
69. Henning, op. cit., p. 106.
70. James, *The German slump*, pp. 71, 206.
71. D. Hertz-Eichenrode, *Wirtschaftskrise und Arbeitsbeschaffung* (Frankfurt, 1982), pp. 147–9; *Wirtschaft und Statistik*, 10, 20 (October 1930), p. 813. On private building during the slump, see F. Blaich, 'Der private Wohnungsbau in den Deutschen Grossstädten während der Krisenjahre 1929–1933', *JNS*, 183 (1969), pp. 435–48.
72. BAK, R2/13640, 17 June 1930, letter from W. Nelke.
73. W. Woytinsky, 'Arbeitslosigkeit und Kurzarbeit', *JNS*, 134 (1931), p. 42.
74. Silverman, op. cit., p. 120. H. Kruschwitz, 'Die deutsche Wohnungswirtschaft seit 1933', *JNS*, 146 (1937), gives a good overview of the successes, and failures, of Nazi residential housing policy. G. Spencely, 'R. J. Overy and the Motorisierung: a

comment', *Economic History Review*, 32 (1979), pp. 100–6, discusses the wider role of building in the Nazi economy.
75. Balderston, op. cit., p. 165.
76. P. C. Witt, 'Finanzpolitik als Verfassungs- und Gesellschaftspolitik. Uberlegungen zur Finanzpolitik des Deutschen Reiches in den Jahren 1930 bis 1932', *GG*, 8 (1982), pp. 400–1, and 'Die Auswirkungen der Inflation auf der Finanzpolitik des Deutschen Reiches 1924–1935', in G. D. Feldman (ed.), *Die Nachwirkungen der Inflation auf die deutsche Geschichte* (Munich, 1985), p. 83.
77. BAK, R2/13640, letter to Dietrich from Koenigsberg, 26 June 1931.
78. BAK, N. L. Lautenbach, G. Colm to E. Trendelenburg, 8 September 1931.
79. 'Z', pp. 168–9.
80. G. D. Feldman, 'Weimar from inflation to depression: experiment or gamble?', in Feldman (ed.), *Die Nachwirkungen der Inflation auf die deutsche Geschichte* (Munich, 1985), p. 391.
81. James, *The German slump*, p. 19.
82. H. James, 'Gab es eine Alternative zur Wirtschaftspolitik Brünings?', *Vierteljahrschrift für Sozialgeschichte und Wirtschaftsgeschichte*, 70,4 (1983), pp. 539–40.
83. James, *The German slump*, p. 160.
84. Borchardt, 'Zum Scheitern . . .', *GG*, 9 (1983), p. 129, n. 12; and Borchardt's contribution to the group discussion in K. D. Erdmann and H. Schulze (ed.), *Weimar, Selbstpreisgabe einer Demokratie. Eine Bilanz heute* (Düsseldorf, 1980), p. 255.
85. K. Hildebrand, contribution to group discussion in Erdmann and Schulze, op. cit., p. 252.
86. P. W. Klein, 'Depression and policy in the '30s', *Acta Historiae Neerlandicae*, VIII (1975), pp. 123–58; F. Weber, 'Die Weltwirtschaftskrise und das Ende der Demokratie in Österreich', in E. Froeschl and H. Zoitl (ed.), *4. März 1933. Vom Verfassungsbruch zur Diktatur* (Vienna, 1984), pp. 37–67; F. Weber, 'Die österreichische Bankenkrise und ihre Auswirkungen auf die niederösterreichische Industrie', in A. Kusternig (ed.), *Beiträge über die Krise der Industrie Niederösterreichs zwischen den beiden Weltkriegen* (Vienna, 1985), pp. 123–46; L. Jonung, 'The depression in Sweden and the United States: a comparison of causes and policies', in K. Brunner (ed.), *The Great Depression Revisited* (Boston, 1981).
87. A. S. Milward's Report to the Bochum Conference in H. Mommsen et al., op. cit., pp. 51ff., remains as pertinent to the present state of Weimar historiography as it was at the time of delivery.

TEN

Images of Fascism: Visualization and Aestheticization in the Third Reich

PETER LABANYI

'Hitler was the first rock star' – thus spoke the pop singer David Bowie. *Triumph of the Will* is, so we are told, one of Mick Jagger's favourite films. To maximize provocation, youth sub-cultures have absorbed Nazi emblems into their codes. To depict the Third Reich as the ultimate boudoir of sexual perversion guarantees a film's box-office success. To sell a paperback, one of the best ways is to put a swastika on the cover. Our own culture's glamorization of fascism is self-revealing. Such morbid exploitation ironically parallels the Nazis' own debasement of culture, which is crystallized in the cliché: 'Whenever I hear the word culture I reach for my revolver' – in fact a slight misquotation from Hanns Johst's play about a nationalist martyr canonized by the Nazis, *Schlageter*. Indeed the definitive comment on the culture of the Third Reich is Ernst Bloch's description of the Nazi as a King Midas in reverse: whatever he touches turns to dirt, including gold.[1] However, that the real issues are differences not so much in the quality but in the *function* of art,[2] is the main burden of my argument throughout what follows. For in the relationship between culture and fascism there is a whole spectrum of complex mediations and interactions to be explored. Given the enormous importance attached to the cultural realm by the Nazi regime, the Johst quotation is misleading; yet, at the same time, its association of culture and violence – the Third Reich's twin-track strategy of domination – is uncannily apt.

The emphasis on the cultural by Nazism brings together a number of historical tendencies: long, medium and short-term. From the late eighteenth century onwards, German thought was saturated with cultural particularism: a belief in the organic rootedness of national culture in the soil of the *Volk*. But after such cultural anticipations had eventually found political fulfilment in national unification, there ensued not a cultural revival but a literally 'pessimistic' sense that the pinnacles attained by German music, philosophy and literature in the late eighteenth and early nineteenth centuries would never again be equalled. Such cultural pessimism was intensified, especially from the 1890s onwards, under the pressure of the Wilhelmine Empire's headlong industrialization and urbanization, by the spectre of the masses, symbolized by the labour movement. It was in *cultural* terms that the euphoria of 1914 was voiced by the liberal and conservative intelligentsia. However, in the wake of defeat, disarmament, reparations and inflation, this soon darkened once more into a sense of cultural decline. From the late 1920s onwards, fuelled by a phobia about the social effects of industrial rationalization and the democratizing ('bolshevist') tendencies of Weimar culture, this gave rise to a renewed modernization crisis. Spiced with an added aggressiveness, the 'Ideas of 1914' were served up again, above all to a petty-bourgeois public even hungrier for illusions. What unites cultural nationalism, cultural pessimism and the prophets of cultural crisis towards the end of the Weimar Republic is the translation of what are political energies and anxieties into cultural terms and, conversely, the escalating enlistment of culture to justify and cloak political violence.

This gives us a provisional answer to the question of how to justify studying Nazi culture when, either there was no such thing, or, to adapt Brecht, to discuss it would be like talking about trees, with the chimneys of Auschwitz smoking in the background. That there is still a taboo surrounding Nazi art was reaffirmed by its omission from the major retrospective exhibition of twentieth-century German painting held in 1985 in London.[3] This taboo was first breached in 1974–5 by an exhibition shown in Frankfurt and other German cities, which caused violent controversy on both left and right – even though the organizers had taken pains to confront Nazi works of art with the documented barbarisms of the regime.[4] However, the breaking of a taboo is, on its own, no justification. The cultural dimension of Nazism demands study not simply because the regime took culture so seriously, nor because, in Walter Benjamin's now overworked but still suggestive phrase, it 'aestheticized politics' but, most importantly, because economic explanations of Nazism have not, on their own, proved to be adequate. To analyse the mechanisms whereby socio-economic discontent was translated into political mobilization we need 'cultural' perspectives, such as those opened up fifty years ago by Ernst Bloch and Wilhelm Reich. For the Depression produced not only material hunger but a 'hunger for meaning' that was no less widespread and, arguably, even more volatile politically. Indeed it is valid to see Nazism as primarily a phenomenon of the superstructure, which left the real economic and class divisions of capitalism largely untouched. For it was in the realm of culture that change could be conjured up and *visually* represented in concrete symbols.[5]

It will be clear that I have blurred the sense of 'culture' by using it to refer not only to works of art and institutions but also to 'a whole way of life': to the values, beliefs and practices of a particular society at a particular time. A major difficulty with culture is that the concept tends to overlap and blend with others: such as, attractively immediate but potentially uncritical, 'everyday life'; more explicitly political and dialectical, 'ideology'; and, more structural and hegemonic, 'public sphere'. Such conceptual difficulties are indicators of real problems, which cannot be defined out of existence; and with Nazism the difficulties are compounded by the understandable temptation to conflate 'culture' with 'propaganda'. In practice, such problems have been avoided by compartmentalization, giving us separate studies of, say, Nazi cinema, art policy, everyday life, etc., but few integrative attempts to examine the diverse functions and meanings of the cultural dimension in the Third Reich.[6]

All societies have an objective 'culture'; bourgeois epochs in particular have had self-conscious and fully formulated ideologies of culture, whose purpose is to lay down the ground-rules within which the production and consumption of meanings takes place. Energized by post-war political upheaval and technological change, Weimar culture at its most radical did challenge the bourgeois formal and ideological canon. But, unlike the revolutionary art of the first decade of the Soviet Union, the Weimar avant-garde was always a sub-culture, operating within a still dominant paradigm, and hence in a precarious position. The Depression merely accelerated long-standing counter-tendencies, exemplified by the racist theories of art of Hans F. K. Günther and Paul Schultze-

Naumburg, which served as a bridge between the Nazis and the turn-of-the-century cultural pessimists, who had themselves already laid great emphasis on art, as exemplified by Julius Langbehn's *Rembrandt als Erzieher*. Success in the 1930 Thuringian provincial elections gave the Nazis a chance to stage a full dress-rehearsal of the coming cultural counter-revolution. This included the founding of a new chair of Race Research, an ordinance against what was called 'Negro Culture', the banning of books, films and plays, the removal of Modernist paintings, and the sacking of art teachers. But, of course, what happened in Thuringia was trifling compared to what was to come after 1933.

The details of the Nazi *Gleichschaltung* of culture will not be recapitulated here; but this is not just for reasons of space. For the danger is that, if one keeps too close to the official documents, one runs the risk of reproducing Nazi culture's own view of itself. In any case, what is the status as historical evidence of the 'documents', or indeed of the 'events' (ceremonies, spectacles, festivals), generated by such a ruthlessly manipulative regime? With reference to Riefenstahl's 'documentary' of an NSDAP rally, Siegfried Kracauer noted:

> . . . from the real life of the people was built up a faked reality . . .; but this . . ., instead of being an end in itself, merely served as the set-dressing for a film that was then to assume the character of an authentic documentary. *Triumph of the Will* is undoubtedly the film of the Reich's Party Convention; however, the Convention itself had also been staged to produce *Triumph of the Will*, for the purpose of resurrecting the ecstasy of the people through it.[7]

Taking the elaborately constructed façade of the Third Reich for its reality has led to the assumption that, for instance, simply because 'co-ordination' was proclaimed, centralized and bureaucratically implemented, a monolithic cultural sphere was the outcome. Such 'intentionalism'[8] is misleading, because not just the gaps between 'documented' ideology and practice but also the polycratic conflicts found elsewhere in the Nazi state made themselves felt here too.

Moreover, the notion of total control by a 'Führer-state' implies an acquiescent population. This merely begs the key question, already raised by Wilhelm Reich: 'Why do the masses allow themselves to be politically swindled?'[9] If we take the images of cheering crowds for the sole reality of the Third Reich, we are merely duplicating the view of Nazi propaganda, for it was Goebbels's media industry that manufactured such images in the first place. Recent research, supported for instance by the reports of the underground SPD, has revised this stereotype. To dominate the minds and actions of its citizens was what the regime *set out* to do; and this is why it established a whole apparatus of organizations to subjugate and colonize consciousness and everyday life, in and out of work, virtually from cradle to grave. But a distinction needs to be made between official 'public opinion' and grass-roots 'popular opinion'.[10] According to the latter, apart from periods of euphoria after the seizure of power and during the Blitzkrieg period, the population was divided and disillusioned, alternating between apathy and restless pleasure-seeking. This reminds us of the normality of everyday life for most citizens of the Third Reich.[11] Some, at least, enjoyed both new career opportunities and consumerism once the economy had recovered, with not just radios (for propaganda purposes), but electrical appliances, cosmetics, caravans and, as a sign of both prosperity and growing psychological tensions, alcoholism. Contrary to official ideology, the Americanism of the Weimar period continued, with Coca-Cola – whose German plants increased tenfold in five years – Hollywood films and, despite bureaucratic controls, swing music.

Orwell's observation that 'all art is to some extent propaganda'[12] usefully reminds us that every form is at the same time a value, that there can be no such thing as an ideologically 'innocent' work. Explicit propaganda in the Third Reich was, however, generally restricted to the modern mass media – press, radio and newsreel (rather than feature film) – whose capacity for rapid response to issues was, for so opportunistic a regime, essential. Even so, Nazi propaganda was less didactic than liturgical and narcotic: an appeal to the collective unconscious. The hypnotic intensity of image and rhetoric was raised to a pitch where questions of plausibility became irrelevant. Bloch explained the success of Nazi oratory by the fact that whereas the Communists, even though they had spoken the truth, had talked about *things*, the Nazis had told lies but to *human beings*.[13] While all cultural production is – whether by intention or omission – affirmative or critical of the dominant values of a society, and thus a work that does not contain any overt propaganda can have an effect comparable to one that does, simply to equate Nazi art with propaganda is to lose sight of the former's specific and more mediated function.

Although there is such a thing as Nazi culture – if we accept that the possession of culture does not entail that a society is 'civilized' – it can be argued that there is no such thing as Nazi art, in the sense of a unique period style. Let us take landscape painting. Not only have portrayals of the unchanging cycle of labour in the fields, in harmony with nature, long been a stock element of European art; the tradition of nineteenth-century genre painting did survive unbroken, especially in Southern Germany. What is significant is that it should have been presented as the 'new' art of the Third Reich. How do we explain this centring of a backward-looking provincial tradition?

The Third Reich contained contradictions at all levels; above all, between its ideology and its practice. These contradictions became blatant in the transition between Nazism as 'movement' and as 'system', as well as in the course of the gearing-up towards a war economy. The outcome was that, on the eve of the war, German society was quite unlike what the Nazis had promised it would be: the rural population was dwindling, industrialization had intensified, and capital concentration was increasing.[14] The contradiction between the social base and the economic function of Nazism was manifest. Also manifest, therefore, was potential for dissent, not only among the working class but also among the Nazis' traditional supporters, the peasantry and the petty bourgeoisie. It was, of course, to the latter two groups that, in different ways, the ideal of a timeless and harmonious rural existence had most appeal. Where it could not overcome contradictions, the Nazi public sphere employed neither rational arguments nor overt propaganda but fell back on aesthetic compensations.[15] Thus the petty bourgeoisie were compensated for the abandonment in economic and social policy of the *Mittelstandsideologie*, whereby the Nazi Party had gained their votes, by the enthronement of middlebrow taste as 'official' art.

In his contribution to the wave of books diagnosing cultural crisis that appeared around 1930, *Civilization and its Discontents*, Freud notes that 'the surrogate satisfactions offered by art are, compared with reality, illusions; but, thanks to the role that fantasy [*Phan-*

tasie] has asserted in mental life, this does not diminish their impact on the psyche'.[16] During Weimar, both the parties and, with one or two distinguished exceptions, also the theorists of the left fatally underestimated fantasy and the role it plays in the shaping of political motivation and allegiance.[17] Material hardship is not calculated to engender sober socio-economic judgement: 'man does not live by bread alone, *especially* when he has none'.[18] Indeed it is Ernst Bloch's brilliant analyses of the 'lack of synchronization' between urban and provincial mentalities during this period – as embodied in the petty bourgeoisie above all – that supply an answer to the critical question of how socio-economic discontent was translated into political mobilization.[19] But his theory of the co-existence of different layers, rhythms and time-scales within any historical moment, his denial that history consists of unilinear progress that leaves previous stages behind, provides insights into the diverse constellations and mechanisms of Nazi culture too. A case in point is why the proscribed artistic styles should have come to include 'Nordic' Modernism as well. The Expressionism of the *Brücke* group in particular was, after all, not only the Germanic form of the Modern Movement; it also articulated – by contrast with Italian Futurism – a rejection of modern material civilization and issued an impassioned summons for a new *spiritual* basis for human existence. In certain respects, this overlapped with elements of Nazi ideology, and two prominent Expressionists in particular, the painter Emil Nolde, who had been a party member since 1920, and also the writer Gottfried Benn, had aligned themselves with Nazism. A less paranoid regime might have exploited such talents instead of eventually shackling them both.[20] The trouble was, Expressionism was an ambivalent phenomenon which contained not only primitivist but also rebellious and indeed utopian energies. Where the former lived on in the shape of the Nazi apparatus of terror, to have incorporated the latter could have threatened the regime's stabilization by stimulating demands that the promise of social revolution become a reality. For the dynamism of Expressionism was dangerously reminiscent of the 'movement' period of Nazism and so, like the SA, it too had to be muzzled.[21]

It is significant that not only Nordic Expressionists were eventually rejected as models for Nazi art but even a quintessentially *völkisch* artist such as Fidus, whose roots lay in Germanic prehistory. It has been argued that such primitivist tendencies were extinguished because they were not compatible with the modernization climate of the armaments drive; but the approved artistic idioms – genre painting, Classicism – were scarcely more in harmony with the technology of twentieth-century warfare. A more satisfactory explanation is that Nordic Expressionism and *völkisch* art, along with German Romantic painters such as Caspar David Friedrich, all articulated a powerful transcendental impulse, which might have encouraged the citizens of the Third Reich to direct their thoughts and wishes beyond the *status quo*. Any utopia is potentially a force for change, and thus must be neutralized or colonized by a totalitarian regime. Accordingly, what passed for Nazi 'art' was, as Bloch noted, in part driven by a 'fear of all images that point to the future'.[22]

Indeed this static quality of the art of the Third Reich reveals that its prime function was to make manifest the existence of an established and stable system, a regime that had attained maturity. Consequently, the most appropriate artistic vocabularies were those that denied the very existence of change: the timeless styles of Hellenic Classicism and of provincializing and backward-looking genre painting. The latter's purpose was, however, not just to reassure the petty bourgeoisie that modernization had never taken place, but also to transmit various ideological themes, especially where social practice had run counter to Nazi promises. These included *Blut und Boden* and the glorification of female domesticity. No less important was the failure to transmit others, such as urban life. By contrast, Classicism served to signify Art itself, to substantiate the claim that the Third Reich had inherited the role of the guardian of Western culture.

The first major exhibition of art approved by the regime was complemented by one showing 'degenerate' art, where 700 of the finest works of Modernism, culled from some 17,000 confiscated in a purge of German galleries, were often literally piled on top of one another in deliberately unfavourable surroundings. The purpose of this 1937 exhibition, which attracted an embarrassing 2 million visitors, was a favourite tactic of Nazi ideology: to integrate by negation. Thus the distortions of Modernism were presented as the objectification of the 'diseased' spiritual condition of Weimar's body politic. The catalogue juxtaposed works by Modernist masters such as Klee with drawings and paintings by schizophrenics in order to demonstrate alleged 'similarities'. By contrast, the sterile academic and anatomical perfectionism of the nudes in the nearby Great German Art exhibition was intended to prove that the Third Reich had succeeded in bringing to a halt the 'crisis' proclaimed by the cultural pessimists. In Hitler's address at the opening of the new 'temple' of German art in Munich, he asserted: 'Never was humanity in its external appearance and in its frame of mind nearer to the ancient world than it is today.'[23] This Hellenizing cult of bodily beauty, health and sport was also celebrated in the Berlin Olympics and Riefenstahl's film of the event.

The opening of the annual Great German Art Exhibition was marked by a special feast day, on which a vast pageant symbolizing 2,000 years of German culture paraded through the festively decorated streets of Munich.[24] The pageant, and therefore supposedly German culture, culminated in marching columns of SA, SS and Wehrmacht. As the rituals and quasi-religious vocabulary associated with art in the Third Reich suggest, one aim of Nazi ideology was to restore to art precisely the aura and the cultic function that, according to Walter Benjamin's well-known argument, it had lost in the age of 'mechanical reproduction' and mass media.[25] The interlocking components of this strategy were, on the one hand, to exploit the styles of art associated in the mind of the bourgeoisie with High Culture and, on the other, to eliminate not just politically hostile art such as the work of George Grosz, but all modes that, like Dadaism and especially montage, followed through the cultural logic of technological change and, as a result, in their techniques problematized the nature of the work of art itself. This Nazi impulse to restore art not only to the *styles* displaced by Modernism but also to its cultic *role* ensured that painting and sculpture could seldom be vehicles for explicit propaganda, even though their effect was often equivalent.

In Nazi painting, nudes generally depict women and tend to be allegorical – such as Adolf Ziegler's 'Four Elements', which hung in the salon of the Führerhaus in Munich – voyeuristic, or even semi-pornographic. The female nude is offered up as an object for male visual consumption, and in the perverse context of fascism it is disturbing to have to admit that some of these paintings still possess a certain erotic power. Male nudes, by contrast, are to be found primarily in sculpture, often of larger-than-life size. The function of works such as those of Arno Breker was often multiple. Classical allusions are exploited so as to dignify and underwrite the racial theme; while there is at the same time a celebration of martial virtues which serves to de-historicize war and define it as a mythical struggle between heroic individuals – such as the Führer – and destiny. But such sculptures also work at a more visceral level. In Nazi painting and sculpture, female nudes are presented as soft, passive, yielding – 'Leda and the Swan' was a favourite theme – while male nudes are hard, assertive, erect. The tight-lipped, tense expressions of 'heroic' males are celebrations of stored-up phallic aggression about to erupt in an orgasm of violence.

Nazi sculpture fabricated a vision of the race of supermen that would one day spring from the Reich's purified blood. It was, therefore, ideologically interdependent with the apparently 'harmless' paintings of the *Blut und Boden* theme. But, of course, this 'positive' Aryan racial message also works in tandem with the 'negative' images of the Jew familiar from Nazi propaganda. This strategy was made explicit in a juxtaposition which appeared in the *Stürmer* (illustration i, p. 161).[26] The logic is clear: if the yardstick of 'humanity' was that embodied in antique sculpture and its imitations, anybody who deviated from it could, if necessary, be classified as 'subhuman' and treated 'accordingly'. There is here again an equation between physical appearance and spiritual essence. Thorak's 'Two Humans' ('Zwei Menschen') was in fact used in an SS pamphlet justifying Nazi genocide in the Eastern territories. It was juxtaposed with a primitivist sculpture of a couple captioned 'Two Subhumans' ('Zwei Untermenschen').[27] But the real complementary images to the idealized nudes are those that show what resulted when the Nazis forcibly brought reality into line with their ideas and themselves reduced 'inferior' races to a sub-human level.

It would, however, be false to suggest that every aspect of the culture of the Weimar years was extinguished under the new regime. Social and economic continuities between the periods before and after 1933 are echoed in the cultural sphere. This applies also to tendencies that are not generally classified as 'conservative'. Thus, whereas Expressionism was eliminated – though not until 1937 – the uncritical Verism of the late 1920s and early 1930s can be detected in some Nazi painting, though the subject-matter is, of course, radically different: rural rather than urban. Even though the Bauhaus was an immediate victim of the regime, functionalism survived throughout the Third Reich – but, significantly, in

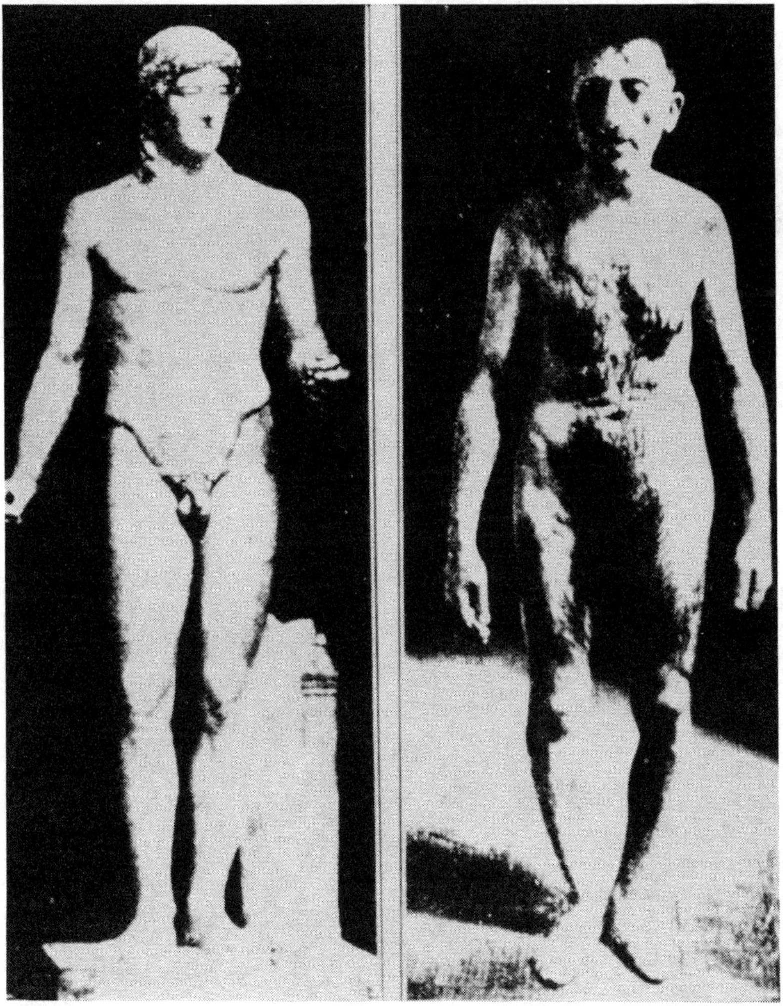

i

ii

iii

iv

v

vi

vii

undilutedly technocratic guise and now confined to factory architecture.

If the social role of painting and sculpture in the Third Reich was essentially marginal, that of architecture was central. Architecture became the dominant art form because it was immediately recognized that a programme of public building could help to revive the economy. But it also became the art of domination because it made the new regime a palpable presence throughout the country. This representative dimension was presented as the justification for projects that had little value for the population. Here too, Classicism was the chosen idiom, as in the 'Temple of Honour' to the so-called 'martyrs' of the Munich Putsch. But the defining feature of Nazi architecture is its gigantism. The grotesque scale is exemplified by the project for a Great Hall as part of the planned reconstruction of Berlin as 'Germania', the imperial capital. The building was to be sixteen times the size of St Peter's in Rome – that city being a constant yardstick for Nazi aspirations – and a new wonder of the world. Its dome was to rise to 290 metres, ten times taller than the Brandenburg Gate. The same new North–South axis, seven kilometres long, was to be spanned by a triumphal arch 120 metres high. This was to serve as a memorial to the German dead in the First World War, every single one of whose 1,800,000 names was to be carved into its granite.

One purpose of such gigantism was the maximum utilization of labour and resources, which is also exemplified in the preference for expensive and archaic techniques and materials, above all natural stone. While the cult of gigantism should not therefore be simplified to the megalomania of a Führer whose passion for planning and building has become a part of the Hitler myth, the scale of Nazi monumental architecture can be seen as setting, in aesthetic terms, the scale of political ambition to which the Third Reich should correspond – in other words to surpass the Roman Empire. However, this imperial architecture preceded – in its conception at any rate – the Nazi Empire. Such buildings served to show the citizens of the Third Reich what, when the time came, they would be dying for. It is almost as if war became necessary, not merely to validate the cult of sacrifice that mobilized loyalty to the regime, but also to justify the construction of war memorials on an undreamt-of scale, as exemplified by the plans for vast 'Castles of the Dead' to mark the extremities of Hitler's conquests. Such reversals of historical logic were endemic. Thus, a serious factor in the planning of monumental architecture was its 'ruin-value'; the aim was to create buildings that would, in hundreds or even thousands of years, in their ruined state resemble the ancient models on which they had been based. This self-conscious obsession with posterity was an attempt to step out of real history and into myth: 'the greatness of the present will', according to Hitler, 'be measurable only in the light of the values it leaves behind'. By focusing on the demands of a 'thousand-year legacy', the 'satisfaction of the wishes and hopes of the present'[28] could be indefinitely postponed. But the inhuman scale of Nazi architecture was not merely representative: it had an ideological function too. For gigantism serves as a shock tactic to free architecture from both humanistic and functionalist criteria and re-invest it with an aura. This enables it to intimidate the masses and thereby – as with the various arenas in the Nuremberg complex – define them in a subordinate relationship to the Führer.

As with Classical painting, the state architecture of Nazism prevents identification, and thereby neutralizes utopian energies in favour of the cosmic ambitions of the regime. It is opposed not so much to functionalism, therefore, as to the largely unrealized social-utopian architectural visions of Expressionism and the early Bauhaus. But there was a third component in Nazi architecture, again inherited from a previous epoch: the *Heimatschutz* style. As a mode of building that was supposedly 'rooted' in the landscape and that employed local materials and craftsmen, this was the architectural equivalent of *Blut und Boden* painting. It was used, among other things, for housing, community buildings and also – as an aggressively ideological style – for the 'Order Castles', schools for the party élite, which were patterned on medieval castles and situated to look as though they were growing out of the mountainside. They were part of a wider tendency to re-feudalize culture, which was expressed in the revival of mural painting, reliefs and tapestries, as well as in the seigneurial pretensions of many members of the Nazi leadership.

This parallelism of Classical, functionalist and archaicizing styles in architecture was itself evidence of the contradictions and lack of 'synchronization' within the regime itself, which simultaneously offered a 'public' façade of timeless grandeur and indomitable power, a material base of modern technocratic rationality, and an ideological never-never land of organic rootedness and tradition.

These three tendencies – the representative, the technocratic and the organic – were fused in the main surviving monument of the Third Reich, the Autobahn network. The simultaneity of differing historical moments is captured in a carefully composed photograph (see illustration ii, p. 162), which brings together not only modern engineering and *Blut und Boden* but also the antique, in the shape of the pillar from a Roman aqueduct standing, as a monument, by the side of the road.

As with the programme of public buildings, the main motivation for the Autobahnen was job-creation: but the project also served to symbolize the achievement of 'folk community' in the way the network fused the different regions of Germany into a nation. But the most revealing feature of the Autobahnen is that they were often deliberately routed through areas of scenic beauty. This was because of the desire to present them as works of art in harmony with nature and, on the model of the great cathedrals of the Middle Ages, inspired by faith and built by craftsmen.[29] This aesthetic dimension was incorporated into the structures themselves, as a façade; as the same photograph shows, bridges, which often retained antique arch forms, were provided with an anachronistic stone cladding to help them to blend with the landscape.

The Autobahnen not only exploited new technology and helped to legitimize the new regime, they were also a logistical achievement. Without the ruthless exploitation of labour – concentration-camp prisoners were, literally, worked to death in quarries to meet the huge demands for natural stone – such projects could never have been carried out. The task of incorporating and controlling the working class in Nazi Germany was undertaken by the Labour Front. But this organization itself rested on a blatant contradiction: whereas its membership comprised both workers and employers, as supposed evidence of classless 'folk community', the employer was given the status of absolute 'Führer' in the workplace. Once again, the means of diverting attention from this, as well as compensating for the intensified exploitation of labour under the regime, were aesthetic.

The 'Strength through Joy' section of the Labour Front served several functions. It was, first of all, intended to fill the leisure vacuum – left by the liquidation of the Weimar Republic's working-class cultural organizations – with theatre and cinema, factory concerts, book clubs, holidays and, of course, sport. The aim, however, was not simply compensatory but the total organization of free time so as to 'abolish the difference between work and culture'.[30] There was nothing utopian about such a project, whose purpose was merely to ensure that work discipline was maintained while labour power was being reproduced. With surprising candour, Labour Front leader Robert Ley admitted that '"Strength through Joy" regularly overhauls every worker, just as one has to overhaul a car engine after a certain number of kilometres'.[31] This was to be carried out on an industrialized scale by a perfectionism of organization. At a proposed holiday plant for 20,000 on the Baltic coast the guests ready for overhauling were to have been – as at Auschwitz – unloaded straight from the trains into the 'blocks' to which the latest consignment of labour power had been allocated. As with many other areas of Nazi ideology and culture, 'Strength through Joy' did go some way towards democratizing leisure and meeting human needs, but merely as a smokescreen for the real purpose of domination and exploitation.

The same is true of the Beauty of Labour bureau, whose complementary aim was to provide an aesthetic façade *within* the workplace. By 1935, over 12,000 plants had been modernized and beautified with lawns and flower-beds – often by the 'voluntary' labour of the employees themselves in their own free time – and working conditions too were improved. But once again the 'beauty' was not simply an attempt to put a 'human' face on capitalist rationality: it was simultaneously – and primarily – *in the service of* this rationality. As Ley himself stressed, Beauty of Labour 'was not a luxury or a gift, but in the last analysis had been transformed into an increase in production and surplus value'.[32] The same lack of synchronization is encountered here too, for the bureau was simultaneously responsible for, on the one hand, *Heimatschutz*-style workers' clubrooms decorated with murals of peasant life and, on the other, for the manufacture of standardized functionalist furniture, crockery and cutlery, and for improvements in the working environment that were based on the latest scientific management research.

What is crucial about the workings of Nazi ideology, and thus also about the function of the aesthetic dimension, is the recognition that it is possible to enlist the real needs of human beings in order to get them to work against their own interests – as Ley said, 'the best social policy is also the best economic policy'.[33] This is what Walter

Benjamin had in mind when he said that fascism grants 'the masses expression (but in no way their rights). The masses have a right to a transformation of property relations; fascism seeks to give them expression in the latter's preservation.'[34]

The instrument used in this strategy is the 'aestheticization of politics'.[35] Its most vivid example is, of course, the realm of spectacle and pageantry stage-managed by the regime, not just at party rallies but at all public occasions. This was necessary because the fascist public sphere cannot overcome the contradictions of the system and is compelled to use often-elaborate aesthetic diversions and façades – in many cases literally. Thus the original caption to the photograph of a Nuremberg rally campsite on p. 162 (illustration iii) read: 'The Swabian Labour Service men have fitted out their tent with the façade of a homely farmhouse', complete with wattle fence enclosing a 'garden' with Christmas trees, a peasant 'mural' and even a 'stork' nesting on the thatched roof.[36] An escape from the realities of the present was evident in the overall atmosphere at Nuremberg (illustration iv, p. 163). Spectacle was systematically fabricated – often by means of modern technology, as in Speer's use of 130 searchlights to create a 'cathedral of light' visible to a height of over 20,000 feet in the night sky. What is most striking about the Nuremberg arenas is not just their enormous size but the austerity of the architectural forms. This was deliberate, because the decorative component was to be supplied by the marching masses, their uniforms and their banners. But what once again bears out Benjamin's analysis is that this was not visible to the participants themselves but only to the Führer – as well as to the eye of the camera, as the well-known photograph on p. 163 (illustration v) shows. The fact that this is a still from *Triumph of the Will* reminds us again of the fundamental tension within Nazism between 'movement' and 'system'.[37] Just as Riefenstahl's film of the 1934 rally counterbalances the rigid geometrical composition by its ceaseless movement, so too the regime itself attempted to give an 'impression of dynamism in a rigid system'.[38]

But this photograph also reveals how, in the process of fulfilling an 'ornamental' function within the arena, the crowds have themselves been reduced to a 'mass ornament'.[39] Indeed the description of the Nazi regime as a *Gesamtkunstwerk*,[40] a total work of art, makes more sense once we recognize that the raw material for 'shaping' is the German people themselves. The mass is now no longer the 'shapeless' threat that had terrified the petty bourgeoisie but 'human architecture' and soldierly 'order'.[41] It is, paradoxically, the imposition of such a *mechanistic* order on the human body that realizes, in purely visual and symbolic terms, the *organicist* fantasy of the state as a body, an organized *Volkskörper* now purged of the alien elements that had infected it.[42]

The whole process is made manifest in Ferdinand Staeger's 'The Front' (illustration vi, p. 163). To us it may now seem like one of the few 'realistic' works of art to emerge out of the Third Reich. The individual is, like a column in a Classical façade, subordinated to an architectonic scheme. Thus Staeger's painting exposes the reality of the 'folk community' as far surpassing the dehumanization that resulted from Weimar mechanization and rationalization – as a protest against which the Nazi movement had presented itself. The figures are clones devoid of all autonomy: the indistinguishable results of production-line technology. This is no doubt why such explicit propaganda paintings were rare. For, if anything, the Nazi system is visualized in too immediate a form.

As we have seen, Nazism exploited the aesthetic dimension in two ways in particular: as a façade to conceal societal contradictions, and, secondly, to give concrete form to the principles of Nazi ideology. 'The Front' exemplifies *both* strategies. It signifies not only achieved social order but also the order of a Platonic perfection. This is also brought out in another painting by Staeger, 'SS Guard',[43] where the upturned faces of all the figures – except for a fat man with a cigar – symbolize not only political but also philosophical idealism: in other words, the divination of an ideal realm that is manifested in the material world by the perfect symmetry of Nazi architecture and town planning, and by the no-less-perfect order of the marching columns of SA and SS (see illustration vii, p. 164). This is made explicit in a passage from the *Völkische Beobachter* in 1931:

> The power of the will and the ultimate secret of this movement will assume living shape (*Gestalt*) in the brown battalions and testify to the enormous power of the National Socialist idea, which is pressing to assume the form of the state. This spirit (*Geist*) and the elemental will that is storming forwards . . . is the strongest political reality that the German nation possesses today.[44]

'Shape', 'form', 'idea', 'spirit': it is characteristic that here *political* terminology is derived from the aesthetics of German Idealism. For the Nazis, the medium was the message: to show something made it real; in the regime's visualized 'beauty' lay its truth.

As this suggests, it is not quite accurate to describe Nazism as technocracy in *Romantic* guise.[45] For Nazism is not just an aesthetic phenomenon but an *aestheticist* one. Indeed, it is fitting that, in the context of crisis around 1930, when socio-economic fears were translated into prophecies of cultural degeneration, fascism, the movement that salvaged capitalism, should not simply re-activate the cultural pessimism of the 1890s but also tacitly incorporate the aesthetic principles – though not, of course, the styles – of the last flourish of bourgeois culture: *l'art pour l'art* and *fin-de-siècle* decadence.

Furthermore, if we grasp aestheticism as a cult of artifice that sets itself apart from the bourgeois ethical code, we can see it as a parallel phenomenon to technocracy, which is a domination of nature that presents itself as value-neutral. These two tendencies of aestheticism and technocracy are brought together in the idea of war,[46] which became a key cultural and ideological battleground during the last years of the Weimar Republic. For Ernst Jünger, *technologized* war is a 'total work of art', which intoxicates all the senses and makes the blood boil in one's veins.[47] The cult of war as an 'inner experience' marks the *nec plus ultra* of Decadence's ceaseless quest for ever more extreme sensations, which can culminate only in nihilism and death. In its terminal crisis, bourgeois culture bursts the crust of civilization to uncover the pulsating, primal energies beneath. As Franz Neumann noted, 'violence not only terrorizes but attracts',[48] and many intellectuals with jaded sensibilities were drawn to Nazism by just this atavistic impulse. It is mirrored not simply in the swastika but in the colours that the movement adopted: brown, the colour of earth and excrement; red, the colour of blood and vitalism; black, the colour of decay and death. The centrality of the aesthetic dimension in the Third Reich should not therefore be understood as, strictly speaking, a 'cultural' phenomenon at all but rather, within the context of 'cultural crisis', as the revolt of a primordial sensuality against 'civilization' itself. As Marcuse has said, extending Freud, 'civilization has subjugated sensuousness to reason in such a manner that . . . if [sensuousness] reasserts itself, [it] does so in destructive and "savage" forms'.[49]

As utilized in war, the supreme destructive force is, of course, technology; and it is striking that 'conservative revolutionaries' such as Jünger should have attacked rationalism and civilization, but not technology. The paradox of such 'reactionary modernism'[50] is consistent with the way in which Nazism perfected rationalistic methods to achieve wholly irrational ends – a contradiction that is echoed, as Neumann noted, in the Nazis' fusion of bureaucratic and charismatic rule. Yet an irrational end is precisely what all technocracy finally leads to, because the monitoring faculty of human reason has been uncoupled from the system. This is mirrored in the dynamics of capitalism itself, where production is geared to exchange rather than use. The means used to bridge the resulting gap between exchange-value and use-value, between a commodity's promise and its reality, are *aesthetic*.[51] Through styling, packaging and advertising, the product is invested with an *aura* that finds an echo in the minds of the consumers. A parallel reliance on the mobilization of illusion helps to explain the primacy of the visual in the cultural strategies of the Third Reich. But whereas the content of Nazi ideology may rely on illusions and fantasies, the *images* it marshals nevertheless appeal to needs that are not imaginary but real: if the needs were not real, the strategies would not be effective.

So the aesthetic dimension of fascism can, ultimately, be understood as a kind of commodity aesthetics.[52] An ideological product – the Führer, folk community, or whatever – is supplied with a brand name and a trade-mark – the swastika – and a product-image is carefully designed. After consumer testing on a local basis, the final product is adapted, packaged and marketed to a mass public that has already been softened up for such a 'campaign' by the modern illusion industries of Weimar – cinema, magazines, advertising – which stimulated desires that could not be satisfied during the Depression years. The point is that aestheticization – and indeed visualization – needed to play such a crucial role because Nazism was not a coherent ideology at all but a multi-purpose ideological commodity whose unity lay not in its substance but in its *forms*: in an immediately recognizable packaging and product-style whose very uniformity served as an instrument for the symbolic integration of the Reich. This gives a fresh meaning to Max Horkheimer's famous admonition that, if you don't want to talk about capitalism, then you can't talk about fascism.[53] Nazism gained mass appeal because it managed to offer something to almost everyone. This was the secret behind the success of the marketing campaign that brought it to power. But as the product itself began to lose favour with the public, its consumption was increasingly enforced by terror.

The final irony is that, today, the Third Reich has itself become one of the most enduringly potent and successful commodities in our own mass culture. In the light of all this, the opening analogy between Hitler, the star commodity of Nazism, and systematically packaged, promoted and marketed rock stars now seems altogether less grotesque. But to have proved David Bowie right after all is too frivolous a conclusion. For there were people in the Third Reich who were not the consumers, nor merely the operatives but, ultimately, the raw material of a fully rationalized production-process, which was geared to extracting the maximum surplus value out of the human body itself, not merely while still clinging to life in the camps but even after death, for industrial conversion into soap, lampshades and other commodities. Of all the images of fascism this was the one that the Nazis did not dare disseminate; but it must always remain the image by which fascism defines itself.

Notes

1. 'Deutsches Verbot der Kunstkritik', in Ernst Bloch, *Vom Hasard zur Katastrophe* (Frankfurt, 1972), p. 168.
2. cf. Hermann Hinkel, *Zur Funktion des Bildes im deutschen Faschismus* (Giessen, 1975).
3. However, the catalogue contains an interesting essay by one of the organizers of the Frankfurt exhibition: Georg Bussmann, '"Degenerate Art" – A Look at a Useful Myth', in Christos M. Joachimides, Norman Rosenthal and Wieland Schmied (ed.), *German Art in the 20th Century: Painting and Sculpture 1905–1985* (London, 1985), pp. 113–24.
4. On the exhibition and the surrounding controversy, see the articles by Olav Münzberg: 'Bericht über die Ausstellung "Kunst im Dritten Reich – Dokumente der Unterwerfung" in Hamburg', and 'Aus Anlass der Ausstellung "Kunst im Dritten Reich – Dokumente der Unterwerfung"', *Ästhetik und Kommunikation*, 19 (April 1975), pp. 59–68, 69–84.
5. The Nazis themselves needed no reminding of this: 'According to its eternal laws, visualization [*Anschauung*] always operates with symbols. . . . Genuine visualization thus . . . embraces the whole of art . . . as a means of representing, via concrete symbols – colours, emblems, sounds – universal essence, a life-myth. . . . The symbol

is, ultimately, the ideal of the Nordic race', Alfred Rosenberg at the 1929 Nuremberg NSDAP rally, quoted in Hildegard Brenner, *Die Kunstpolitik des Nationalsozialismus* (Reinbek, 1963), p. 276. Such ideas of the primacy of sensual and intuitive *Anschauung* over conceptual cognition were at the time being systematized by Ludwig Klages.

6. The problems raised by the study of Nazi art are outlined by John Heskett in 'Art and Design in Nazi Germany', *History Workshop*, 6 (1978), pp. 139–53. Reinhard Merker's well-illustrated *Die bildenden Künste im Nationalsozialismus* (Cologne, 1983), attempts to integrate accounts of Nazi ideology in general, cultural policies and practices, and artistic production. George L. Mosse, *Nazi Culture: A Documentary History* (New York, 1966), provides a wide-ranging collection of primary material on culture grasped as 'whole way of life'. What is still required for an adequate evaluation of the meanings and functions of the 'cultural' in the Third Reich is to combine the above two perspectives and measure them against detailed contextual research.
7. *From Caligari to Hitler* (Princeton, 1947), p. 301.
8. In a most stimulating article, 'Intention and Explanation: A Current Controversy about the Interpretation of National Socialism' (in Gerhard Hirschfeld and Lothar Kettenacker (ed.), *The 'Führer State': Myth and Reality* (Stuttgart, 1981), pp. 12–40), Tim Mason argues that historians of Nazism must, if they are to understand a document's *function*, go beyond a literal reading and take into account both its context and its concealed or (often calculatedly) symbolic meanings. This is no less true of Nazi pronouncements on culture, the domain of symbols and societal representations. Bloch, for instance, interprets Goebbels's 1937 prohibition of 'art criticism' as in reality directed at anyone who might wish to criticize the regime itself; cf. op. cit., pp. 163–5.
9. Wilhelm Reich, *The Mass Psychology of Fascism* (London, 1972), p. 36.
10. cf. Ian Kershaw, *Popular Opinion and Political Dissent in the Third Reich* (Oxford, 1983).
11. cf. Hans Dieter Schäfer, *Das gespaltene Bewusstsein. Deutsche Kultur und Lebenswirklichkeit 1933–1945* (Munich, 1981), pp. 114–62.
12. *The Collected Essays, Journalism and Letters of George Orwell*, Sonia Orwell and Ian Angus (ed.), vol. 2 (Harmondsworth, 1970), p. 276.
13. 'Kritik der Propaganda', Bloch, op. cit., p. 197.
14. cf. David Schoenbaum, *Hitler's Social Revolution* (New York, 1966).
15. On the fascist public sphere cf. Eike Hennig, 'Faschistische Öffentlichkeit und Faschismustheorien', *Ästhetik und Kommunikation*, 10 (June 1975), pp. 107–17, and 'Faschistische Ästhetik und Faschistische Öffentlichkeit', in Berthold Hinz et al.

(ed.), *Die Dekoration der Gewalt. Kunst und Medien im Faschismus* (Giessen, 1979), pp. 9–15; also the discussion between Peter Brückner, Oskar Negt et al., 'Perspectives on the Fascist Public Sphere', *New German Critique*, 11 (Spring 1977), pp. 94–132.

16. Sigmund Freud, *Civilization, Society and Religion*, The Pelican Freud Library, vol. 12 (Harmondsworth, 1985), p. 262 (translation adapted).
17. cf. Oskar Negt and Alexander Kluge, *Öffentlichkeit und Erfahrung* (Frankfurt, 1972), p. 386; English translation forthcoming.
18. Bloch, op. cit., p. 196.
19. Ernst Bloch, 'Nonsynchronism and the Obligation to its Dialectics' (an extract from *Erbschaft dieser Zeit*), *New German Critique*, 11 (Spring 1977), pp. 22–38; cf. also the introduction by Anson Rabinbach, which brings into focus 'the power of fascism as cultural synthesis', ibid., p. 5.
20. Gottfried Benn was to vent his disappointment with the cultural realities, as against the promise, of Nazism in vitriolic terms in the essay 'Kunst und Drittes Reich', *Gesammelte Werke*, vol. 3 (Wiesbaden, 1968); cf. esp. pp. 877–84.
21. cf. 'Gauklerfest unter Galgen', Bloch, *Vom Hasard zur Katastrophe*, pp. 235–41.
22. ibid., pp. 103–4.
23. Quoted in Mosse, op. cit., p. 15.
24. cf. Wolfgang Hartmann, 'Der historische Festzug zum "Tag der deutschen Kunst"', in *Die Dekoration der Gewalt*, pp. 87–100, which contains several other excellent contributions.
25. cf. Walter Benjamin, 'The Work of Art in the Age of Mechanical Reproduction', *Illuminations* (London, 1976), pp. 223ff.
26. Reproduced in Bill Kinser and Neil Kleinman, *The Dream that was no more a Dream: A Search for Aesthetic Reality in Germany 1890–1945* (New York, 1969), p. 118.
27. Reproduced in Robert Cecil, *Myth of the Master Race: Alfred Rosenberg and Nazi Ideology* (London, 1972), opposite p. 199.
28. Hitler's 1935 cultural address, reprinted in Berthold Hinz, *Die Malerei des deutschen Faschismus* (Frankfurt, 1977), p. 152.
29. As Fritz Todt, who masterminded the Autobahn programme, himself put it: 'The following are the features that make a road as a totality into an artwork that brings the environment joy through its intrinsic beauty and harmony with the environment: The direction of lines is bound to the land. Construction remains true to natural forms. Workmanship is based on the craftsman's principles of building and implantation in the earth', quoted in Jeffrey Herf, *Reactionary Modernism: Technology, Culture and Politics in Weimar and the Third Reich* (Cambridge, 1984), pp. 104–5.
30. Quoted in Roswitha Mattausch and Brigitte Wiederspahn, 'Das Bauprogramm der Deutschen Arbeitsfront – die Umwelt der Arbeiter', in *Kunst im 3. Reich. Dokumente der Unterwerfung*

(Frankfurt, 1979), p. 208. This volume, a reissue of the catalogue of the 1974 Frankfurt exhibition, is strongly recommended.
31. Quoted in ibid., p. 212.
32. Quoted in Anson Rabinbach, 'The Aesthetics of Production in the Third Reich', *Journal of Contemporary History*, vol. XI, no. 4 (October 1976), p. 64.
33. Quoted in ibid., p. 48.
34. Benjamin, op. cit., p. 243 (my translation).
35. ibid., p. 244 (my translation).
36. cf. Kinser/Kleinman, op. cit., p. 37.
37. cf. Klaus Theweleit's imaginative and suggestive interpretation of this conflict between 'order' and 'flow' – and of much else besides – in his remarkable sexual–political investigation of the psychic mechanisms underlying fascism, *Male Fantasies*, vol. 1 (Cambridge, 1987).
38. Negt/Kluge, op. cit., p. 278.
39. cf. Kracauer, op. cit., p. 302.
40. cf. Rainer Stollmann, 'Faschistische Politik als Gesamtkunstwerk', in Horst Denkler and Karl Prümm (ed.), *Die deutsche Literatur im Dritten Reich* (Stuttgart, 1976), pp. 83–101.
41. The art historian Hubert Schrade described the march-past at the 1933 NSDAP rally as follows: 'Huge masses of humanity had gathered. But these had not streamed together in unruly mobs. The summons of a shaping will . . . had compelled them to subject themselves and submit to a strict form, a primal form of existence obligated to the community, a soldierly formation. It was, thus, an old soldierly custom when the Führer and Chief of Staff inspected the formations. And yet, after an epoch of disorder, it must have seemed to us as something quite new', quoted in Brenner, op. cit., p. 119. It is significant that the whole process is conceived in aesthetic terms: chaotic raw material is 'shaped' into an ordered 'form' by a creative 'will'.
42. In the words of the Nazi art historian Werner Hager, 'As people learn once again to move in a united manner or even simply to stand still, an invisible hand begins to mould and shape them. A new sense of the body develops, even if only in the everyday raising of the hand in the Hitler salute, but experienced in its most intense form in the compelling shape of collective bearing to be found in parades and ceremonies', quoted in Joseph Wulf, *Die bildenden Künste im Dritten Reich: Eine Dokumentation* (Berlin, 1966), p. 241.
43. Reproduced in Hinz, op. cit.
44. Quoted in Hans-Gerd Jaschke and Martin Loiperdinger, 'Gewalt und NSDAP vor 1933. Ästhetische Okkupation und physischer Terror', in Reiner Steinweg (ed.), *Faszination der Gewalt. Politische Strategie und Alltagserfahrung* (Frankfurt, 1983), p. 144.
45. cf. Rolf Peter Sieferle, *Fortschrittsfeinde? Opposition gegen Technik und Industrie von der Romantik bis zur Gegenwart* (Munich, 1984),

esp. pp. 206–24.

46. cf. Walter Benjamin, 'Theories of German Fascism', *New German Critique*, 17 (Spring 1979), pp. 120–8.
47. For an acute and extremely stimulating study of Jünger's pre-1939 work, its aesthetic premises and wider implications, cf. Karl-Heinz Bohrer's *Die Ästhetik des Schreckens* (Munich, 1978).
48. Franz Neumann, *Behemoth: Structure and Practice of National Socialism* (London, 1942), p. 328.
49. Herbert Marcuse, *Eros and Civilization* (London, 1969), p. 152.
50. cf. Herf, op. cit.
51. cf. Wolfgang Fritz Haug, *Critique of Commodity Aesthetics* (London, 1986), pp. 131–5.
52. According to Neumann the 'superiority of National Socialist over democratic propaganda lies in the complete transformation of culture into saleable commodities', op. cit., p. 357.
53. cf. 'Die Juden und Europa', *Zeitschrift für Sozialforschung*, vol. VIII (1939), nos. 1/2, p. 115.

Notes on illustrations

i. *Der Stürmer*, 7 January 1943; reproduced in Kinser/Kleinman (cf. note 26), p. 118, described as 'A racial comparison'.
ii. Autobahn; reproduced in Kinser/Kleinman, p. 37; from Karl Springenschmid and Anton Hadwinger (ed.), *Frohes Schaffen. Ein Hausbuch deutscher Jugend*, no. XVI (Leipzig).
iii. Tent at Nuremberg rally; reproduced in Kinser/Kleinman, p. 37; from Hanns Kerl (ed.), *Reichstagung in Nürnberg*, vol. IV (Berlin, 1936).
iv. Watchtower constructed for a Nuremberg rally; reproduced in Kinser/Kleinman, p. 40; from *Reichstagung in Nürnberg*, vol. V (1937).
v. Nuremberg rally, 1934 (still from Leni Riefenstahl, *Triumph des Willens*); reproduced in Schäfer (cf. note 11); from Leni Riefenstahl, *Hinter den Kulissen des Reichsparteitags-Films* (Munich, 1935), p. 95.
vi. Ferdinand Staeger, 'The Front'; reproduced in Hinz (cf. note 28), plate 135 (copyright Ullstein Bilderdienst, Berlin).
vii. Marching column; from Stefan Lorant, *Sieg Heil! Eine deutsche Bildgeschichte von Bismarck zu Hitler* (Frankfurt, 1979), p. 251.

ELEVEN

Germany's Way into the Second World War

EBERHARD JÄCKEL

Like almost all historical phenomena, Germany's path towards the Second World War can be explained in several ways, and interpretations depend very much on the individual historian's perspective. In this chapter I will propose four different approaches to answers to the question of how and why Germany went to war.

The first is simply that Hitler was determined on war, he had a programme which involved territorial expansion, mainly in Eastern Europe and chiefly at the expense of the Soviet Union. The objective was *Lebensraum* (or living space) or, in economic terms, the quest for raw materials, oil, food and arable soil for generations to come. Hitler's ultimate aim of conquest was reinforced by a structured list of steps which had to be taken on the way towards this goal. Among these were his alliances or agreements with Italy and Britain and also the preliminary campaign against France which he envisaged before launching the ultimate war of conquest. As far as Hitler was concerned the invasion of Russia on 22 June 1941 marked the real beginning of the Second World War.

Hitler also had one other aim: the elimination of the European Jews, beginning with those in the Soviet Union. This objective was linked closely with the policy of *Lebensraum*. On the very same day on which the German army moved into the Soviet Union, thereby beginning in earnest the conquest of living space, the *Einsatzgruppen* or SS police followed the military units and began the campaign of killings which marked the occupation of Russia.

This explanation of the war is important but insufficient. It is hardly conceivable that a war can be accounted for simply by the fact that one man, however powerful, wanted to bring it about. Human beings do not act solely out of personal motives; they act also under certain conditions. They cannot do everything they want to do, and what they want to do they do only when they can. An individual such as Adolf Hitler could have acted as he did only as a result of certain conditions or circumstances.

So, the next approach to the question of why Germany went to war would involve studying the conditions which enabled Hitler to follow his own ideas and to implement his programme. I will divide this second approach into three sub-explanations. The first of these, a point on which I will reflect only very briefly, was internal German circumstances. To a certain extent, of course, Germany had to be ready to follow Hitler. Rearmament was an essential pre-condition for war, and the German war machine was of a very high standard. While in theory Hitler was commander-in-chief and was able to order that war machine to go into action, in practice he had to engage in a complex and difficult process of persuasion and conviction. Hitler had to convince his military advisers that his programme was in Germany's interests, and he did not always find this easy. In the summer of 1940 he argued his case for war against Russia in the context of the Battle of Britain; he assured his generals that Britain's last hope lay in Russia and they must take that hope from her. His war against the Soviet Union was presented as a means of defeating Britain, whereas in reality his goal was the conquest of *Lebensraum*.

External as well as internal German conditions permitted Hitler to unleash the Second World War, and one must ask why the other European powers were unable to prevent him from launching the war which he had so openly proclaimed in the 1920s and which he was so visibly preparing in the 1930s. Why, for example, could Britain and France not forestall Hitler's aggression? The most popular answer is still the one expressed in the theme of the first volume of Winston Churchill's memoirs: 'How the English-speaking peoples through their unwisdom, carelessness and good nature allowed the wicked to rearm.' Others have developed Churchill's approach further in criticizing and denouncing the policies of appeasement. Appeasement and lack of resolution are seen as one condition of the war, or as one explanation of it.

More detailed answers are provided by studies of the diplomatic, social and economic history of the inter-war period. Such examinations usually stress factors such as the demographic weakness of France and her exhaustion after the slaughter of the First World

War, the post-war economic crisis, American isolationism, and the anti-Communism which inhibited the Western powers from concluding a defensive alliance with the Soviet Union early enough to prevent the outbreak of war. The conditions which enabled Hitler to launch his campaign of conquest – first of all his determination to do so, and secondly the internal conditions within Germany – were reinforced by external conditions within Europe, by the lack of determination or by the inability of the other powers to prevent a war.

The last factor to be examined is an even more fundamental condition of the Second World War; it can prompt us to reflect on Hitler's role and perhaps to see it in a different light. The Second World War was not a German war alone but a world war, a global conflict, and so the historian's approach has to be global as well. If we say that Hitler's war was a war of territorial conquest or of territorial expansion we must not overlook the fact that two other countries sought similar wars for territorial expansion at the same time, and even started them before Hitler started his.

Japan expanded into Manchuria in 1931 and then opened hostilities against China in 1937. This war of aggression, beginning in 1931, has a background which can be traced back through the whole history of modern Japan as far as the Meiji Restoration of 1868. Japan's attempts at conquering living space for herself in Chinese territory received their first expression in the war against China in 1894–5, then in the war against Russia in 1904–5, and once more during the First World War. Although this conflict was mainly a European affair it had important repercussions in Asia since the absence of European competitors permitted Japan to expand into the Chinese mainland. This process culminated in the attack on the North-Eastern province of Manchuria in 1931, the fully fledged war against China in 1937, and ultimately into war with the United States after the attack on Pearl Harbor in December 1941.

Italy's attempts at territorial expansion were similar to Japan's. Mussolini launched his war of conquest against Ethiopia (or Abyssinia) in 1935, and this campaign, too, had a long pre-history dating back to Italian efforts to annex Ethiopia at the end of the nineteenth century. These ended in 1896 with a severe Italian defeat at Adowa. In the case of Italy as well as of Japan a long-term aim of territorial expansion was revived in the 1930s and 1940s.

Whereas Hitler favoured such moves by Japan and Italy and

concluded alliances with them, in particular the tripartite pact of September 1940, it cannot be claimed that he provoked these wars in East Asia and East Africa. Neither, of course, can it be claimed that they provoked his war which he had envisaged many years before. None the less, there do seem to be similarities or parallels. On the one side the Second World War was characterized by the regional hegemonial ambitions of Germany, Italy and Japan, all three of which tried to acquire new living space and a new predominance through conquest of areas adjoining their national territory. Japan called hers the 'Greater East-Asia Co-Prosperity Sphere', and a map of Japanese conquests by mid-1942 reveals a wide perimeter centred on the Japanese islands and extending to the West into the Chinese mainland and to the South as far as the islands in the Pacific and modern Indonesia. It was intended to be one living space or area of conquest.

Germany, of course, made a similar attempt to achieve what after 1938 Hitler called the *Grossdeutsches* Reich, or, in the latter stages of the war, the *Grossgermanisches* Reich, a greater Germanic empire. The map of Europe in 1942 reveals the frontiers of a vast German empire approximating to Hitler's ultimate goal. At the same time Mussolini extended the use of the term *il mare nostro* from the Adriatic to the Mediterranean as Italian *aspirazioni* or aspirations became more extensive. North African territories such as Libya and Tunisia provided a link between Italy in the North and Ethiopia in the South, and the colonies formed a new living space which Mussolini sometimes called the new *Impero Romano*, the new Roman Empire.

During the Second World War these three expansionist states stood opposed to three other states which had no territorial ambitions: Britain, France and the United States of America. Their defensive attitude was clearly expressed in what later became their joint programme, the Atlantic Charter of 14 August 1941. France had already been defeated by then, while America had not yet formally entered the war. In the Atlantic Charter the British and American heads of government, Churchill and Roosevelt, declared as their first point that their countries would seek no aggrandizement, territorial or otherwise. This remained one of their aims, and although their countries emerged victorious from the war they did not exploit their position for any territorial expansion worth mentioning.

The Soviet Union was in a different position from the three expansionist states of Germany, Italy and Japan, and also unlike Britain, France and the United States which fought to preserve the *status quo*. It did not enter the war to acquire new territory, but simply because it had been attacked; this was the only reason for its involvement. Unlike the Western allies, however, the Soviet Union made ambitious use of the war for territorial aggrandizement. Already in 1939–40, protected by its treaty with Germany, the Hitler–Stalin pact, it had embarked on an expansionist policy. Its territorial gains at the moment of victory were important. In 1945, at the end of the Second World War, Russia won back more or less all the areas which had been lost in Asia after her defeat by Japan in 1905, in particular Sakhalin and the Kuriles, as well as those which had been lost in Europe after 1917. Incidentally, at the three-power conference in Yalta, in a document said to have been drafted especially at Stalin's wish, it was laid down that Russia would be given back those areas which had been taken from her following 'the treacherous attack by Japan in 1904'; even in February 1945 Stalin had not forgotten the Japanese attack of 1904, made at a time when the two states were not at war with each other. Soviet expansionism may be called revisionist expansionism, whereas the three aggressors – Germany, Italy and Japan – fought for new conquests, for territories they had never controlled before.

We are faced with a tripartite division of the great powers involved in the Second World War. The three which desired to change the territorial *status quo* in their favour, Germany, Italy and Japan, were ranged against three others which were satisfied and defensive. In between them stood the Soviet Union. Its special position was illustrated by its shift of alliance in 1941. With a certain amount of justification it may be claimed that the Soviet Union had sided with Germany between August 1939 and June 1941. Then, having been attacked by Germany it changed sides and entered into an alliance with Britain and the United States.

There are certain relevant similarities in the history of the seven great powers, certain parallels between Germany, Italy and Japan on the one hand and Britain, France and the United States on the other. The first three nations had entered upon the stage of world politics at almost the same time, about 1870. Effectively they had not existed before they came into being as great powers. Germany and Italy had been divided into several different political units, and between the policies of the three regimes, and I certainly do not wish to overlook or minimize Germany's particular responsibility, her exceptional aggressiveness and brutality. Yet, as historians, we are bound to be intrigued by the basic analogy.

How are we to assess Hitler's role in this global perspective? Undoubtedly he developed a programme of his own, and this was his personal and individual achievement, but this programme must have matched some of the deeper tendencies and ambitions of his country and his time. We have to recognize that Hitler's programme and his determination were reinforced by a number of circumstances; by internal circumstances in Germany, external conditions in Europe and finally the global conditions which embraced Italy and Japan as well as Germany. These are fundamental points which concern not only the role of the individual in history but also historical understanding in general. There is no final and convincing answer to these problems, but it is important to balance Hitler's objectives on the one hand with, on the other, the three different sets of conditions which made it possible for him to lead Germany into the Second World War.

Japan's self-imposed isolation had only recently been replaced b its exposure to foreign contacts. This was followed rapidly by th Meiji restoration which, though formally dated to April 1868, was actually a lengthy process beginning in the 1870s.

At the time when these three new or younger powers entered world politics the four other great powers had long been in existence and had already an extended period of territorial expansion behind them. Russia and the United States had achieved this mainly by penetrating their respective continents from coast to coast. The United States grew westwards from the original thirteen colonies until it reached the Pacific, while in the course of the sixteenth, seventeenth and eighteenth centuries Russia expanded from its medieval heartland of Moscow across the Urals and Siberia to Vladivostok. Britain and France gradually built up their great colonial empires. All the great powers might be called expansionist in these phases of their history; indeed it might even be said that every state which comes into existence is expansionist in the beginning.

After the First World War, however, the Western powers changed their attitudes and they established the League of Nations which would act as an instrument for preserving the *status quo*. After some years this new post-war balance of power was challenged by the three future aggressors, Germany, Italy and Japan. All of them had been dissatisfied by the outcome of the war, even though Italy and Japan had been among the victors. All three experienced economic crises, social unrest, political instability and the establishment of authoritarian regimes. This pattern began in Italy with the advent of fascism in 1922; Germany's turn came in 1933, and Japan's history in the 1930s was marked by a long process in the course of which the parliamentary regime was abolished and replaced by a military dictatorship. All three left the League of Nations under protest, Germany and Japan in 1933 and Italy following suit in 1937. They then launched new campaigns of expansion which culminated in the Second World War.

Such a broad, worldwide perspective forces us to look differently at Hitler's role in launching the Second World War. There existed in Italy and Japan, as well as in Germany, a long-standing tendency towards territorial expansion. This led both countries into wars of conquest and expansion which were at least comparable to Germany's. I do not wish to overlook or minimize the differences

TWELVE

The War, German Society and Internal Resistance

PETER HOFFMANN

Hitler wanted war from the moment of his appointment as chancellor in January 1933. He announced his intention to go to war just four days after his appointment, in an address to senior armed-forces officers in the Armed Forces Ministry in Berlin.[1] In November 1937 he ordered the army to be ready for war against Czechoslovakia on 1 October 1938.[2] Feverish diplomatic activity and British and French military preparations against Germany forced him to settle for the minimal demand of occupation of the Sudeten region; but he occupied Bohemia and Moravia on 15 March 1939, and Slovakia became a client state.[3] Believing his agreement with the Soviet Union on the fourth partition of Poland gave him a free hand, and an alliance strong enough to keep the Western Powers out of the war, Hitler misread, or chose to ignore, the British reaction, thereby provoking a new world war.[4]

The campaign against Poland began on 1 September 1939.[5] It was successful, though flawed by supply problems, but it was characterized by the policy which Hitler had announced in his address to senior commanders on 22 August 1939:

> Genghis Khan has sent millions of women and children into death knowingly and with a light heart. History sees in him only the great founder of states. As to what the weak Western European civilisation asserts about me, that is of no account. I have given the command and I shall shoot everyone who utters one word of criticism, for the goal to be obtained in the war is not that of reaching certain lines but of physically demolishing the opponent. And so for the present only in the East I have put my death-head

> formations in place with the command relentlessly and without compassion to send into death many women and children of Polish origin and language. Only thus can we gain the living space that we need. Who after all is today speaking about the destruction of the Armenians?[6]

These threats were carried out in Poland, and protests from highly placed commanders, such as General Blaskowitz and Admiral Canaris, were without effect.[7]

Britain and France declared war on Germany on 3 September, and Australia, New Zealand, South Africa and Canada followed.[8] They could not save Poland, nor was this the principal object of their intervention. This was the defeat of Germany. Soon it became apparent that Hitler and Stalin had agreed on more than the partition of Poland. The Red Army occupied Eastern Poland after the German victory, and the Soviet Union concluded 'assistance' treaties with Estonia, Latvia and Lithuania, which had been relinquished in the Hitler–Stalin Pact to the Soviet 'sphere of influence'. Finland refused to accept Russian conditions and was attacked by the Soviet Union on 30 November 1939.

Hitler ordered the German armed forces to prepare an attack against France, since neither France nor Britain seemed inclined to accept his 'peace offers', in which he proposed to keep what he had and let bygones be bygones. They refused to give him a free hand for more conquests. Weather conditions and insufficient preparations forced a series of postponements of the attack in the West. As Britain appeared ready to move to assist Finland, and to try to prevent German ships from using Norwegian territorial waters as a sea lane for iron-ore shipments from Sweden, Hitler began to feel ill-at-ease about his northern flank and about iron-ore supplies from Sweden. He ordered the occupation of Denmark and Norway to begin on 9 April 1940.

On 10 May 1940 the German armies crossed the borders of the Netherlands, Belgium and France, advancing from stunning attacks to devastating victory. The Netherlands and Belgium capitulated in May, and an armistice was concluded between Germany and France on 22 June; a British force of some 200,000 was semi-encircled at Dunkirk but escaped across the Channel.

Hitler then attempted to drive Britain out of the war both by threatening and half-heartedly preparing for an invasion, and by a major air offensive, but these efforts failed and were abandoned. A German submarine offensive against Britain inflicted serious losses, but on the whole it was frustrated by the British fleet and by American naval support. German–Italian efforts to dominate the Mediterranean Sea and North Africa were similarly unsuccessful.

Even before the 1940 air offensive against Britain had reached its greatest intensity, Hitler had ordered the preparation of an attack on the Soviet Union. While German preparations were proceeding, Hitler had sent his foreign minister, von Ribbentrop, to negotiate with the Russian foreign minister, Molotov, about a further division of spheres of influence in South-Eastern Europe.[9] Political developments in Yugoslavia and an Italian invasion of Albania and Greece caused Germany's southern flank to weaken, drawing her into a Balkan campaign in the spring of 1941 which delayed the attack against the Soviet Union.

This attack began on 22 June 1941. It was accompanied by genocidal measures on a vast scale against the political infrastructure of the Soviet Union, against the 5.7 million Soviet prisoners-of-war (of whom 3.3 million lost their lives) and against the Jews in Russia and in Eastern Europe, of whom at least 5.1 million were murdered. These measures had long been in preparation.

Numerous scholars have for years been locked in dispute over the question of whether a central will (Hitler's) had planned, directed and guided the extermination programme from the beginning of Nazi rule, or whether it was the result of a gradual accumulation of spontaneous bureaucratic and individual actions. There is general agreement on two aspects: one, that the extermination policy was impossible without Hitler as a central factor; the other, that there was a large degree of co-operation on the part of individuals and agencies who became involved, in almost all cases involuntarily, with the process.[10] Hitler's central role, however, could be denied only if substantial evidence of his personal decisions at crucial junctures were ignored. The events of 1938 in particular signalled his re-entry into the decision-making process.

In the war crisis of 1938 anti-Jewish violence was intensified in a government-ordered pogrom such as the cities of Germany had not seen since the Middle Ages. At the same time the spectre of the war which Hitler was planning brought to the dictator's lips public threats, on 30 January 1939, against the Jews of all Europe.[11] The start of the war in September 1939 was coupled with the so-called euthanasia programme, which turned out to be a preparatory stage for the mass-murder of Jews in concentration camps. Impatience accelerated events; the German troops who invaded Poland were followed immediately by special SS and police units who conducted large-scale shootings of intellectuals, priests, partisans and Jews – just as Hitler had threatened to do in his speech before senior military commanders on 22 August 1939.[12]

At the end of the Polish campaign, and in the face of interventions and protests by army commanders,[13] the killings had to be scaled down and conducted in a more 'regular' manner, under acceptable pretexts such as sabotage or espionage. The campaign against the Soviet Union, however, opened up new possibilities, and this time the preparations for mass killings, particularly of Jews, were much more elaborate. They were written and introduced in a fashion designed to avoid or to mute protests from the regular army, not entirely successfully. The commanders of *Einsatzgruppen* and *Einsatzkommandos* (mobile killing squads) encountered few difficulties with German military authorities; frequently they may have been surprised at the amount of co-operation they received. The crucial orders for what became known as the Holocaust were given by Hitler, Himmler, Goering and Heydrich in the months immediately preceding the attack on Russia to August/September 1941.[14] Hundreds of thousands were shot, and the military commanders, engaged in fierce battle in a vast foreign land, against an ever-more-formidable enemy, did not see how they could stop the killings. The huge Russian hinterland was thinly controlled by German forces, while vast territories had been traversed but not occupied. The military commanders' concern was more to ensure that these areas were controlled so that supply trains were not blown off the tracks than with what the SS and police and local militia were doing.

The majority of the more than 5 million Jews who were killed died in six special death camps in Poland and in the Ukraine: at Chelmno, from December 1941 to March 1943, 150,000 Jews; at Belzec, from the winter of 1941 to the spring of 1943, an estimated 550,000; at Sobibor, from April/May to June 1942 and from March to August 1943, 200,000; at Treblinka, from July 1942 to October 1943, 750,000; at Oswiecim (Auschwitz) from September 1941 to 28 November 1944, 1,000,000; at Majdanek, 200,000 people, 50,000 of them Jews. Cautious estimates of the numbers of Jews killed by mobile death squads and in other open-air shootings run to 1.3 million. At least 800,000 were killed through ghettoization and general privation, and another 250,000 in camps with smaller killing operations and in some Romanian and Croatian camps where local militias carried out large-scale massacres.[15]

German advance units reached the outskirts of Moscow, but by December 1941 the German invasion had collapsed in early rains, snow and frost. On 6 December, Hitler knew the war was lost.[16] Field Marshal von Brauchitsch, commander-in-chief of the army, resigned, and Hitler took direct command of the army.

Japan attacked Pearl Harbor on 7 December 1941, and Hitler declared war on the United States four days later, for reasons which are still obscure. The United States had been involved in the European war, to all intents and purposes for some time. Hitler formalized this state of affairs, thereby permitting the United States to develop her full force against both Japan and Germany. Hitler seems to have hoped for a victory over the Soviet Union while the Americans were heavily committed in the Pacific Ocean. But he failed in the East, and the United States had resources for serious commitment in both the Pacific and the Atlantic.[17] The year 1942 ended with the disaster of Stalingrad, where the entire German 6th Army was annihilated and close to 100,000 soldiers taken prisoner; it ended also with a contracting and in the long-term untenable position of the Afrika Korps (which went into captivity in May 1943); and it ended with the failure of German efforts to prevent the United States from sending supplies to Britain across the Atlantic.

In spite of the enormous efforts of the German military and home fronts, and in spite of constant increases in arms production, German forces were fighting on too many fronts and had not the strength to force a decision at any of them. A new offensive in Russia in the summer of 1943 (Zitadelle, 5-13 July) failed at Kursk[18], and by 12 July 1944 the German Army Group Centre in Russia was smashed, with 350,000 men lost, and the Red Army units had come within a few miles of the German border.[19] The submarine offensive did not stop American supplies and troops from crossing the Atlantic, and the American and British forces built up a growing superiority on the seas and in the air. Germany's only major ally in Europe, Italy, fell into disorder with the *coup d'état* against Mussolini in July 1943; in September Italy changed sides, and Germany had another front to defend.

The Western allies mounted their long-awaited invasion of France in June 1944, broke out of their bridgehead, occupied Paris in August and reached the Rhine in the autumn. During the desperate last nine months of the war there was no diminution of the scale of fighting and slaughter. Hitler's last gamble, the Ardennes offensive of December 1944–January 1945 could not, however, succeed against the overwhelming military forces and material might that were thrown against Germany.

Hitler hoped for nothing short of a miracle. He ended his life as a gambler, in total disregard for 'his' nation and for the lives he destroyed and continued to destroy in senseless prolongation of the war, and he pursued to the end his obsession that he must destroy the Jews. Finally, when most of Germany was in enemy hands, and the Red Army was closing in on the Reich chancellery bunker in the centre of Berlin, Hitler took his own life.

Society's responses to war present a paradox. Initially, President Roosevelt and Chancellor Hitler experienced the same difficulties in marshalling popular support for war.

On 5 November 1937 Hitler announced plans for conquest before the heads of the armed forces, much in the manner of Frederick the Great's *Träume und chimärische Pläne*, as political dreams to be realized when the opportunity arose.[20] As Hitler spoke, his war minister, his commander-in-chief of the army and his foreign minister objected that Germany could not confront the major powers of the world in the forseeable future; the commander-in-chief of the navy is not recorded as having spoken, and the head of the air force raised indirect objections.The bare fact was that Hitler did not receive any support for his ideas at the highest level. He concluded that he would have trouble with such half-hearted advisors and by February 1938 the three principal objectors had lost their posts.

Three of the highest-ranking functionaries of the regime had said no to Hitler's wishes. As Field Marshal von Manstein said in the Nuremberg Trial on 10 August 1946: 'Under a dictatorship, a dictator cannot permit himself to be forced, because the moment he gives way, his dictatorship ends.'[21] General Ludwig Beck, the chief of the general staff, understood this, too, and he tried to back up his protests against Hitler's war plans in 1938 by organizing a collective refusal of the senior commanders to carry out orders if Hitler ordered an attack on Czechoslovakia. Beck also understood that such a confrontation must lead to Hitler's fall. But his efforts had been pre-empted by Hitler's dismissal of General von Fritsch as commander-in-chief of the army, in January 1938, and by the appointment of General von Brauchitsch as his successor, whom Hitler had bribed. Brauchitsch did not support Beck's protest, and Beck was forced to resign.[22]

The response of the population at large was similar to that of the chief military and political leaders. They flatly refused to cheer when the 2nd Motorized Division from Stettin was marched through the streets of Berlin, on 27 September 1938.[23]

> The hundreds of thousands of Berliners pouring out of their offices . . . ducked into the subways, refused to look on, and the handful that did stood at the curb in utter silence unable to find a word of cheer for the flower of their youth going away to the glorious war. It has been the most striking demonstration against the war that I've ever seen. . . . They are dead set against war.

Thus wrote in his diary William L. Shirer, the American news correspondent.

Hitler knew he must do something about this situation, and told members of the press corps on 10 November 1938 in Munich:

> Circumstances have forced me to speak almost only of peace for decades. . . . Somehow I believe that this record, the pacifist record, has played itself out here. . . . Now the truth must be stated, and the entire people must learn to believe so fanatically in the final victory that any defeats we might suffer would be viewed only from the superior consideration that this was temporary.[24]

Methods of war tend to become steadily more brutalized. The United States resorted to unrestricted submarine warfare against Japan in 1941. In 1917 German unrestricted submarine warfare against her enemies' suppliers had been held to be immoral and provided the United States with a cause for entering the war. The so-called strategic bombing offensive against the civilian population of Germany killed several hundreds of thousands of civilians, without any demonstrable effect on the outcome of the war.[25]

This can be attributed in part to increased potential resulting from technological developments, to more powerful explosives and greater firing power. It is also a result of greater numbers of people being involved in war activities because of the vast population increase since the nineteenth century. But the fundamental problem is the fact that governments have such difficulty in finding popular support at the outset of war.

Uncontrollable forces are unleashed in nationalized, universal draft armies. They are the 'forces of the depths' which King Frederick William III of Prussia feared when universal military service was advocated by Scharnhorst and Gneisenau, the forces he himself later called upon in the Proclamation of Kalish in March 1813.[26] Restraint had been a necessity when armies were small and expensive, when professionals confronted professionals. Now the reservoir was inexhaustible, amateurs fought amateurs as people became intoxicated with killing and with the justice of their cause. Were they not defending their women and children, their homes, their homelands? It is these sentiments, untempered by professional coolness, that make popular-army soldiers so brutal. It was this same brutality, however, and the non-military killing operations, which helped produce the resistance movements in Germany.

No regime will ever govern wholly unopposed. A dictatorship necessarily forces the opposition underground. Underground opposition may be no more than residual, or it may crystallize into a dangerous conspiracy for the overthrow of the government.

Phases and centres of resistance

Underground opposition in Germany developed in phases from 1933 to 1945. First there was an initial phase in which opposition practised in the Weimar Republic continued to function but was suppressed, outlawed and destroyed gradually, by the secret police. Communists and socialists were rendered ineffective as organized sources of opposition, although numerous individuals carried out heroic acts of defiance, resistance and sabotage against the Nazi regime.

The numbers speak most loudly. According to a Gestapo summary, 162,734 persons were being held in 'protective custody' for political reasons in April 1939, 27,369 were under indictment for political offences, 112,432 had been sentenced for political offences; by this time 225,000 people had been sentenced to average gaol terms of slightly less than three years. Between 1933 and 1945 about 3 million Germans were held in concentration camps or prisons for political reasons. Tens of thousands were executed after being sentenced by a court, and more perished from mistreatment, privation, torture and murder in camps and prisons.[27]

These numbers reveal the potential for popular resistance in German society, and also what happened to it.

A few groups managed to keep intact beyond the 1930s, among them those connected with the war organization of the Soviet military intelligence service *Rote Kapelle*; this group operated for about a year from 1941 to 1942, with moderate success, before it was destroyed by the Gestapo. The other organizations which can be said to have presented something more than sporadic opposition were the Catholic Church and the Lutheran Confessing Church.

Many Catholic clergymen defended courageously the rights guaranteed in the Concordat of July 1933.[28] The Lutheran Confessing Church was an important secession from the Established Church which had become dominated by pro-Nazi clergymen. Its members could not accept that the secular Führer should take precedence over Jesus Christ, they insisted on the pure Gospels and although they were less united on this point, they also opposed the persecution of Christian converts from the Jewish faith.[29] A number of institutions and individuals in both the Catholic and the Lutheran Confessing Churches remained effective throughout the twelve Nazi years as underground networks, aiding many people in need and in flight from the authorities. Members of both Church hierarchies put up courageous opposition, in individual cases quite openly, to the campaign of murder against the mentally ill and the feeble, the Jehovah's Witnesses, Gypsies, and Jews. Bishop von Galen of Munster preached publicly against the murder of the mentally ill and other crimes, and Bishop Wurm of Württemberg wrote half a dozen letters to governmment ministers and to Hitler himself during the war years denouncing the murders of these mental patients and the Jews.[30] But Hitler let them be, postponing the final reckoning with the Churches until after the war.[31]

This sort of opposition was no more than an irritant to the regime. Full knowledge of the crimes was rare and uncertain,[32] and the majority of the population were motivated to support the Nazi regime, through propaganda, nationalism and police terror. No dictatorial regime in the twentieth century has been overthrown from within so long as it commanded the loyalty of the armed forces.

A new political resistance crystallized in 1938, during the Blomberg–Fritsch crisis. The removal of the two senior military leaders was a new blow to the integrity of the armed forces; the other principal factor was the threat of European war. The new centre formed around the chief of the general staff of the army, General Beck, and in the Military Counter-Intelligence Agency of Admiral Canaris.[33] Beck planned to lead senior commanders in a *coup d'état* against Hitler, but failed in August 1938 because General von Brauchitsch denied Beck his support, whereupon Beck resigned. His successor, General Halder, carried on with plans to topple the regime if Hitler drove Europe to war. But this time the unreadiness of the British government led to a compromise which culminated in the Munich Agreement in September. The opposition did not regroup in any serious way until the general war involving the Western Powers had become an acute menace once more when, after the defeat of Poland, Hitler ordered an attack upon France for the beginning of November, 1939.

Some people were resolved to act at any time to bring down the regime by any means. They can be divided into those who believe that organized action, a *coup d'état*, would be necessary if the Nazi system were to be eliminated, and there were those who would have been content to eliminate the chief criminal, thinking the regime would not survive his fall. The first group needed support from nationalist elements, and they could hope to receive it only in the most extraordinarily menacing circumstances. Those in favour of eliminating Hitler regardless of tactical considerations made a number of attempts which failed.

A Swiss theological student, Maurice Bavaud, tried in November 1938 to kill Hitler during the annual commemoration of the failed Putsch of 1923.[34] At the same place and time, the Swabian cabinet-maker Georg Elser planned and carried out an attack in 1939, in which he very nearly succeeded in killing Hitler.[35] Several other assassination plots were hatched in 1939, but they also failed.[36]

The most active centre of resistance during the war was in the military intelligence service. Some of those involved were Admiral Canaris, Colonel Oster, Dr Josef Müller, Dr von Dohnanyi, the Reverend Dietrich Bonhoeffer, Dr Gisevius, Karl Ludwig Baron von Guttenberg and Helmuth Count von Moltke.

They pursued contacts in 1939–40 with the British government via the Vatican; Pope Pius XII himself acted as mediator.[37] They proposed to overthrow Hitler and change the German government if Britain offered reasonable conditions; but they could not follow their plans through. As preparations advanced General Halder had become less apprehensive about the German army's chances of success.[38] Moreover, the conditions for peace negotiations conveyed or hinted at by the British side may have seemed so unfavourable as to preclude support from nationalist elements in the German army.[39]

This is illustrated by the analysis of his own position by General Halder, the Chief of the General Staff of the Army from 1938 to 1942. Halder had risked his life by conspiring to overthrow Hitler in 1938. But in November 1939 he made the following points to one of the conspirators who tried to press him to take action against Hitler: it would violate tradition; there was no successor; the young officer corps was not reliable; the mood in the interior was not favourable; it could not be tolerated that Germany was permanently a 'people of helots' subservient to England; (concerning Hitler's war plans) Ludendorff, too, in 1918 had launched an offensive against general advice, and historical judgement did not condemn him. He, Halder, therefore did not fear the later judgement of history either. Furthermore, whatever hopes had been cherished of winning over General von Brauchitsch had been misplaced from the start.

Despite many efforts, the centre in the military intelligence service could not raise enough support for further *coup* attempts until the Stalingrad catastrophe in 1943. In the meantime the centre was active in saving Jews and other potential victims, as well as in maintaining and establishing contacts with enemy powers. Saving Jews was its undoing, and the centre was broken up by the arrests of Dohnanyi, Müller, Bonhoeffer and Oster in April 1943.[40]

Another resistance centre functioned, particularly during 1942 and 1943, in the high command of the Army Group Centre in Russia, whose headquarters were near Smolensk. They co-operated closely with the Abwehr centre, and members were instrumental in bringing about two assassination attacks in March 1943, in co-ordination with the preparations of the Abwehr centre. The most prominent members were General von Tresckow, Lieutenant von Schlabrendorff and Colonel Baron von Gersdorff, but several others – Boeselager, Kleist, Waldersee – played important roles. This centre ceased to be effective after Tresckow's transfer in 1943.[41]

Another centre existed in Paris, where key figures in the military government of France and Belgium were ready to contribute to an uprising. The Paris centre functioned best of any of them on 20 July 1944: its members arrested the entire Gestapo establishment there and were ready to execute them when the news of the failure in Berlin arrived.[42]

There were other groups, consisting of current or former high-ranking civil servants, politicians and officers. One of these groups, containing diverse elements, was headed by Dr Goerdeler, the former Mayor of Leipzig, General Beck, former ambassador Ulrich von Hassell, and the Prussian minister of finance, Dr Popitz. They co-operated with certain former leaders of the Christian trade unions. By 1943 they had established a working relationship with the so-called Kreisau Circle.[43]

This centre had formed around Helmuth Count von Moltke who worked under Admiral Canaris, and around some of his friends, including Peter Count von Yorck. Its members, unable although not unwilling to engage in direct action against the regime, concerned themselves with preparations for the time after Hitler's death. Nine of the nineteen members were socialists, five were clergymen and several were serving in the armed forces.[44]

From August 1943 to July 1944 the Abwehr centre was suceeded as the driving force in the resistance by the Stauffenberg centre in the Home Army command. Its basic method was the same as the one that the Abwehr group, the cell in the Army Group Centre command, and conspirators in the Home Army had envisioned but had not yet refined: to deploy the Home Army against the regime once Hitler had been killed.[45]

In the last months before the final *coup* attempt, contacts were sought with the Communist underground, weak though it was. There was no unanimity concerning these advances, neither in the military nor in the civilian wings of the resistance conspiracy. But the contacts did go ahead.[46]

Internal and external support for the overthrow of Hitler from within

In all phases of the resistance movement, internal and external support was crucial for the overthrow of Hitler's regime.

Resistance activities might have been effective if they had been broadly based within the nation, or if key military leaders could have been persuaded to support a *coup d'état*. Sociologically, all categories and levels of the population were represented in the resistance: ordinary soldiers, professionals, factory workers, trade union leaders, diplomats, government ministers, civil servants, generals, priests and Lutheran ministers. Politically, the entire spectrum from left to right was represented. But in quantitative terms, representation was insignificant. The resistance did not fully represent the nation: broad support was lacking, and it could not be generated in the existing conditions. In general terms, the regime was accepted. The true nature and magnitude of its crimes eluded the comprehension of the majority; the campaigns of mass murder threatened only minorities.[47] The immediate threats were the ubiquitous secret police, death at the fronts, and allied aerial bombing raids. The war was sustained by nationalism, by an effective propaganda machine, and by secret-police terror.

Attempts to find an underground 'mass basis' for anti-government action were made throughout the twelve years of Nazi rule, only to be outflanked again and again by the Gestapo machine. In the Kreisau Circle, Dr Carlo Mierendorff had called repeatedly for co-operation with the Communist underground in 1943.[48] Final efforts to establish a broad base for the overthrow of the Führer were made on 22 June 1944.[49] The socialists and Kreisau Circle associates, Dr Julius Leber and Professor Adolf Reichwein, met in a Berlin physician's apartment with members of the Communist underground central committee, Anton Saefkow and Franz Jacob. The rudimentary underground popular front remained élitist; neither the socialists nor the Communists commanded a mass following. The conspirators were betrayed by a Gestapo infiltrator, and were arrested on 4 and 5 July.

All groups involved in the conspiracy professed to seek the re-establishment of the rule of justice and human decency, and all declared themselves against a revival of the conditions of the Weimar Republic which had produced Hitler's dictatorship.[50] The stress placed on individual liberty, social reform and democracy, however, varied considerably. There were those who demanded the socialization of all means of production and a dictatorship of the proletariat; there were those who wanted a liberal democratic republic; and there were those who believed frankly that a more authoritarian constitution, possibly a monarchic one, would be most suitable.

It would be easy to dismiss out of hand the proposals at the extremes of the spectrum, and to find fault with those in between. But the drafts which have become known were designed to achieve a transition from the police-state dictatorship to a state in which personal liberty and the rule of justice were guaranteed. The transition had to be achieved during the most ferociously fought war the world had known, with Germany vastly outnumbered and fighting off dangerous enemies on all sides.

Before the conspirators' drafts for a constitutional transition are criticized, they ought be examined for their intentions. Some plans were drafted for the immediate transition, while others were designed for the long-term political education of German society. None of the drafts that have come to light were designed as definitive constitutions.

While the anti-Hitler forces shared the goal of removing the dictator, they did not share long-range political objectives. They all sought to prevent the restoration of conditions that had brought Hitler to power, but a coalition of all the anti-Nazi forces had to be temporary. Total coalition is the negation of political liberty and would have amounted to fascism. But free and general elections could not be held immediately after Hitler's fall. Nazism had to be rooted out, and society had to be educated in democratic procedures.

The question of whose ideas might have prevailed was a matter of timing. In 1940 or 1941, an anti-Nazi regime in Germany could have relied on a strong military position, and presumably would have been rather on the conservative side. In 1943 or 1944, an anti-Nazi regime would have been faced with a much more difficult external and internal situation, but it would also have found it necessary to rule authoritatively for a time.

This was more a question of the military situation than of conservative names on prospective cabinet lists. The lists prepared by the conspirators, in any case, show few variations from about 1940 to 1944; Beck and Goerdeler were always regarded as the leading personalities, and the principal socialists associated with the Kreisau Circle appeared on the lists as well. There was a shift towards the left when Leber and Leuschner gained more prominence in the 1944 lists; on the other hand, Tresckow and Stauffenberg found their way on to lists only in 1944.

The attitude of Germany's enemies would determine to a large extent what sort of regime could survive in Germany after Hitler's fall. In 1940, it was entirely unknown whether Britain and America would force upon Germany another Versailles Treaty, or whether they would accept some accommodation which would have left Germany in possession of some of Hitler's conquests. In 1943, with the principle of unconditional surrender established beyond a doubt, and with Germany clearly losing the war, the prospect was the occupation of Germany by the Red Army. That would not have left an anti-Nazi government with much room for manoeuvre.

The obvious conclusion from the circumstances described above had already been drawn by most of the leading conspirators, by some of them as early as 1938: that only elements of the armed forces, preferably in collaboration with the police, had the ability to neutralize the Nazi Party forces, the SS in particular, and any loyal army units, and to occupy key government and other power positions in the state.

'Effective resistance' may now be defined as 'resistance capable of eliminating Hitler's and his party's power'. This is not to disparage other resistance efforts. It means simply that they were not effective, and had no prospect of being so. Military power would be the only means to overthrow Hitler's regime, since mass action such as strikes and the like could not be organized in a terrorist police state. Effective resistance in Germany, however, had to come from the most nationalist, conservative elements in the German state. The resistance in Germany had to *overcome* nationalism in the ordinary sense in order to become active and effective; members had to some extent to deny their own feelings of patriotism.

This distinguishes the German resistance from resistance movements in countries occupied by German forces where resistance and nationalism did not conflict. All other resistance movements also received allied encouragement and support; the German resistance did not.

Methods of securing support within the country and the mobilization of the Home Army against the regime for the *coup d'état* in Germany may be divided into several categories:

1. The demonstration to potential supporters in the armed forces that Germany had better prospects of surviving as a nation in her existing territory if Hitler and his clique were removed. This would

give legitimacy and a hope of political survival to the conspiracy and to those who associated themselves with it.

2. The person to whom all soldiers had sworn a personal oath of loyalty and obedience, and to whom most felt honour-bound, must be eliminated. This would enable commanders and soldiers to follow the orders of generals and colonels leading the *coup d'état*.

3. A further aspect of their plans reveals a great deal about the state of mind of German society, and about the conspirators' judgement of it. The Home Army was to be mobilized (operation 'Valkyrie') on the basis of the pretence that corrupt elements within the Nazi Party and the SS had assassinated the Führer in order to put themselves in power, and that they were stabbing the fighting forces in the back; in this situation the army would assume executive power to maintain order.

However, the first general orders and proclamations to be sent out by teleprinter and broadcast by radio were to stress a profound repudiation of all that the previous regime had done and stood for. One is faced again with the contradictory position of a group of people at once repudiating crime, and bound in loyal support to the chief criminal. If it could not be argued that Germany could survive better without Hitler than under his rule, military support for a *coup d'état* would be hard to find. The deception involved in operation 'Valkyrie' was not certain to work if high-level military support was lacking.

The attitude of Germany's enemies, however, determined their war aims. British war aims were expressed in the terms of the British–Polish alliance of 25 August 1939 and in its secret protocol, in Prime Minister Chamberlain's House of Commons speech of 12 October 1939, and in communications passed between German conspirators and the British government through the Vatican in 1939–40.[51] In these communications the British government insisted on 'security for the future', and a decentralized and federal Germany. Since the Treaty of Versailles had not produced 'security', complete disarmament and control of Germany were required. Sir Francis d'Arcy Osborne, the British minister to the Vatican, told Pope Pius XII on 16 February 1940 that he could not see how there could be peace with Germany so long as the German military machine remained intact.

The British–Soviet Agreement of 12 July 1941 excluded negotiations or the conclusion of an armistice or treaty of peace 'except by mutual agreement'. This was confirmed by all allied powers, now including the United States, in the Washington Pact of 1 January 1942. This stipulated 'total victory' before any agreement with Germany could be reached, and the incorporation of the 'Atlantic Charter' that Prime Minister Churchill and President Roosevelt had agreed upon on 14 August 1941. The Charter aimed at the disarmament of Germany, and the Washington Pact at her unconditional surrender.[52] When foreign secretary Anthony Eden was in Moscow in December 1941, Stalin sketched for him the division of Germany and Europe. In July 1942 the War Cabinet approved the general principle of the transfer to Germany of German minorities in Central and South-Eastern Europe after the war 'where this seems necessary and desirable', referring to the expulsion of the German populations from East Prussia, Upper Silesia, and by implication at least from West Prussia. It was estimated that from 3 to 6.8 million Germans were to be expelled.[53]

In view of such war aims the allied powers could not be expected to offer any assurances to resistance emissaries about acceptable treatment of Germany after Hitler's elimination, nor could they be expected to promise to hold back their armies and air forces while a *coup d'état* was in progress in Germany. What may have looked like such a concession in February 1940 was probably no more than an admission that immediate military action was not within the power of the allied governments.

Churchill instructed Eden with regard to any kind of peace feelers, on 20 January 1941, as follows: 'Your predecessor was entirely misled in December 1939. Our attitude towards all such inquiries or suggestions should be absolute silence.'[54] At the Moscow Conference in October 1943 the governments of Britain, America and Russia agreed 'to inform each other immediately of any peace feelers which they may receive from the Government of, or from any groups or individuals in, a country with which any of the three countries is at war'.[55]

Before the landing and breakthrough of American and British forces into central France unconditional surrender such as the allied powers demanded meant in effect the occupation of Germany by the Red Army. In view of Russian activities in countries they occupied, and in view of German activities in Russia, this was unacceptable to any prospective non-Communist German government seeking to supplant Hitler's dictatorship. Consequently, innumerable secret missions emanated from the resistance to seek assurances that 'unconditional surrender' would not be insisted upon in case of a successful *coup d'état* by the resistance.[56]

There were those like Goerdeler who wanted solid concessions concerning Germany's territorial integrity; those like Trott who tried to leave the door open for negotiations while trying to secure maximum concessions with which to argue the case of revolt to German military men; and those like Bonhoeffer who were willing to accept any allied dictate afterwards but wanted only enough support to make the revolt possible.[57] But the answer of the allies was the same to all of them.

Nevertheless the conspirators acted. They did so, unlike all other anti-Nazi resistance movements, without any support or encouragement from the powers allied against Nazi Germany. Several assassination plans and attacks were launched in February, March and December 1943, and in February, March and July 1944. They were based on the conviction that it was mandatory to go forward in order to end the killing, and because the honour of Germany demanded such an action even if the territorial integrity and independence of Germany could not be preserved.[58] If nothing else, the planned *coup* would document the existence of an Other Germany which did not acquiesce in the crimes committed in her name.[59]

The 20 July 1944 coup d'état

The above view is reinforced by a look at the manner in which the leader of the conspiracy in July 1944 proposed to proceed.[60] He was Colonel Claus Count von Stauffenberg, chief of staff in the Home Army command. He had been preparing to lead the Home Army to support a *coup d'état* once a member of the conspiracy had assassinated Hitler. There was no lack of volunteers – men like Bussche, Gersdorff, Tresckow, Schlabrendorff, Strachwitz, Breitenbuch, Kleist were among them – but there was a lack of people with access to Hitler *as well as* a willingness to assassinate him. By July 1944 it had become clear that the assassination, the key to everything else, would not be carried out unless Stauffenberg himself acted as assassin. But the odds against him were staggering.

The plan required Stauffenberg to move Home Army units into vital positions and government centres at once, as soon as Hitler had been killed.[61] The Home Army command and government centres were in Berlin, while Hitler's headquarters were either near Salzburg in Austria or near Rastenburg in East Prussia, in either case about 500 kilometres from Berlin. From a military standpoint the plan was absurd: a commander had to be on duty at the front. Three hours would elapse between the assassination and the return of the assassin to Berlin – if he did return. He had to try to survive the assassination attempt and return to the *coup d'état* centre, because it had become clear that no one could lead it in his absence.

Stauffenberg was forced therefore to use explosives with a timed fuse. He had been wounded in Africa and he had lost a hand and two fingers on the other hand, as well as an eye. Apart from needing to leave unobtrusively before the explosion and to survive it, he would have been unable to use a pistol with any confidence. As it turned out, he was interrupted by an orderly while setting the fuse; it is likely that this caused him to leave with only half of the explosives he had brought with him. The bomb, which should have been designed to kill all those present at Hitler's conference, including Hitler, killed only one person immediately; three others died later.[62]

There was no reasonable hope that an assassin could escape from the security zones of Hitler's headquarters after any explosion, and particularly after an attack on the Führer. But Stauffenberg did escape, by bluffing his way through. He reached Berlin against all odds; no attempt was made to intercept the aeroplane that carried him, either *en route* or on arrival. Unpredictably, all the major obstacles were overcome on 20 July 1944, but the unavoidable delay caused by Stauffenberg's flight to Berlin – and, of course, the survival of Hitler – could not be compensated for.

Despite initial successes, particularly in Paris and in Vienna, the *coup d'état* never gained enough momentum. Later that day Stauffenberg and three of his comrades were shot in Berlin, General Beck took his own life, and almost 200 other resisters were subsequently hanged. Claus Stauffenberg's brother was hanged, resuscitated and hanged again, several times, and all the hangings were filmed for Hitler's personal viewing.[63]

Stauffenberg and his friends had known that the chances of success were as good as naught. They acted in the face of overwhelming odds, without substantial hope of succeeding in killing Hitler or seizing control of Germany. They had even less hope of surviving politically for more than a few days or weeks, and therefore no hope of putting into effect their reconstruction ideas, for they had no chance of avoiding the occupation, amputation and division of Germany by enemy forces. They had known this, and they had faced it. But General Beck, General von Tresckow, Dietrich Bonhoeffer, Claus and Berthold Stauffenberg all agreed that the assassination had to be attempted at all costs; even if it failed, the attempt to seize power in Berlin had to made. What mattered now was no longer the practical purpose of the *coup*, but to prove to the world that the men of the resistance dared to take the decisive step and give their lives for their beliefs. They sacrificed their personal honour for the honour of Germany. As Berthold Stauffenberg put it: 'The most terrible thing is knowing that it cannot succeed and that we must still do it for our country and our children.'[64] His brother Claus put it similarly: 'I know that he who will act will go down in German history as a traitor; but he who can and does not will be a traitor to his conscience. If I did not act to stop this senseless killing, I should never be able to face the widows and orphans of the war.'[65]

The self-sacrifice of resistance members has given German society a moral perspective in which it can face up to its recent history. The conspirators of 20 July 1944 became the most visible representatives of the thousands who had stood up against crime and evil. Despair is tempered by a glimmer of faith in human decency.

Notes

1. *Völkischer Beobachter*, Munich edn, 6 Feb. 1933; Thilo Vogelsang, 'Neue Dokumente zur Geschichte der Reichswehr', *Vierteljahrshefte für Zeitgeschichte*, 2 (1954), pp. 434–5; Karl Dietrich Bracher, Wolfgang Sauer, Gerhard Schulz, *Die nationalsozialistische Machtergreifung. Studien zur Errichtung des totalitären Herrschaftssystems in Deutschland 1933–4*, 2nd edn (Cologne/Opladen, 1962), p. 719.
2. *The Trial of the Major War Criminals before the International Military Tribunal*, vol. XXV (Nuremberg, 1947), pp. 433–9, 445–7.
3. Karl Dietrich Erdmann, *Die Zeit der Weltkriege* (Gebhardt, *Handbuch der Deutschen Geschichte*, 9th edn by Herbert Grundmann, vol. 4) (Stuttgart, 1976), p. 479.
4. *Akten zur deutschen auswärtigen Politik 1918–1945*, Series D 1937–1945, vol. 7 (Baden-Baden, 1956), nos. 228, 229.
5. See Herbert Michaelis, 'Der Zweite Weltkrieg 1939–1945', in Leo

Just, *Handbuch der Deutschen Geschichte*, vol. IV, 2 (Konstanz, 1953–), pp. 3–356; Erdmann, pp. 498–591.

6. *Documents on British Foreign Policy 1919–1939*, 3rd series, vol. VII (London, 1954), no. 314, pp. 257–9. See also versions in *Trial*, XXVI (1947), documents PS 798 and 1014; *Trial*, XLI (1949), document Raeder-27; *Nazi Conspiracy and Aggression* (US Government Printing Office, Washington, 1946), vol. VII, document L3; Winfried Baumgart, 'Zur Ansprache Hitlers vor den Führern der Wehrmacht am 22. August 1939: Eine quellenkritische Untersuchung', *Vierteljahrshefte für Zeitgeschichte*, 16 (1968), pp. 120–49; Peter Hoffmann, *Widerstand, Staatsstreich, Attentat. Der Kampf der Opposition gegen Hitler*, 4th edn (Munich/Zurich, 1985), pp. 143, 702, n. 55; Peter Hoffmann, *The History of the German Resistance 1933–1945* (London/Cambridge, Massachusetts, 1977), pp. 109, 566, n. 56.
7. Franz Halder, *Kriegstagebuch*, vol. I (Stuttgart, 1962), p. 160; Helmuth Groscurth, *Tagebücher eines Abwehroffiziers 1938–1940* (Stuttgart, 1970), pp. 239, 245, 247.
8. *The Times*, Royal edn, 4 Sept. 1939, p. 8; 7 Sept. 1939, p. 6; 11 Sept. 1939, p. 8.
9. *Akten zur deutschen auswärtigen Politik 1918–1945*, Series D 1937–1945 (henceforth *ADAP* D), vol. XI, 1 (Bonn, 1964), nos. 325–9, pp. 448–78; *Documents on German Foreign Policy*, Series D (henceforth *DGFP* D), vol. XI (London, 1961), pp. 533–49, 550–70.
10. Eberhard Jäckel and Jürgen Rohwer (ed.), *Der Mord an den Juden im Zweiten Weltkrieg. Entschlußbildung und Verwirklichung* (Stuttgart, 1985), passim; Raul Hilberg, *The Destruction of the European Jews*, rev. edn (New York, 1985), passim; Christian Streit, *Keine Kameraden. Die Wehrmacht und die sowjetischen Kriegsgefangenen 1941–1945* (Stuttgart, 1978), pp. 9–10.
11. Lionel Kochan, *Pogrom 10 November 1938* (London, 1957); Max Domarus, *Hitler. Reden und Proklamationen 1932–1945. Kommentiert von einem deutschen Zeigenossen.* (Neustadt a.d.Aisch, 1963), pp. 1047–67.
12. See note 6.
13. See note 7.
14. Jäckel/Rohwer, passim; Helmut Krausnick, Hans-Heinrich Wilhelm, *Die Truppe des Weltanschauungskrieges. Die Einsatzgruppen der Sicherheitspolizei und des SD 1938–1942* (Stuttgart, 1981), passim; Ino Arndt, Wolfgang Scheffler, 'Organisierter Massenmord an Juden in nationalsozialistischen Vernichtungslagern. Ein Beitrag zur Richtigstellung apologetischer Literatur', *Vierteljahrshefte für Zeitgeschichte*, 24 (1976), pp. 105–35; for Majdanek: A[lfred] C[attani], 'Dokumentation eines Kriegsverbrecherprozesses', *Neue Zürcher Zeitung*, Fernausgbae Nr. 284, 6 Dec. 1984, p. 9.
15. Hilberg, op. cit., pp. 1219–20.
16. Rudolph Binion, '*. . . daß ihr mich gefunden habt*'. *Hitler und die*

Deutschen. Eine Psychohistorie (Stuttgart, 1978), p. 71, cites a note of General Alfred Jodl which he dictated in the Nuremberg prison: 'Earlier than any other person in the world Hitler felt and knew that the war was lost.' Percy Ernst Schramm, *Hitler als militärischer Führer. Erkenntnisse und Erfahrungen aus dem Kriegstagebuch des Oberkommandos der Wehrmacht* (Frankfurt/M., 1965), pp. 67, 154.

17. See Eberhard Jäckel, 'Die deutsche Kriegserklärung an die Vereinigten Staaten von 1941', in *Im Dienste Deutschlands und des Rechtes. Festschrift für Wilhelm G. Grewe* (Baden-Baden, 1981), pp. 117–37; Samuel Eliot Morison, *The Two-Ocean War: A Short History of the United States Navy in the Second World War* (Boston/ Toronto, 1963).
18. Ernst Klink, *Das Gesetz des Handelns. Die Operation 'Zitadelle' 1943* (Stuttgart, 1966).
19. cf. note 5, also for the remainder of the survey of the Second World War.
20. *DGFP* D, I (1949), no. 19, pp. 29–39; Friedrich der Grosse, *Die Politischen Testamente* (Berlin, 1922), pp. 63–9 ('Politische Träumereien'), 229–40 ('Träume und chimärische Pläne').
21. *Trial*, XX (1948), p. 624.
22. cf. Peter Hoffmann, 'Ludwig Beck: Loyalty and Resistance', *Central European History*, XIV (1981), pp. 340–8.
23. William L. Shirer, *Berlin Diary: The Journal of a Foreign Correspondent 1934–1941* (New York, 1941), pp. 142–3; see also Alfred Ingemar Berndt, *Der Marsch ins Grossdeutsche Reich*, 4th edn (Munich, 1940), p. 222; Paul Schmidt, *Hitler's Interpreter* (Melbourne/London/Toronto, 1951), p. 105.
24. Wilhelm Treue, 'Rede Hitlers vor der deutschen Presse (10. November 1938), *Vierteljahrshefte für Zeitgeschichte*, 6 (1958), pp. 175–91.
25. Henry L. Stimson, 'The Nuremberg Trial: Landmark in Law', *Foreign Affairs*, 25 (1946–7), p. 189; Statistiches Bundesamt (ed.), *Statistisches Jahrbuch für die Bundesrepublik Deutschland. 1960* (Stuttgart/Mainz, 1960), pp. 78–9.
26. G. H. Pertz, *Das Leben des Ministers Freiherrn vom Stein*, vol. 2 (Berlin, 1850), pp. 178–88, vol. 3 (Berlin, 1851), pp. 298–322; Peter Paret, *Clausewitz and the State* (New York/London/Toronto, 1976), p. 138.
27. Günther Weisenborn, *Der lautlose Aufstand. Bericht über die Widerstandsbewegung des deutschen Volkes 1933–1945* (Hamburg, 1962), pp. 30–2; Eric H. Boehm (ed.), *We Survived: The Stories of Fourteen of the Hidden and the Hunted of Nazi Germany* (New Haven, 1949), p. VIII; Gabriel A. Almond, 'The German Resistance Movement', *Current History*, 10 (1946), pp. 409–527; *Trial*, XXXVIII, pp. 362–5; Rudolf Pechel, *Deutscher Widerstand* (Erlenbach/Zurich, 1947), pp. 326–38; Walter Hammer, *Hohes Haus in Henkers Hand. Rückschau auf die Hitlerzeit, auf Leidensweg und Opfergang Deutscher Parlamentarier*, 2nd edn

(Frankfurt/M., 1956), p. 114; Annedore Leber, *Das Gewissen entscheided. Bereiche des deutschen Widerstandes von 1933–1945 in Lebensbildern*, 4th edn (Berlin/Frankfurt/M., 1960), p. 21.
28. John S. Conway, *The Nazi Persecution of the Churches 1933–45* (London, 1968), passim.
29. See Conway, op cit., passim; Eberhard Bethge, *Dietrich Bonhoeffer* (London, 1970), passim.
30. Heinrich Portmann, *Cardinal von Galen* (London, 1957); Gerhard Schäfer (ed.), *Landesbischof D. Wurm und der nationalsozialistische Staat 1940–1945* (Stuttgart, 1968).
31. Adolf Hitler, *Hitler's Secret Conversations 1941–1944* (New York, 1953), pp. 117, 332, 447–51; Henry Picker, *Hitlers Tischgespräche im Führerhauptquartier 1941–1942*, 2nd edn (Stuttgart, 1965), pp. 176–8, 436–9.
32. Michael Balfour and Julian Frisby, *Helmuth von Moltke. A Leader Against Hitler* (London, 1972), pp. 215–24 (Moltke to Lionel Curtis, 25 March 1943); Lawrence D. Stokes, 'The German People and the Destruction of the European Jews', *Central European History*, 6 (1973), pp. 167–91.
33. cf. Hoffmann, *History*, pp. 69–96; Hoffmann, 'Beck', pp. 332–50.
34. Peter Hoffmann, 'Maurice Bavaud's Attempt to Assassinate Hitler in 1938', in George L. Mosse, (ed.), *Police Forces in History* (London, 1975), pp. 173–204; Klaus Urner, *Der Schweizer Hitler-Attentäter* (Frauenfeld/Stuttgart, 1980).
35. Anton Hoch, 'Das Attentat auf Hitler im Münchner Bürgerbräukeller 1939', *Vierteljahrshefte für Zeitgeschichte*, 17 (1969), pp. 383–413; Johann Georg Elser, *Autobiographie eines Attentäters* (Stuttgart, 1970); Hoffmann, *History*, pp. 256–8.
36. Groscurth, op. cit., pp. 222–3; Hoffmann, *History*, pp. 129, 136, 255–7.
37. Kurt Sendtner, 'Die deutsche Militäropposition im ersten Kriegsjahr', *Vollmacht des Gewissens*, vol. 1 (Frankfurt/M./Berlin, 1960), pp. 456–7; Peter Ludlow, 'Papst Pius XII., die britische Regierung und die deutsche Opposition im Winter 1939–40', *Vierteljahrshefte für Zeitgeschichte*, 22 (1974), pp. 299–341; Josef Müller, *Bis zur letzten Konsequenz. Ein Leben für Frieden und Freiheit* (Munich, 1975), pp. 130–7; Hoffmann, *History*, pp. 158–69.
38. Groscurth, op. cit., pp. 241, 247.
39. See note 37; Groscurth, op. cit., p. 236; Halder, op. cit., p. 133.
40. Hoffmann, *History*, pp. 292–5.
41. Hoffmann, *History*, pp. 278–89.
42. Wilhelm Ritter von Schramm, *Conspiracy Among Generals* (London, 1956).
43. Hoffmann, *History*, pp. 178–202, 348–72.
44. Ger van Roon, *Neuordnung im Widerstand. Der Kreisauer Kreis innerhalb der deutschen Widerstandsbewegung* (Munich, 1967); Eng. abridged edn: *German Resistance to Hitler: Count von Moltke and the Kreisau Circle* (London, 1971); Balfour/Frisby, op. cit., passim.

45. Hoffmann, *History*, pp. 278–311.
46. Roon, op. cit., pp. 589–90; Hoffmann, *History*, pp. 362–4.
47. Stokes, op. cit., passim; Balfour/Frisby, op. cit., pp. 215–24.
48. Roon, op. cit., pp. 589–90.
49. Hoffmann, *History*, pp. 362–4.
50. Gerhard Ritter, *Carl Goerdeler und die deutsche Widerstandsbewegung*, 3rd edn (Stuttgart, 1956); Eng. abridged edn: *The German Resistance: Carl Goerdeler's Struggle against Tyranny* (London, 1958); Hans Mommsen, 'Social Views and Constitutional Plans of the Resistance', in Hermann Graml et al., *The German Resistance to Hitler* (London, 1970), pp. 55–147.
51. *Agreement between the Government of the United Kingdom and the Polish Government Regarding Mutual Assistance, London, 25 August, 1939*, Cmd. 6144 (London, 1939); publ. in *The Times* (Royal edn), 26 Aug. 1939, p. 9; publ. again with secret protocol as Cmd. 6616 (London, 1945); *ADAP* D, vol. VII (Baden-Baden, 1956), nos. 228, 229; *Parliamentary Debates*, 5th series, vol. 352 (Commons), 12 Oct. 1939, cols. 563–5; Ludlow, op. cit., pp. 330–8.
52. *Agreement between His Majesty's Government in the United Kingdom and the Government of the Union of Soviet Socialist Republics providing for Joint Action in the War against Germany* (with Protocol), Moscow, 12 July 1941, Cmd. 6304 (London, 1941), also publ. in *The Times* (late London edn), 14 July 1941; *Foreign Relations of the United States. Diplomatic Papers 1941* (*FRUS*), vol. 1 (Washington, 1958), pp. 367–9; *Roosevelt and Churchill: Their Secret Wartime Correspondence* (New York, 1975), pp. 153, 186, 234; *FRUS* 1942 (Washington, 1960), pp. 1–38; *FRUS. The Conference at Washington, 1941–1942, and Casablanca, 1943* (Washington, 1968), pp. 362–76; *The Times* (late London edn), 15 Aug. 1941; *War Cabinet 84 (42), Conclusions*, 19 Aug. 1941, p. 223, Public Record Office, London (PRO), Cab. 65/19.
53. Detlef Brandes, *Grossbritannien und die Exilregierungen Polens, der Tschechoslowakei und Jugoslawiens vom Kriegsbeginn bis zur Konferenz von Teheran*, Habilitationsschrift, Freie Universität (Berlin, 1984), pp. 352–9, cites War Cabinet, W.P. (42) 280, 2 July 1942, PRO Cab. 66/26.
54. PRO, FO 371/26542/(C 610), FO 371/26543/C10855, PREMIER 4/100/8; the first two items were published partially in *Dokumente zur Deutschlandpolitik*, 1st series, vol. 1, ed. Rainer A. Blasius (Frankfurt/M., 1984), p. 269.
55. *FRUS* 1943, vol. 1, pp. 680, 687, 737, 752–4.
56. cf. Hoffmann, *History*, pp. 205–48.
57. Peter Hoffmann, 'Peace through *Coup d'État*: The Foreign Contacts of the German Resistance 1933–1944', *Central European* History, XIX, June 1986.
58. Hoffmann, *History*, pp. 263–89, 322–32.
59. ibid., pp. 373–94.
60. ibid., loc. cit.

61. ibid., pp. 301–11.
62. ibid., pp. 373–411; Peter Hoffmann, 'Warum misslang das Attentat vom 20. Juli 1944?', *Vierteljahrshefte für Zeitgeschichte*, 32 (1984), pp. 441–62.
63. Hoffmann, *History,* pp. 412–534, for the course of the *coup d'état* and its aftermath.
64. Annedore Leber, *Das Gewissen steht auf. 64 Lebensbilder aus dem deutschen Widerstand 1933–1945*, 9th edn (Berlin/Frankfurt/M., 1960), p. 126; Eng. edn, *Conscience in Revolt* (London, 1957).
65. Joachim Kramarz, *Stauffenberg: The Life and Death of an Officer, 15th November 1907–20th July 1944* (London, 1967), pp. 122, 185.

2006
1998
8

98
22
76